The Scottish Peaks

Plate 1 Liathach in snowy raiment

W. A. Poucher, Hon. F.R.P.S

The Scottish Peaks

A pictorial guide to walking in this region and to
the safe ascent of its most spectacular mountains with
246 photographs by the author, 33 maps and 74 routes.

Ninth Edition

Frances Lincoln

Frances Lincoln Ltd
4 Torriano Mews
Torriano Avenue
London NW5 2RZ
www.franceslincoln.com

First published in Great Britain 1965 by Constable and Company Ltd
Copyright © 1965 by William Arthur Poucher
Eighth edition 1998
Ninth edition re-originated from the original photographs and
published by Frances Lincoln in 2005

British Library Cataloguing in Publication data
A catalogue record for this book is available from the British Library.

Printed and bound in Singapore

ISBN 071112 2406 4

9 8 7 6 5 4 3 2 1

*Hillwalking and scrambling carry certain risks. If you have any doubts
about your ability to conduct these activities you should consider engaging a
qualified guide or instructor to lead you or to instruct you in the techniques
required to travel safely in the mountains. Your use of this book indicates
your assumption of the risks involved, and is an acknowledgement of your
own sole responsibility for your safety.*

Contents

Notes on the routes 100

Detailed directions for 74 routes 102

Preface to the ninth edition

The Scottish Peaks first appeared in 1964 and until this edition was published by Constable, but now Frances Lincoln have taken over this task and will, I am sure, continue in the same tradition. As an example of their approach to the task, they have used today's technology to re-originate all the available photographs and so improve their quality.

Since it was first published it has been regularly updated, originally by my late father, until in his 90s he was no longer able to travel to Scotland. So, for the eighth edition two well-known Scottish mountaineers, Kevin Howett and Tom Prentice shared this task as it was felt too big a job for just one man, considering the scope of the work.

In spite of the routes being updated, it is still possible for slight changes to appear due to erosion, rock falls and other natural causes and if such variations are noticed by a user of this guide it will be most helpful if they would let me know so that they can be included in any future edition of this work.

As all visitors to mountainous areas will know, many footpaths have, over the years, become so eroded that repair or reinstatement was urgently required. On many hills this work has been carried out; I urge walkers to keep to any such improved or diverted paths in the interest of conservation and, on paths that have not yet been repaired, to walk on the worn part or on stony ground so as not to increase the damage already done.

I would draw readers' attention to a booklet, *Tread Lightly*, produced by the British Mountaineering Council in co-operation with the Mountaineering Council of Scotland, with financial support from the Nature Conservancy Council. This booklet covers many aspects of the correct conduct on and around the fells, which is summed up by the phrase: 'Take nothing but photographs, leave nothing but footprints.'

It should be noted that the routes described and illustrated herein have been frequented over the years without objection, but they do not necessarily constitute rights of way. If in any doubt, the reader should contact the owner of the land and ask permission to cross it before embarking on their walk. This is most important in view of the outbreaks of vandalism which have occurred in recent years and have resulted in damage to fences, hedges, gates, walls, cairns and shelters in moutain districts; this is not only deplorable but also contrary to the accepted Country Code.

It was my father's opinion that the best time to visit the Scottish hills was in the spring, not only because the weather is then most favourable, but also because the midges can be quite insufferable after May. In view of the number of accidents that occur every year, I would remind readers that mountaineering can be a risky sport, but that all the routes in this book are within the powers of any fit and experienced mountain or hill walker, whereas some of them may well be dangerous to the ordinary pedestrian.

Finally, I would urge leaders of school and youth parties not to venture on these hills unless the weather is favourable; moreover, they should always insist upon everyone wearing boots and proper clothing and carrying the various items mentioned in the section devoted to 'Safety Considerations'. If they do this they will not only reduce the risk of accidents, but also avoid the, often needless, call for Mountain rescue.

A Route Card will be found at the end of the book which is used in Scotland. This should be completed by all walkers as in the event of an accident it will facilitate Mountain Rescue. However, it is important to complete route cards properly and not to alter routes without notification to the establishment where the original route has been left. I also draw the attention of readers to the section at the end of Sense on the Scottish Hills.

The maps were drawn by Martin Collins.

John Poucher
Gate Ghyll, High Brigham
Cockermouth, Cumbria
2005

After Mr Poucher's death in August 1988, at the age of 96, his son and daughter-in-law felt that as he had loved Scotland, and particularly Skye, so much it would be appropriate for there to be some form of memorial to him in the area. So with the agreement of the proprietor, a memorial seat was presented to the Sligachan Hotel, and it now stands in its gardens. The seat bears a plaque which reads:

IN MEMORY OF
WALTER POUCHER 1891–1988
A RENOWNED MOUNTAIN PHOTOGRAPHER
WHO LOVED THE WILD PLACES

Introductory notes

For many decades Scotland has been the treasured venue of the angler, who, often coming from distant places to engage in this fascinating sport, has delighted in fishing for salmon on its famous rivers, and on occasion also for trout on the innumerable lochs and lochans that grace this wild and beautiful country. Before the Second World War its mountains were the special preserve of the connoisseur, largely because of their remote situation from the Midlands and the South of England, although Scotsmen themselves, living on the doorstep so to speak, have climbed them and revelled in their beauty with pride and gusto for many years. However, for some years now there has been an increased interest in mountain walking, ridge wandering and rock climbing, but it has been concentrated mainly in the regions between Arran and Lochaber, doubtless owing to their ready accessibility. But in more recent years the remote and magnificent peaks of the North Western Highlands have attracted greater attention and due to the almost universal use of the motor car they are now more easily reached and explored. This approach has been facilitated by the improved road conditions; for while it was an adventure to drive over them in the 1950s almost all of them have now been resurfaced, and although they are mostly single-track, with ample passing places, they give fair access to a large number of the peaks cited in this work.

Nowadays many of our young people have ample funds available for holidays, and since youth hostelling and camping are an inexpensive form of travel there is no valid reason why the Highlands, the Cairngorms and Skye should not become as cherished centres as others in Britain. Energetic young men and women who have a special predilection for hill country may well choose Lochaber for their first visit, and on arrival they will raise their eyes to the peaks and imagine themselves standing by one of the summit cairns, inhaling the invigorating mountain air and scanning the glens far below, the chain of engirdling hills and the distant glimmering seas. Come what may, they lose no time in setting out to climb one of them, and on reaching their objective gain that satisfaction that comes only after the ardours of the ascent. It is highly probable that Ben Nevis will be their first conquest, not only because it is the monarch of all our British hills, but also because they believe it will disclose the finest and most comprehensive panorama on account of its dominating altitude. On achieving this ambition they quite naturally speculate upon the merits of the views from the other high peaks in this region, and after talking over the question with their friends they will in all probability continue their exploration by climbing Bidean nam Bian, or walking over the ridges of the Mamores, or perhaps even traversing the exciting crest of Aonach Eagach.

And it is here that I must draw attention to the differences between the Scottish Peaks and those of English Lakeland and Snowdonia. Hill walking experience in these two regions can be invaluable, but it must be borne in mind that not only are the summits of lesser altitude than those of the Highlands, but they are all fairly close together and easily reached from the network of roads that pattern both districts. In many parts of Scotland, and particularly so in the Cairngorms, the peaks are usually a very great distance from the starting point and may necessitate walking over vast stretches of moorland that is often dappled with bog. Moreover, when they are reached the ascents are longer and frequently more arduous, so that good planning, an early start and at least two companions are essential for safety. For in the event of an accident one can stay with the victim while the other goes for help, and in some places long tramps are involved to reach a spot where assistance can be obtained. Although the wearing of brightly coloured clothing may not be to everyone's taste, it might help rescuers to locate a casualty more rapidly.

On returning home our young friends will often ponder over this advice and their own experiences, and especially so if they have been captivated by the spirit and mystery of the hills. The map will doubtless be unfolded at frequent intervals, and by tracing the routes thereon they will re-live these happy times. If they climbed Bidean nam Bian by way of Ossian's Cave and Aonach Dubh their thoughts will follow that pleasant route from Glen Coe and Loch Achtriochtan with the first summit soaring overhead, their surprise at the spectacular view of Aonach Eagach on the other side of the glen on attaining the cairn, the tramp along the broad ridge to Stob Coire nan Lochan whose superb situation opens up magnificent scenes in all directions with a first view of Ben Nevis to the north above Aonach Eagach, the scramble across the narrow ridge that rises to the dominating peak of the group, with splendid prospects of the two buttresses on the right, followed by the exhilaration of standing by the highest cairn in Argyll with a whole kingdom spread out at their feet.

A close inspection of the map will suggest to our friends several other routes to this lofty peak, and curiosity will induce them to speculate upon their respective merits. Would the easier route by way of An t-Sron have been as interesting? Perhaps it would have been more thrilling to have made the ascent from Loch Achtriochtan by the Dinner Time Buttress, or what of the more circuitous route by the Allt Coire Gabhail? Then another line of thought may develop: for they had seen a grand array of peaks engirdling the horizon from Bidean and they will speculate again upon the merits of the panoramas from their summits, to realise with surprise that a lifetime is scarcely too long in which to become acquainted with them all.

The cogitations of our young friends will follow a normal course and they will do exactly the same as the rest of us did in our novitiate; for they will formulate the plans for their next holiday long before it is due. Next time they may decide to stay perhaps in Glen Torridon and explore its enclosing hills;

but which ones? To solve this problem they will often get out the map, and while scanning it with happy anticipation compare it with the various guide-books which describe this marvellous countryside. There they will *read* what their authors have so lucidly written, but much will inevitably be left to their imagination.

It is here that my long experience of the Scottish Peaks will help to solve their problems; for by consulting this volume in conjunction with my other works devoted to the Highlands, the Cairngorms and Skye they will not only be able to choose their centre with certainty, their routes to the peaks in the vicinity in accordance with their powers as hill walkers, and the subjects for their cameras if they happen to be photographers, but they will also be able to *see* beforehand through the medium of my camera studies precisely the type of country that will satisfy every one of their needs.

Scotland's mountains

The Scottish hills, in general, are subject to more severe weather conditions than the rest of the UK. Indeed it is not uncommon to experience snow on the summits during the middle of summer, or conversely in other years to find scorching hot conditions when heat-stroke would be a hazard. The unpredictability of the weather (sudden and unexpected changes from warm sunshine to cold, rain or even blizzard), the scale of the hills and the distances to be covered in tackling the summits of some hills, mean that it is unwise to venture out without knowing what you can expect to encounter. You should also ensure that you have clothing and equipment that are suitable for the expected worst conditions, not just for the feel of the weather at the car-park.

There can be an enormous difference in tackling the same hill at different times of the year or by different routes. In summer the Scottish peaks described here can generally be ascended armed with no more technical equipment than suitable walking boots and clothing to protect you from rain and cold. An ascent will not necessarily involve any rock climbing or the need for a rope (except perhaps the Cuillin, Aonach Eagach and some other ridges). It all depends upon how you wish to reach your summit cairn: for instance, in good weather any able-bodied person can walk up to the summit of Ben Nevis by the well-trodden path from Achintee; for a more demanding ascent to the same summit you could ascend Carn Mor Dearg, then cross the famous arête before finally ascending the steep flanks of the great North East Buttress; while the rock climber could take Tower Ridge from Coire na Ciste or any of the more technical and difficult routes which festoon the savage walls of the North Face.

To accomplish any of these you must be in fit condition, so

it depends on your sporting instincts, your experience, your knowledge of your mountain and how you wish to enjoy your day out in this superb countryside.

However, to tackle any of the routes in this guide in the depths of winter means encountering a much tougher, though very exciting experience. Conditions can be extremely cold and even violent. Strong winds, blizzard, 'white-out' snow conditions, very deep snow or very hard névé or high avalanche risk are all possible. The Cairngorm plateau, for example is often described as having arctic weather conditions in winter and a simple walk in such conditions becomes more akin to mountaineering that is more usually associated with bigger mountain ranges in other parts of the world, such as the European Alps.

Although Scotland lacks the height or permanent glaciers of such mountain ranges, walking in the Scottish hills in winter should be regarded as mountaineering and walkers should ensure that they have the clothing and technical equipment that are applicable for such an activity and know how to use them.

The winter hills

Snow may fall on the hills above the 3,000-foot (914-metre) contour at any time of the year, but it does not tend to stay long outside the winter months, excepting in the deep recesses of high north-east corries. By October and November, the high mountains begin to accumulate their winter raiment and significant precipices encircling the high corries acquire a white mantle and tremendous cornices grow from ridges and the edges of summit plateaux, to hang over the cliffs. Accumulated snow can remain on north-east slopes, corries and in the gullies well into April. Indeed winter snow and ice climbing can still be had sometimes in May on Ben Nevis.

The walker venturing out during this period not only requires more technical mountaineering equipment but must take more care in selecting a route that takes account of snow conditions in order to allow safer movement in the hills.

The natural world of the hills is an environment of uncertainty, of factors beyond our control, and even the most experienced mountaineer will be learning anew throughout his or her life. Of all the hazards that one may encounter that could lead to an accident, it is still true that the greatest cause of accidents in the hills is a simple slip. Although some slips are unavoidable, many that result in an accident are due to people not being prepared for the conditions. Statistics show that most people injured are actually well equipped so knowing how to use the equipment effectively and when to use it is therefore very important.

Scrambling – to rope up or to go solo?

Virtually all the Scottish peaks can be ascended without necessarily involving any rock climbing or the use of a rope. There are however, those where use of the hands is necessary and these are mentioned (there is often a walking alternative to bypass such obstacles). Using your hands as well as your feet on such terrain is called scrambling and is potentially one of the most hazardous aspects of enjoying the hills as the activity lies at the blurred distinction between walking and rock climbing. As a general rule, most rock climbers would probably use ropes and protection equipment for anything other than easy climbs. As a result rock climbing is generally quite safe. A rock climber undertaking scrambling will be well within any physical and mental limits and so will be relatively safe. An inexperienced walker attempting a scramble would probably be at the limit of his/her experience, and as scrambles tend to be in exposed positions the consequences of a slip are more severe.

Two novices using a rope to give themselves confidence on such ground will probably just double the peril. In such a situation it is better to be with a more experienced colleague who can give guidance. The use of a rope is only of any help if those using it know how to – tying-on, belay techniques etc. It is better to plan ahead, know what hazards your expedition may encounter and make provisions to deal with them.

Ski mountaineering

The use of ski on the British hills is not often possible, save in a severe winter when snow lies heavily on their slopes, and even then it is preferable to run over snow carpeting long grassy declivities rather than boulder-strewn ground. The greater altitude of the Scottish peaks is a decided advantage in that they are more likely to be snowbound for longer periods and so facilitate the enjoyment of this exhilarating sport. Of all of Scotland's hills, the Cairngorm mountains offer the best chance to indulge. The Cairngorms ski facilities at The Lechdt, Glen Shee and Cairn Gorm itself allow downhill skiing but when the whole of the massive chain is snowbound it is admirably suited for ski mountaineering and due to the distances involved in travelling across the Cairngorms this mode of transport can be the best option in times of heavy snow. Experienced Scottish skiers are fortunate to be able to take advantage of these conditions so near their homes.

Rock climbing

This is a sport engaged in nowadays by a very large number of enthusiasts and it has been cited as the fastest growing sport of the 1990s. Those who live south of the border are accustomed to regard such cliffs as Scafell in Lakeland and Clogwyn Du'r Arddu in Snowdonia as the acme of British big cliffs. Those travelling north are enthusiastic in their praise of the peaks of the Cuillins, in Skye, the great cliffs of Ben Nevis and such Glen Coe hills as Buachaille Etive Mor and Bidean nam Bian, but these are only a few of the possibilities in Scotland, a country with a wide variety of rock types and whose huge mountain cliffs contain much rock still unclimbed. The development of new routes and whole new areas continues apace.

Anyone with an interest in trying this exhilarating pastime is advised to seek some guidance. If you have a friend who is experienced, ask him/her to explain the techniques and the use of the equipment so you can put the theory into practice. Joining a local climbing club may give you an opportunity to meet like-minded people with whom you can develop your climbing. Alternatively, go along to one of the many indoor climbing centres, enrol in a climbing course there or at an outdoor activities centre. There are also many books on the subject of teaching yourself the basics and in Scotland the Rock Climbing Guidebook Series produced by the Scottish Mountaineering Club will show you where to put it all into practice.

Disclaimer
Finally, remember that mountaineering (including hill walking in winter) is a hazardous activity with a chance of injury or even death. The risks can be minimised by knowledge, skills and experience, and it is up to individuals to take responsibility for themselves, even when out with more experienced people, in order to increase their own safety.

Access to Scotland's mountains for recreation
There has been confusion over the rights and laws concerning access to the mountains of Scotland for some years now, both amongst those living outside Scotland and amongst residents as well as past guidebook writers. The term 'Freedom to Roam' is used a lot in connection with Scotland now. This remains a moral right only until the Land Reform (Scotland) Act is fully implemented and is associated with traditional mountain freedoms dating back to before the nineteenth-century sporting estates started using the hills exclusively and preventing access to others.

The main legal constraint on access has been cited as the Law of Trespass. This is a civil matter and any prosecutions can only be concerned with criminal activity whilst out on the hills, such as damage. There has been, and still is, dispute about the interpretation of the civil law regarding trespass and the rights of a landowner to remove you from land, and on the other hand, whether hill walkers can in any way be regarded as trespassers. However, there is a criminal law element in the 1865 Trespass Scotland Act that makes it an offence to 'encamp' or light fires without the landowner's permission. Camping wild in the hills will rarely, however, be actively prevented as long as it is undertaken responsibly and with respect for the personal privacy of local people. A code of conduct for wild campers is available from the Mountaineering Council of Scotland (MCofS).

More recently, in 1994, the Criminal Justice and Public Order Act created a criminal offence of 'Aggravated Trespass' to prevent 'intentional disruption or obstruction' of sporting shooting activities. The government has given assurances that this will not be used against hill walkers, but there is no specific clause that precludes its use in this way. The MCofS has produced an information leaflet about the freedom to roam and this particular act.

Whatever the outcome of current debate and argument about the law, there is, since 1996, an agreement between landowning and recreational interests about access in the form of a Concordat on Access. This was agreed through the Access Forum set up by Scottish Natural Heritage (SNH). The statements are self-explanatory and if all walkers and all landowners interpret them sensibly then there should be few incidents of conflict. The Concordat is available from SNH or the MCofS. The main principles are:

- Freedom of access exercised with responsiblity and subject to reasonable constraints for management and conservation purposes.
- Acceptance by visitors of the needs of land management, and understanding of how this sustains the livelihood,

culture and community interests of those who live and work in the hills.
- Acceptance by land managers of the public's expectation of having access to the hills.
- Acknowledgement of a common interest in the natural beauty and special qualities of Scotland's hills, and the need to work together for their protection and enhancement.

The mountain environment

In the spirit of the Access Concordat, it is incumbent on walkers to act responsibly towards the mountain environment. Everyone has heard of the Country Code but few know the detail. On the other hand, walkers and climbers as a group exhibit particular concern for the environment and have been at the forefront of protecting Scotland's mountain heritage; it was a climber, Percy Unna, who bought and then gave the Glen Coe estate to the National Trust for Scotland to protect it for all time for the nation. Unna's 'rules', conditions he expressed about the future management of the estate, have for many years been regarded as worthy conservation ideals; the great mountaineer Bill Murray, whose books *Mountaineering in Scotland* and *Undiscovered Scotland* have inspired generations of climbers, was espousing conservation ideals after World War Two, when they were unfashionable.

We derive great joy from the mountains, and so inherently share a concern over their well-being, and we can all help by educating ourselves about issues such as disturbance to nesting birds, wild flowers, toilet hygiene in the hills, path erosion, fires; we can all help by leaving no trace of our passing bar footprints.

The Access forum has produced a booklet entitled 'Care for the Hills: guidance on the careful use of Scotland's hills and mountains for open-air recreation'. A distilled message taken from this has also been produced as a leaflet, bearing the same name, which acts as a new version of the Country Code specific to the Scottish mountains. These are available from SNH. The MCofS also produces information about hygiene and health in the hills.

Bibliography

Among Mountains by J Crumley
A Century of Scottish Moutaineering by W D Brooker
The Cuillin of Skye by H B Humble
Friends in High Places by Cairngorms Mountain Rescue Team
Hamish's Mountain Walk and *Climbing the Corbetts* by H Brown
Munros in Winter by M Moran
Mountaineering in Scotland and *Undiscovered Scotland* by
     W H Murray
Weir's World by T Weir
Cairngorms Scene and Unseen by S Scroggie
Glen Coe, The Changing Moods by A Thomson
The Nature of Scotland by M Magnusson and G White
The First Fifty, Munro Bagging Without a Beard by M Gray
*A High and Lonely Place, The Sanctuary and Plight of the
     Carngorms* by J Crumley
Native Stones by D Craig
Bell's Scottish Climbs by J H B Bell
Always a Little Further by A Borthwick
Calculated Risk by D Haston
Call Out by H MacInnes
One Man's Mountains by T Patey

Safety considerations

Climb if you will, but remember that courage and strength are nought without prudence, and that a momentary negligence may destroy the happiness of a lifetime. Do nothing in haste; look well to each step; and from the beginning think what may be the end.

Edward Whymper

Equipment

Anyone who ventures out on to the hills without proper equipment is asking for trouble, and since the weather is one of our greatest hazards it is wise, indeed imperative, to be prepared for sudden and unexpected changes, from warm sunshine to rain to blizzard, by wearing proper boots and clothing, as well as other essentials which I shall enumerate in these pages.

Boots

Your feet are your mode of transport so it is important to take care of them. The long distances and the varied sorts of terrain you will encounter on the Scottish peaks, from acidic peat bogs to boulder fields and scree, means good footwear that gives support and protection is important. Various types of walking, fell running or trail shoes are now available. Many have cushioned soles and deep treads and can be very comfortable on 'soft' terrain and easy paths in summer, their stiffened heel cups helping to keep the foot from slipping and twisting in the shoe. Sports sandals of similar design are useful in very hot weather too.

But once on to the 'hard' terrain on the more rock-covered peaks, boots give much better support and protect the ankles from damage. There are numerous makes and styles available to choose from. The essential criterion when choosing a pair of boots is that they will do the job you require of them and for this you will have to decide what sort of conditions you intend to use them in.

There are boots available with uppers made of leather or synthetic fabric or plastic (usually with padded inner boots in the latter's case). The soles of boots are usually made from some form of moulded rubber material, with Vibrams being the most commonly recognised brand-name, and there are newer versions of trail-type shoes and boots with 'sticky-rubber' of the sort used in climbing footwear.

There are even various kinds of sole designs. They all purport to give security on grass or rock, in wet or dry conditions, but in reality they all have their limitations and it is the wearer who must be ever vigilant. The leather boots (choose one-piece uppers if possible) tend to be stiffer and heavier than fabric boots, whilst fabric ones are very comfortable to wear at all times but stand up less well to wear and tear in rocky terrain. Both have their place in the hills at different times. Plastic boots are relatively lightweight, generally comfortable but cause some people foot-cramp as the soles are fully stiffened and allow no flexing of the foot. They are, however, ever waterproof, very warm (good in winter but not summer) and need no 'breaking-in' – a feature of the heavier leather boots.

If winter walking is contemplated then boots with stiffened soles to accommodate crampons are needed. All plastic boots obviously fit this criterion as they are fully stiffened. Other boots have differing degrees of stiffening by containing $\frac{1}{2}$, $\frac{3}{4}$ or full shank metal or plastic plates in the sole. This alters the boot's flexibility and what type of crampon, if any, can be fitted. The style of crampon attachment to the boot will also determine what boot is chosen as crampons with 'step-in' bindings need a 'welt' round the edge of the boot at the heel and toe for the crampons to fix to; strap-on types do not.

Unfortunately for the walker, it would be ideal to have

different types of boot for different occasions. Personal finances will preclude this for most people and a compromise choice will have to be made on type, quality and style. A lightweight pair for summer and a more robust pair that takes crampons for winter would be ideal if you can afford it. However, never compromise on comfort and always buy the best you can afford. Take advice from books, shops, articles in the outdoor magazines and other, experienced walkers.

Clothing

The choice of purpose-made clothing for the outdoors is bewildering and what is chosen in the end may be a matter of personal taste. The following basic information is just a guide.

The layering system

To cope with the extremes of weather one can meet throughout a day in the hills it is the generally held belief that a layering system of interchangeable garments is the best. A base-layer, next to the skin, has the function of moving body moisture away to keep the skin dry. This process is called 'wicking'. So-called 'thermal underwear' is the garment used, usually a man-made polyester fabric, although silk and wool are the more natural versions. Cotton does not 'wick' perspiration but holds it and as soon as you stop moving it cools and becomes uncomfortable and chilling. There are synthetic material 'sports bras' for women which are far better than cotton ones. Thermal underwear includes leggings.

The mid-layer is the most variable and several garments can be worn together depending on the temperature. The choices are between fleece jackets of varying thickness, down-filled jackets or wool sweaters and shirts – whichever is your own personal preference. Down clothing is the warmest and packs small but it should not be subject to a soaking or it becomes useless. For the legs the trend is to wear shorts in warm weather (even when raining) and synthetics such as stretch nylon, polycotton or microfibre fabrics, which are comfortable, windproof and hard-wearing, when the temperature decreases (and the wind chill increases).

The outer shell-layer is the most important. This is your main defence against wet, cold conditions. Most waterproofs manufactured for the outdoor market are made from 'breathable' fabrics, either microporous (a membrane with minute holes, e.g. Goretex and Sympatex) or hydrophilic (the membrane is coated with a substance that transfers vapour molecules, e.g. Entrant). In theory, these allow water vapour out but do not allow rain in. They depend on a temperature / humidity difference between the inside and out. The best of each type are as good as each other, and are better than polyurethane-coated nylon which although 100% waterproof does ensure you get wet from your sweat. However, many walkers expect too much from these garments and hope to be free from condensation at all times, and are therefore disappointed when they operate below par under some extreme environmental conditions (or when the differential works the wrong way or is non-existent).

The design and construction of the garment are probably more important to worry about. Things to consider are: fully taped seams, built-in hoods with good protection but reasonable visibility, double protection flaps on the main front zip, sleeves with articulated elbows and adjustable cuffs.

An alternative is 'ventile' material, either cotton or man-made. These work by mimicking the waterproof system of animal fur. Ventile cotton has better breathability than the above types, but is heavy and the outer layer gets soaked in water and requires drying each night. The man-made version, NBA, e.g. Paramo NBA by Nikwax, does not have this problem and seems to work extremely well. They also have a longer 'hill life' as they can be reproofed easily.

Finally, waterproof 'overtrousers' complete the package. You can buy either trouser or salopette styles. The latter are best for winter as they give extra protection to the back (especially the kidney area) and chest. Again look for sealed seams in membrane types, and articulated knees are a must. Knee-length zips make putting them on over boots easier.

A single-layer system

There is one manufacturer, Buffalo, who is defying the general trend by advocating a single layer approach when it comes to really foul weather. Made from polyester pile and a Pertex nylon shell, the combination of trouser or salopette, shirt and jacket allows maximum breathability and wicking whilst giving protection from the wind and most rain conditions. Those who have used it are converts to the cause and claim that it works better than other garments in the most awful of Scotland's weather conditions – heavy rain and wind in near freezing temperatures. Most shell clothing cannot stand up to continuous exposure to such conditions.

Accessories

Once encumbered in any of the above clothing there remain only the little nooks and crannies to plug, through which rain and cold would otherwise seep. Hats are essential in winter and very useful in summer on cold days on the tops. Fleece types are less itchy than wool and designs include peaked caps and drop-down ear muffs. Gloves, or mitts, are another winter essential and again come in fleece or wool, with waterproof covering or not. Carrying spares is a good idea. A scarf can often be more than just a luxury item. Gaiters are also useful for boggy ground or wet weather, and will be invaluable in winter to keep snow out of boots.

The last essential item, although not a garment, is a rucksack to carry sundry spares, food and drink, maps, spare clothing, head-torch with spare batteries, emergency shelter or bivi bag, basic first aid kit, glacier glasses for winter sun and other winter gear. There is a bewildering number of different makes and styles of rucksacks to choose from. Before you are attracted to any particular style you must first decide what size of rucksack you will require. Sizes are categorised by volume capacity in 'litres'. Anything below 15 litres is only useful for summer rambles. A rucksack size of 20 to 30 litres would be fine to carry everything you need for a summer hill walk. For winter walking you will need between 30 and 50 litres to cater for the increased amount of equipment. To fill a rucksack bigger than that with the equipment needed for just a day walk in winter will probably slow you down so much that it jeopardises your safety.

The designs available offer choice to suit your personal preferences: side pockets or not, mesh holders, adjustable volume lids, twin compartment sacks, compression straps, hip belts and chest straps. The pros and cons of each of these design features are not as important as other features that enable a rucksack to be used effectively. The essentials to look for are a padded back of some sort for comfort, solid shoulder strap attachments, ice axe loops and crampon straps (away from the back of your neck!) that are essential for a winter walking rucksack and quality materials with sound, double stitching. All rucksacks, however well made, will leak at some stage in very heavy rain and it is advisable to also buy a liner of some sort. One of the most important points to consider when buying your rucksack is to get one that properly fits your back length. Most manufacturers make the medium to larger rucksacks in differing lengths or with adjustable back systems and it is a good idea to fully test the rucksack in the shop when you are buying it by filling it with something heavy. That way you get a better idea of the fit.

Packing your rucksack for a day trip may seem like common sense, but it is a bit of an art form, especially in winter. Heavier items are better packed in the upper half of the rucksack to distribute the weight better on your back. Items that may be used intermittently all through the day need to be easily at hand (in side pockets, lid pockets or mesh pockets or in the top of the main body of the rucksack), whilst items such as emergency food, clothing and bivi bags can be placed in the base. In winter conditions there is no sense in storing crampons in the base of the rucksack as when the time comes on the hill when they are needed you will not want to pull everything out to get to them. The same can be said about a helmet if you are carrying one.

Winter equipment: what? how? and when?

An ice axe will prove invaluable in winter but it is essential to learn how to use it. This is best achieved by practising in a safe, controlled situation; it is too late to start learning when you find yourself hurtling down a steep snow slope, above a line of crags. An ice axe can be used effectively to stop such a slide, but a brake (self-arrest) must be applied very quickly after a stumble as a walker clothed in waterproof shell clothing accelerates extremely fast on snow. The axe can also be used for balance security when traversing or descending a steep snow slope, and for cutting steps in harder patches of snow (névé) for short sections. It can also be used for belaying when using a rope. There are many different kinds of axe including specialist ones for extreme ice climbing with 'banana' picks, quick -release wrist loops and interchangeable heads. So-called 'walking' axes tend to be slightly longer with less complex picks, usually with droop heads and an adze, and can be used more easily for self-arrest. There are pros and cons with a wrist-sling attachment on walking axes to prevent losing them, as in the event of not arresting a slide, the axe becomes a lethal weapon that flails about you if still attached. Some people simply prefer to try not to drop it!

A pair of crampons packed with the sack as a matter of course on a winter trip will prove very useful. They give additional security on steep snowed-up ground and make passage over hard névé much less hazardous. They take time to get used to walking with – tripping over your crampons would be just as bad as slipping on the snow – but are worth persevering with as they save time and effort when used at the right times. Ice axe braking with crampons on should be practised with caution on a very safe slope.

It is extremely important to ensure that crampons and boots attach to each other as a solid unit; the styles should be compatible. Crampons should be fitted to the boots, before setting out on a trip. As the array of boot and crampon types is so great a coding system for compatibility has been introduced by some manufacturers for guidance. Advice should be available from the shop, or from the Mountaineering Councils.

Over half the accidents involving head injuries are fatal and there are instances of falls down craggy hillsides where a helmet can be shown to have helped. Most climbers wear a helmet on a winter climb to protect the head from falling ice from above. They will also keep the helmet on for the descent from the cliff. If walkers are considering undertaking one of the routes that require scrambling under winter conditions, they may wish to consider the use of a helmet for those parts of the expedition where they feel most at risk. It should be borne in mind, however, that a long fall will result in multiple injuries, so reducing the chance that you will fall in the first instance is better.

Forward planning

One of the great joys of hill walking is the freedom to be where you want, by your own choice, and to be responsible for yourself. You should set out with the intention of looking out for your own well-being, assessing the hazards that you encounter and dealing with them by making your own decisions. Setting out with the idea that if you get into trouble then someone else will be around to rescue you will not contribute to your own safety.

Make sure you can cope with any potential hazard (including

weather) by gaining the skills needed (and realising your own deficiencies); plan your day's activities in advance (not necessarily in detail but you should certainly do risk assessment associated with what you plan to do and make a note of possible alternatives along the route should problems occur) then, whatever the journey throws at you, the result will be less likely to involve an accident or rescue.

Planning ahead means:

- Finding out as much as possible about the route you intend to take,
- Gaining a weather report so you know what is in store,
- In winter, watching the weather reports for days (or weeks) prior to a trip to assess snow conditions and avalanche risk and so plan the detailed route to compensate,
- Ensuring you have the necessary clothing and equipment,
- Knowing your limitations and increasing your skills before pushing into situations beyond your experience.

Navigation

Statistics gathered by mountain rescue teams based on the details of call-outs have indicated that the cause of many accidents can be traced back to a navigation error at some point. Usually this is when the weather is foul and visibility is poor; or at night, or in a blizzard – or worse, in a white-out. Disorientation and uncertainty lead to further mistakes which can compound to result in an accident. If you work your way out of such a situation before catastrophe then you've experienced an 'epic' you should learn from. Navigation in the hills in clear weather does not depend on the ability to interpret a map or use a compass correctly. It is possible to see the route, and any hazard. As soon as the weather gets bad, however, then these skills become essential. This is something that cannot be learnt at the last minute, nor only in the house or classroom. You have to ingest the essence of it, practise at low level in good weather, then practise in bad weather. Hopefully by the time you encounter weather that could lead to an epic you will know what to do and be confident you are doing it right.

Learning to relate what is on a map to what is on the ground will come with practice and experience. There is no short-cut. Navigating in a white-out taking bearings, or even back-bearings, to fellow walkers, whilst pacing out distances, is extremely difficult to do with any accuracy, but it could save your life.

Maps and compasses are therefore the walker's and climber's friends. It is often true that those who would regard themselves as experienced in the hills are singularly lacking in navigation technique. Perhaps they have simply never yet been caught out in weather that has tested their ability.

The 'traditional' compass that relies on the magnetic forces around us is the most reliable as there is little to go wrong. It is also true that to use it one will have to be able to interpret a map well. The navigation devices relying on satellite positioning – Geographical Positioning Systems (GPS) – seem at first sight to take the hassle out of learning to navigate and may be very tempting for novices. This is not the case, however, and as there is more to go wrong (e.g. batteries) they should not be seen as substitutes for a normal compass and the ability to use it. A GPS is a good companion to a walker already skilled in the use of a compass.

It is not within the scope of this book to go into detail about navigation skills. There are numerous books on the subject already and readers are recommended to refer to the bibliography on p. 37 for a list of some which would be helpful. These books all give very detailed information about the various techniques required and purchase of one of them would be a good starting point for learning navigation.

The sort of skills that you will require to be safe in any weather conditions include the ability to interpret a map's information and link it to reality on the ground (what the map symbols mean and what the contours indicate for the nature of the slope); measuring distances on the map; working out grid references on a map from which to take bearings; orienting the map to north; taking bearings of a proposed route from the map for use whilst walking (taking account of magnetic variation); taking bearings from the ground (sightings to a nearby or distant landmark) and relating them accurately to the map in order to help navigate in the required direction; pin-pointing your position using a technique known as a resection and estimating how long a route (and stages of a route) will take (taking into account changes in terrain and the amount of ascent – 'Naismiths Rule' and 'Tranter's Variations').

In particularly poor weather a whole selection of other techniques will also prove helpful (indeed they may prove indispensable to life) including working out your own personal pacing and being able to pace out stages of a route when visibility is very poor; being able to travel on a back-bearing (including a bearing from one of your walking party in extremely poor visibility) and other techniques such as 'aiming off', 'attack points', 'sweep searching' and 'box searching', and being able to understand and interpret the 'aspect of slope' to help avoid hazards when you become 'lost'.

It is strongly recommended that walkers learn detailed navigation for all weathers. A book can enlighten you to the theory but only by doing it will you gain in expertise and therefore confidence. Going on a course at an outdoor centre or one run by a British Mountain Guide or Mountain Instructor would prove very valuable indeed.

In the event of an accident
Accidents in the chaos of the natural environment of the hills can happen even to the most experienced of mountaineers – the greatest cause of accidents is the simple slip – and if one should occur to a member of your group, then you will be in a much better position to act appropriately if you set out with a

positive attitude about self-reliance and mutual help amongst walkers. This is an essential first principle and will lead to safer walkers who do not rely on others to get them or their friends out of trouble. Assessing the situation and making informed judgements about what to do are part of this. If it is possible to aid the casualty down the hill without risk of further injury to them or those helping, then it should be attempted. It will also depend on the weather, the terrain, the time available and the distance from other help. Even in Glen Coe it could be five hours before help arrives.

If the casualty cannot be moved for fear of aggravating the injury or increasing shock, or in the event of spinal injuries, then they should be made comfortable (bivi bag or other shelter and insulated from the ground), their location on the map verified, and if there is some urgency, someone should go for help whilst another person stays with the casualty. If the party only comprises two people it is best to stay with the casualty and see if there is a chance of signalling for help. The International Distress Signal may attract attention (light or whistle): six long blasts in quick succession followed by a one minute pause, then repeated over and over again until help arrives. Only when it is urgent should the casualty be left.

Being forced to make such decisions can be very frightening when you are unprepared. You owe it to yourself and your companions to be better informed about emergency first aid. Attend a mountain first aid course, or at the very least one sutable for health and safety at work.

When a member of the party has gone for help, they should contact the police in the first instance (by telephone dial free on 999) and give details of the location of the casualty (6 figure grid reference), a description of the location, the accident and the time it occurred, the name of the casualty and next of kin, and the nature of the injuries. The police will instigate appropriate rescue through voluntary ground teams or RAF or naval helicopters if conditions allow and it is thought essential.

Leaving details of your route

Some walkers may like to leave details of their route with someone with the intention of helping the rescue services know where
to start searching should an accident occur. You could leave
'route cards' giving details of the actual route being considered,
the number in the party, their experience and the equipment
carried, with a responsible adult (family, friend). If you are far
from home and wish to leave such details with the landlady of
your B&B, hostel or bunkhouse owner, etc. then only do so if
those persons are prepared to accept such responsibility and
only after agreement as to when they should raise the alarm.
Remember that non-walkers or climbers may become unduly
worried when you are not back at a specified time when in fact
your day just took longer than anticipated and you are not
actually in any distress. It is best not to be too tied to a schedule
in this way, so allowing you to feel free to decide to change
objective during the trip or even when on the hill if you wish.

Mobile phones

These are being carried by more and more walkers nowadays
as a safety back-up in case of accidents. They will undoubtedly
save time in instigating a rescue, but they should not be relied
upon as they require line-of-sight to a transmitter to operate.
There are many areas of Scotland where the topography of the
hills means this is impossible and they will not work; most
corries for example. There have also been instances of walkers
abusing the use of mobile phones by calling the rescue services
for trivial reasons. Mountain Rescue Teams and the mountaineering representative bodies urge walkers to use their phones
only when emergency help is required and not for general
information or for help for anything less than an emergency.

Getting information in Scotland

There are many courses in all aspects of walking and mountaineering available from a variety of sources. There are numerous

clubs which offer a friendly environment in which to gain experience. The Mountaineering Council of Scotland, the national representative body for walking, mountaineering, climbing and x-country skiing in Scotland, offers an information service to members and non-members. Benefits of membership include cheap skills courses (winter and navigation) at the National Outdoor Training Centre, Glenmore Lodge, and mountain first aid courses. Similar benefits are offered by the British Mountaineering Council for those living in England and Wales and the Mountaineering Council of Ireland, in Eire and Northern Ireland.

Weather Information

At the time of writing the following weather information is available from the Met Office (Web page www. metoffice.com) which should be visited in case there have been subsequent changes:

West Highlands covering the areas of the Trossachs, Argyll, Lochaber, the north-west Highlands and Skye – MetFAX 09060 100 405 (£1 per minute) Premium rate phone 09068 500441 (60p per minute)

East Highlands covering the areas of the Grampian mountains east of Rannoch Moor and including the Cairngorms – MetFAX 09060 100 406 (£1 per minute) Premium rate phone 09068 500442 (60p per minute)

BBC TV Scotland: Mountaineering forecasts follow selected news broadcasts.

Radio Forecasts:
BBC Radio Scotland 92.4–94.7 FM; regular coverage following selected news broadcasts.
Nevis Community Radio 96.6 FM; regular reports 7 a.m.–9.35 a.m. including avalanche risk in winter.

Moray Firth Independent Radio 96.6–97.4 give general
weather forecasts after each news bulletin.

Avalanche Information
At present the Scottish Avalanche Information Service
(SAIS) is available by telephone on 01479 861363. The
SportScotland Avalanche Co-ordinator is Blyth Wright Tel.
01479 861264.
The five avalanche forecast areas are: Glencoe, Lochaber,
Creag Meagaidh, Northern Cairngorms and Southern
Cairngorms.

Bibliography
Avalanche Awareness by Epp and Lee
The Handbook of Climbing by A Fyffe and I Peter
Mountaincraft and Leadership by E Langmuir
Mountain Hazards by Walker
Mountain Navigation Techniques by Walker
Safety on Mountains by BMC
Safety on the Hills by Walker
Scotland's Winter Mountains by M Moran
Weather for Hillwalkers and Climbers by Thomas
The Hillwalker's Handbook by Ashton
Mountain Navigation by P Cliff
Mountain Weather by D Pedgley
A Chance in a Million (Scottish Avalanches) by Barton
The Basic Essentials of Hypothermia by Forgey
Emergency Medical Procedures for the Outdoors
First Aid on Mountains (BMC) by Bollen
Medical Handbook for Mountaineers by Steele
Mountaineering First Aid by Mitchell

Useful addresses

The following entries are correct at the time of writing but as Telephone and Fax numbers, in particular, seem to change on a regular basis it would be wise to check them as required.

The Mountaineering Council of Scotland
The Old Granary, West Mill Street, Perth PH1 5QP
Tel. 01738 638 227. Fax. 01738 442 980

British Mountaineering Council
177–179 Burton Road, West Didsbury, Manchester M20 2BB.
Tel. 0870 010 4838

The Ramblers Association (Scotland)
Kingfisher House, Auld Mark Business Park, Milnathort, Kinross. Tel. 01577 861222. Fax. 01577 861333

Scottish Youth Hostels Association
National Office, 7 Glebe Cresent, Stirling FK8 2JA
Tel. 01786 891400. Fax. 01786 891350

Scottish Natural Heritage (Publications)
The Pubications Officer, Battleby, Redgarton, Perth PH1 5EW
Tel. 01738 444177. Fax. 01738 458613

The Scottish Tourist Board
28, Ravelstone Terrace, Edinburgh EH4 3TP
Tel. 0131 332 2433. Fax. 0131 343 1513

National Trust for Scotland
28 Charlotte Square, Edinburgh EH2 4ET
Tel. 0131 243 9300

John Muir Trust
41 Commercial Street, Edinburgh EH6 6JD
Tel. 0131 554 0114. Fax. 0131 555 2112

Scottish Wildlife Trust
Cramond House, Cramond Glebe Road, Edinburgh EH4 6NS
Tel. 0131 312 7765. Fax. 0131 312 8745

The Scottish Rights of Way Society
24 Annandale Street, Edinburgh EH7 4AN
Tel. 0131 558 1222

Glenmore Lodge National Outdoor Training Centre
Glenmore, Aviemore, Inverness-shire PH22 1AV
Tel. 01479 861248. Fax. 01479 861212

Scottish Mountain Leader Training Board
Glenmore, Aviemore, Inverness-shire PH22 1QU
Tel. 01479 861248

Caledonian MacBrayne Ferries
Head Office: The Ferry Terminal, Gourock PA19 1QP
General enquiries Tel. 01475 650100. Fax. 01475 635235.
Car Ferry reservations Tel. 08705 650000. Fax. 01475 635235.

Munro's classification of the Peaks

Classified lists of all the Scottish Peaks were worked out by the late Sir Hugh T. Munro and are known as Munro's Tables. The complete Munro's Tables with explanatory notes appear in 'MUNRO'S TABLES', published by the Scottish Mountaineering Trust, the volume also contains sections covering the 'CORBETTS'. the 'DONALDS' and the 'GRAHAMS' and should be consulted by readers who are interested in the subject.

There are two arrangements, the first according to districts and the second in order of altitude. Both give the O.S. 1:50000 series map number and the former also gives the map reference of each top.

The number of Scottish Peaks whose height exceeds 914 metres (or 3000 feet) is surprisingly large. If the islands off the west coast of the mainland are included, according to the 1997 edition, there are 284 separate mountains and some 511 tops in all rising above this altitude.

The reason for this distinct classification is that one mountain may have two or three tops and yet be part of the same range. For instance Carn Mor Dearg to the east of Ben Nevis is 1220 metres high and the culminating southerly point of a lofty ridge running roughly north-south. To the north of this summit is an excrescence on the ridge known as Carn Dearg Mead-honach, 1179 metres. This point rises above the general line of the ridge sufficiently to warrant its being named and is known as a separate top. Carn Mor Dearg is the ninth highest mountain but only the eleventh top, the other being the twenty-first top.

Heights of some Scottish Peaks referred to in this book arranged in order of altitude over 914 metres: A = separate mountain; B = top. Heights are given in metres; c denotes a contour.

A	B	Height	Name	Group or District
1	1	1344	Ben Nevis	Lochaber
2	2	1309	Ben Macdui	Cairngorms
3	3	1296	Braeriach	Cairngorms
4	4	1291	Cairn Toul	Cairngorms
5	6	1258	Sgor an Lochain Uaine – The Angels' Peak	Cairngorms
6	7	1244	Cairn Gorm	Cairngorms
7	8	1234	Aonach Beag	Lochaber
8	9	1221	Aonach Mor	Lochaber
	10	1221	Carn Dearg	Lochaber
9	11	1220	Carn Mor Dearg	Lochaber
	12	1215	Cairn Lochan	Cairngorms
11	15	1197	Beinn a'Bhuird-North Top	Cairngorms
	16	1184	Sron na Lairige	Cairngorms
13	18	1182	Beinn Mheadhoin	Cairngorms
	21	1179	Carn Dearg Meadhonach	Lochaber
	23	1176	Stob Coire an t-Sneachda	Cairngorms
16	24	1174	Ben More	Perthshire
18	27	1165	Stob Binnein (Stobinian)	Perthshire
20	29	1155	Derry Cairngorm	Cairngorms
21	30	1155	Cac Carn Beag	Lochnagar
23	32	1150	Bidean nam Bian	Glen Coe
27	41	1130	Binnein Mor	Mamores
28	42	1130	Ben Lui	Agylll-Perth Boundary
30	44	1128	Creag Meagaidh	Loch Laggan
31	45	1126	Ben Cruachan	Argyll
	49	1120	Carn Etchachan	Cairngorms
	56	1115	Stob Coire nan Lochan	Glen Coe
	62	1110c	Sron Riach	Cairngorms

45	65	1108	Meall a'Bhuiridh	Black Mount
	67	1107	Stob Coire nam Beith	Glen Coe
	71	1104	Stob Dearg-Taynuilt Peak	Cruachan
50	75	1100	Creise	Black Mount
	77	1099	Clach Leathad	Black Mount
51	78	1099	Sgurr a'Mhaim	Mamores
55	83	1090	Stob Ghabhar	Black Mount
	89	1083	Cuidhe Crom	Lochnagar
63	97	1078	Ben Starav	Loch Etive
	109	1068	Stob Coire an Lochain	Stobinian
70	110	1067	Sgurr Fhuaran	Kintail
72	112	1062	Bidein a'Ghlas Thuill	An Teallach
73	115	1060	Sgurr Fiona	An Teallach
75	118	1055	Spidean a'Choire Leith	Liathach
83	131	1047	Carn an t-Sagairt Mor	Lochnagar
	132	1047	Corrag Bhuidhe	An Teallach
	140	1044	Carn an t-Sagairt Beag	Lochnagar
95	151	1037	Carn a'Mhaim	Cairngorms
99	156	1032	Am Bodach	Mamores
	160	1030c	Lord Berkeley's Seat	An Teallach
105	168	1027	Sgurr na Ciste Duibhe	Kintail
107	171	1024	Sgorr Dhearg	B.a'Bheithir
108	172	1023	Mullach an Rathain	Liathach
110	175	1021	Stob Dearg – Buachaille Etive Mor	Glen Coe
	183	1017	Sgurr Creag an Eich	An Teallach
120	193	1010	Ruadh-stac Mor	Beinn Eighe
121	194	1010	The Saddle	Kintail
	197	1009	Drochaid Glas	Cruachan
130	207	1004	The Devil's Point	Cairngorms
134	213	1002	Sgurr na Carnach	Kintail
	218	1001	Sgor an Iubhair	Mamores
137	219	1001	Sgorr Dhonuill	B.a'Bheithir
140	225	999	Stob Ban	Mamores
141	227	998	Ben More Assynt	Assynt

143	231	998	Stob Diamh	Cruachan
	237	996	Stob a'Ghlais Choire	Black Mount
154	247	992	Sgurr Alasdair	Skye Cuillin
	250	990	Sgurr nan Spainteach	Kintail
162	260	986	Sgurr Mhor	Beinn Alligin
164	263	986	Inaccessible Pinnacle – Sgurr Dearg	Skye Cuillin
166	268	982	An Gearanach	Mamores
170	273	981	Slioch – North Top	Loch Maree
	276	980	Meikle Pap	Lochnagar
	277	980	Sail Mhor	Beinn Eighe
	278	980	Stob Garbh	Cruachan
	280	979	Glas Mheall Mor	An Teallach
	285	978	Sgurr Thearlaich	Skye Cuillin
	288	976	Coinneach Mhor	Beinn Eighe
183	296	974	Beinn Sgritheall (Sgriol)	Kintail
	298	974	Meall Coire na Saobhaidhe	Lochnagar
185	303	973	Sgurr a'Ghreadaidh	Skye Cuillin
	307	970	Sgurr Ban	Beinn Eighe
188	315	967	Sgor nam Fiannaidh	Aonach Eagach
	317	966	Meall na Dige	Stobinian
	318	966	Sron an Isean	Cruachan
190	319	965	Sgurr na Banachdich	Skye Cuillin
191	320	964	Sgurr nan Gillean	Skye Cuillin
	324	963	Sgurr na Forcan	Saddle
	325	963	Sgurr nan Fhir Duibhe	Beinn Eighe
193	326	963	Sgurr Thuilm	Glenfinnan
	335	960	Glas Mheall Liath	An Teallach
	337	960	Stob Cadha Gobhlach	An Teallach
200	342	958	Bruach na Frithe	Skye Cuillin
201	345	958	Stob Dubh – Buachaille Etive Beag	Glen Coe
	360	954	Sail Liath	An Teallach
212	364	953	Meall Dearg	Aonach Eagach
	367	952	Beinn Fhada	Glen Coe

217	373	948	Sgurr Mhic Choinnich	Skye Cuillin
	377	947	Sgorr Bhan	B.a'Bheithir
	378	947	Sgurr Sgumain	Skye Cuillin
226	387	945	Stob a'Choire Odhair	Black Mount
	390	943	Am Bodach	Aonach Eagach
	404	940	Stob Coire Leith	Aonach Eagach
	421	935	Sgurr a'Fionn Choire	Skye Cuillin
242	423	934	Am Basteir	Skye Cuillin
	425	934	Sgurr an Tuill Bhain	Slioch
252	441	928	Bla Bheinn (Blaven)	Skye
	447	927	Am Fasarinen	Liathach
256	449	927	Ben Hope	Sutherland
	459	926	Sgurr Thormaid	Skye Cuillin
265	464	924	Sgurr nan Eag	Skye Cuillin
268	470	922	Tom na Gruagaich	Beinn Alligin
	487	912	Meall Cuanail	Cruachan
277	490	918	Sgurr a'Mhadaidh	Skye Cuillin
281	502	916	Beinn a'Chleibh (Clee)	Ben Lui
	503	916	'Bhasteir Tooth	Skye Cuillin

Although the heights over 914 metres shown above may not agree with those shown on current O.S. maps, they have been used throughout the book as a constant.

Glossary of Scottish place-names

Sassenachs usually find some difficulty in understanding and pronouncing the various Gaelic names given to many of the different topographical features in the Highlands, while several of those in Skye have always been an insoluble enigma because their spelling is frequently obscure and their correct pronunciation most perplexing. When it is realised for instance that Mhadaidh is pronounced *Vatee* or Thuilm *Hulim*, or even the more common Dearg *Jerrag*, it will be obvious that unless the speaker is familiar with the Gaelic tongue he is scarcely ever understood by the native. The position, however, is further complicated by the number of apparently correct spellings for one and the same place; the Cuillin, for example, may be spelt in a variety of ways, all of which would seem to be acceptable to the Gaelic scholar. I have therefore included a short list which I hope will be useful to visitors, but should any of them desire further information I would refer them to my *Magic of Skye* which contains an extensive monograph on Nomenclature.

Aber, Abar, Obar, mouth or confluence of a river
Abhainn, Ambuinn, river. Usually *Avon*.
Achadh, field, park. Usually *Ach*.
Ailean, a green place; plain
Airidh, sheiling
Aisir, a rocky defile or pass
Allt, burn, brook, stream. Conventional forms: *Ald, Alt, Auld, Ault*

Aoineadh, a steep promontory or brae
Aonach, a height, a ridge
Ard, Aird, a high point, promontory
Ath, a ford; also a kiln
Avon, conventional form of *Abhainn*, q.v.

Baile, town. Usually *Bal, Bali*
Ban, white, fair.

Barp, conical heap of stones, a chambered cairn

Barr, a point, top, extremity.

Bard, a poet, a dyke, enclosure, ward

Beag, little, small. Conventional form, *Beg*

Bealach, breach, pass, gap, col

Beinn, a mountain. Conventional form, *Ben*

Beith, a birch tree

Bian, a hide (of cattle)

Bidean, a pinnacle

Binnean, or *Binnein*, a pinnacle or little mountain

Blar, a plain, battlefield

Bo, plural *Ba*, cow, cows

Bodach, an old man, hobgoblin, spectre

Both, Bothan, a hut, booth or bothy

Braigh, top, summit. Usually *Brae, Bread*

Bruaich, a bank, brae, brim, steep place

Buachaille, a herdsman, a shepherd

Buidhe, yellow, golden coloured

Cadha, a pass, steep path

Cailleach, a nun, old woman, a witch

Cam, crooked, bent, one-eyed

Camas, bay, bend, channel

Caol, strait, firth, narrow. Other form *Kyle*

Caolas, alternative Gaelic form for the above

Carn, a heap of stones, cairn

Carr, broken ground

Ceann, head, headland. Usually *Ken, Kin*

Ceo fog, mist

Ceum, a step

Cill, a cell, church. Usually *Kil*

Cioch, a pap, woman's breast

Clach, a stone

Clachan, stones, hamlet

Cladh, a churchyard, a burying place.

Clais, a hollow

Cleit, a ridge, reef; rocky eminence

Cluain, a field pasture, green plain, meadow

Cnap, a knob, hillock

Cnoc, a knoll. Usually *Knock*

Coill or *Coille*, a wood, forest

Coire, a cauldron, kettle, circular hollow. Other form *Corry* or *Corrie*

Creag, a rock, cliff. English form: *Craig*

Crioch, boundary, frontier, landmark

Cro, a sheep-fold, pen

Crom, bent, sloping, crooked

Cruach, stack, heap, haunch
Cul, the back, a nook

Dail, a field. In Norse, a dale
Dearg, red
Doire, grove, hollow
Druim, the back, ridge.
    Usually *Drem, Drom, Drum*
Dubh, black, dark. Other
    form: *Dhu*
Dun, a fort, castle, heap

Eagach, notched
Ear, east
Eas, a waterfall. Other form:
    Easach, a cascade
Easg, bog, fen, natural ditch
Eilean, an island

Fad, long, e.g., *Bienn Fhada*,
    long mountain
Feadan, narrow glen
Fearn, an alder tree
Feith, bog, sinewy stream, a
    vein
Fiadh, a deer
Fuaran, a perennial spring,
    well

Garadh, a fence, dike, garden
Garbh, rough. Other spelling,
    Garve
Gearr, short
Geal, white, clear, bright
Gearanach, a wall-like ridge

Geodha, a narrow creek,
    chasm, rift, cove
Ghabhar or *Gobhar*, a goat
Glac, a hollow, dell, defile
Glais, a stream, burn
Glas, grey, pale, wan; green
Gleann, narrow valley, dale,
    dell; usually *Glen*
Gob, point, beak
Gorm, blue, azure, green
Gualann, shoulder of a
    mountain or hill

I, an island
Inbhir, confluence, place at
    the meeting of river and
    sea. Other form: *Inver*, c.f.
    Aber
Iubhair, yew tree

Kyle, see *Caol* and *Caolas*

Lag, a hollow in a hill.
    Usually *Logan, Logie*
Lairig, the sloping face of a
    hill, a pass
Leathad, a slope, declivity
Leathan, broad
Leithir, a slope
Liath, grey
Linne, pool, sound, channel
Loch, a lake, arm of the sea
Lochan, small loch
Lon, a marsh, morass
Lub, a bend, fold, curvature

Mam, a round or gently rising hill

Maol, headland, bald top, cape

Meadhon, middle, central

Meall, knob, lump, rounded hill

Moine or *Mointeach*, moss-land, mossy

Monadh, moor, heath, hill, mountain

Mor, great, large, tall. English form: *More*

Muileann, mill

Muir, the sea

Mullach, a rounded hill

Odhar, dapple, drab, dun-coloured, sallow

Ord, a round, steep or conical hill

Os, outlet of a lake or river

Pit or *Pet*, farm, hollow

Poll, a pool, pond, pit

Rathad, a road, way

Reidh, plain, level, smooth

Riabhach, drab, greyish, brindled, grizzled. Other form: *Riach*

Roinn, a point, headland, peninsula

Ros, a point, promontory. Other form: *Ross*

Ruadh, red, reddish

Rudha, promontory. Usually *Ru, Rhu, Row*

Ruigh, a run for cattle, shieling, land sloping

Sail, a heel

Sean, old, aged, ancient

Sgorr or *Sgurr*, a peak, conical sharp rock. Sometimes *Scaur*

Sgreamach, rocky

Sith, a fairy. *Sithean*, a fairy hillock or knoll

Slochd, a deep hollow

Sneachd, snow

Socach, snout

Srath, a valley, plain beside a river, strath

Sron, nose, peak, promontory. Other form: *Strone*

Sruth, a stream, current. Usually *Struan*

Stac, a steep rock, conical hill

Stob, a point

Stuc, a pinnacle, peak, conical steep rock

Suidhe, sitting, resting place

Taigh or *Tigh*, a house. Usually *Tay, Ty*

Tairbeart, an isthmus. Other form: *Tarbet, Tarbert*

Tir, country, region, land. Other form: *Tyr*

Tobar, a well, spring, fountain. Usually *Tober*

Tom, a hillock, mound

Torr, a mound, heap, hill

Tulach, knoll, hillock, eminence. Anglicized forms: *Tilly, Tully, Tulloch*

Uachdar, upper-land. Usually *Auchter, Ochter*

Uaine, green

Uamh, a cave, a grave

Uchd, ascent, face of a hill

Uig, a nook, bay

Uisage, water, rain.

The Scottish centres

Accommodation and travel

In the following list I have given the principal centres of accommodation from which the Scottish Peaks cited in this book may be most conveniently reached. It should be borne in mind that in the remote parts of mainland Scotland, particularly in the north-west, accommodation can be scarce and the nearest available may be a considerable distance from the starting point for reaching your mountain. It is therefore not surprising that camping is much favoured by walkers and in regions such as the Coigach Peaks a centrally placed camp would facilitate access to the surrounding hills and save time compared with staying in Ullapool which is at least 15 miles/24 km distant.

Walking and climbing tourism is now recognised as generating a large amount of income for remote communities and as a result the development of suitable accommodation is increasing. The options are:

Bunkhouses

There is now a good network of privately run low-cost accommodation throughout Scotland, including may of the islands, in the form of basic but comfortable bunkhouses. They offer either shared dormitory-style bunk-beds or family and small-sized rooms.

Information is available in the excellent publication *The Independent Hostel Guide*. This is available in shops or from the Mountaineering Council of Scotland (MCofS). The Gatcliff Trust operate a series of bunkhouses on the islands.

Youth Hostels

The Scottish Youth Hostels Association operates numerous hostels throughout Scotland. They are open to members of the association.

Hotels, and B&B guest houses

Up until the 1960s the most readily available accommodation in many areas of the Highlands was in hotels. Some of these were much frequented by walkers and climbers and even today still have strong associations with mountaineers. In some areas of the north-west hotels offer the only option besides camping or guest houses. One of the problems with many B&Bs and hotels has been that they do not offer the facilities required by walkers (drying rooms for wet clothes, early breakfast, packed lunch and late evening meal options, local information on walks and weather or a pick-up point service for walkers without their own transport). The Scottish Tourist Board, in association with the Mountaineering Council of Scotland and The Ramblers (Scotland), have started a 'Walkers Welcome' scheme to encourage proprietors to offer these facilities. The scheme started in 1997. Look out for the Walkers Welcome sign when booking accommodation. Details are available from Tourist Information Centres or from the MCofS Information Service.

Huts

Many of the mountaineering and walking clubs in Scotland operate huts for their own members and individual members of the MCofS and BMC. Membership details and details of over 25 such huts can be obtained from the MCofS in Scotland or the BMC in England.

Where to base yourself

I have arranged the Routes in this guide from south to north of the Highlands, beginning with Arran and ending with Ben Loyal, thence followed by the Cairngorms and finally by the Cuillin of Skye. For convenience of reference I have followed the same plan for describing the nearest centres to each range of hills. (N.B. Scottish Tourist Board Tourist Information Centres are abbreviated to TIC.)

The Isle of Arran is reached by Caledonian MacBrayne passenger and car ferry from Ardrossan on the Ayrshire coast, south of Glasgow, to Brodick on the island. Another ferry operates from Lochranza in the north of the island to Claonaig on the Kintyre Peninsula of Argyll (summer only). Hotel and B&B accommodation abounds on Arran as it has traditionally catered for the holiday plans of Glaswegians. On summer weekends these can all be fully booked. Contact the TIC in Brodick for details and bookings. Tel. 01770 302 140. There are a few bunkhouses; Corrie Croft in High Corrie below Goat Fell is the most useful. Wild camping is possible in some of the remote glens and there is a good formal campsite at the base of Glen Rosa at the start of many of the walks. There are Youth Hostels at Lochranza in the north and Whiting Bay in the south.

Ben Arthur (the Cobbler) is best reached from Arrochar, where there is a hotel and guest houses and which can be reached by rail from Glasgow. There is a good campsite operated by the Forestry Commission at Ardgarten at the base of the hill and a Youth Hostel here too. This is only 4 miles/6.4 km from Arrochar. The Inverarnan Hotel, 12 miles/19.3 km distant at the head of Loch Lomond, has been a traditional stopping-off point for walkers. For the local TIC at Arrochar tel. 01301 702 432.

The Crianlarich Peaks comprising Ben More and Stob Binnein are most easily reached from Crianlarich, which is itself easily reached by rail from Glasgow. There is a Youth Hostel here and a Scottish Club Hut. The hills can be reached from Balquhidder, on Loch Voil to their south, where there are two hotels. The Kingshouse Hotel on the A82 near Balquhidder has a Ramblers' Bar.

Ben Lui is usually gained from either Tyndrum or Dalmally, each of which can be reached by rail. There is a formal campsite at Tyndrum which even has an indoor swimming pool next door. The hotels here are large and expensive. For the TIC in Tyndrum tel. 01838 400 246.

Ben Cruachan may be most conveniently ascended from the village of Lochawe on the banks of the loch of the same name. The nearest railway station is Dalmally on the Glasgow to Oban line and there is a regular bus service between the two. There are guest houses and hotels in Lochawe and Dalmally. If based further afield in Oban to the west or Tyndrum to the east, then private transport would probably be required. Oban is a fairly large town with all amenities. Tyndrum has a campsite (with an indoor swimming pool!), several cafés and hotels. Over the Pass of Brander towards Oban, is a large caravan and campsite with an excellent café cum restaurant open late into the evening in summer.

The Black Mount is reached from the south from the Inveroran Hotel, on Loch Tulla, and the Bridge of Orchy Hotel on the A82, 3 miles/4.8 km distant. The Bridge of Orchy can be reached by rail and the hotel operates a bunkhouse and has a great bar offering good food. From the north, the Kingshouse Hotel, on Rannoch Moor, offers excellent accommodation, climbers' bar and food.

Buachaille Etive Mor is just opposite the Kingshouse Hotel. There are also Scottish Club Huts in nearby Glen Etive.

Bidean nam Bian and Aonach Eagach are best approached from the Glen Coe side. The Clachaig Inn sits at the west end of the Aonach Eagach and has excellent climbers' facilities, bar, food etc. They often run mountaineering events and slide shows through the winter and have an excellent selection of 'real ale' and a real ale festival every year. There is a Youth Hostel in Glen Coe and several campsites including the Red Squirrel (which also has a bunkhouse) next to the hostel, half a mile/0.8 km from the Clachaig Inn. Camping 'wild' next to the Clachaig Inn in summer is now banned due to pollution problems. When staying in any of these, transport to the upper part of the glen would be an advantage – there being no local bus service.

Beinn a'Bheithir overshadows the Ballachulish Hotel near the Ballachulish Bridge over Loch Leven. There is ample self-catering cottage accommodation in the area, open year round. There is also an MCofS/BMC Hut in North Ballachulish (over the bridge) and several Club Huts in the area. A bunkhouse can be found in nearby Onich, but these are some distance from the hill and transport would be needed.

Garbh Bheinn rises in Ardgour, the region to the west of Loch Linnhe, and is best reached by car ferry from Onich to Corran on the other side. Sailings are every hour or so; more frequent and running later in summer. From the ferry it is over 6 miles/9.7 km to the starting point of the walk. There is little accommodation closer than Onich or the hotel at Corran.

The Mamores form an extensive range of hills between Loch Leven and Glen Nevis, and its eastern peaks are best reached from Kinlochleven. This village is undergoing dramatic changes with the closure of the large aluminium smelter. Plans are afoot to establish better facilities for walkers, including bunkhouse, bar and information centre. At present little exists. The western peaks of the Mamores are better reached from Glen Nevis. This involves a 6 mile/9.7 km walk down the glen from Fort William. There is a bus service in summer. There are formal campsites, bunkhouses and Scottish Club Huts in Glen Nevis as well as a Youth Hostel, concentrated in the lower half of the glen; also numerous self-catering and B&B cottages/flats in Fort William. The TIC can help with the latter, tel. 01397 703 738.

Ben Nevis dominates Fort William and the accommodation available is described above, apart from the famous CIC Hut (belonging to the Scottish Mountaineering Club) in the northern corrie of the Ben itself.

Creag Meagaidh rises to the north-west of Loch Laggan between Spean Bridge and Newtonmore. There are hotels, including the backpackers' hotel, at Roy Bridge some 12 miles/19.3 km west of the hill. There is also a bunkhouse at Tarsit a little nearer and two Scottish Club Huts 12 miles/19.3 km to the east. Creag Meaghaidh is a National Nature Reserve but there are no restrictions on access.

The Saddle flanks the south side of Glen Shiel on the road towards Kyle of Lochalsh. Its northern spur can be approached easily from Shiel Bridge where there is accommodation at the Kintail Lodge Hotel at the head of Loch Duich or the Youth Hostel on the south shore of Loch Duich at Ratagan. However, the usual approach is up the Forcan Ridge at the south-eastern end, entailing a drive 3 miles/4.8 km up the glen.

The Five Sisters of Kintail flank the northern side of Glen Shiel and since its terminal peak overlooks Loch Duich, it may be approached from any of the accommodation given for the Saddle. If the traverse is to be done from east to west then there is the Cluanie Inn at the east end. The TIC at Portree on Skye may have information about other accommodation: tel. 01478 612 137.

Beinn Bhan forms the main mass of the Applecross penin-sula north of the Kyle of Lochalsh. This is the land of the single-track road with passing places. It can best be reached from a base in either Lochcarron to the south, where there is a hotel (or a bunkhouse further afield at Achnashellach Station), or Torridon to the north where there are local hotels and B&Bs – see **Beinn Damh** below. Lochcarron can be reached by rail from Inverness. There are then local bus services but the best form of public transport is the post-bus which interconnects every village in the area. Contact the Gairloch TIC for accom-modation details, tel. 01445 712 130.

Beinn Damh, Liathach and Beinn Alligin are all clustered around the head of the sea-loch, Upper Loch Torridon. A base in or around Torridon or Shieldaig is best. The Loch Torridon Hotel lies at the base of Beinn Damh and the path to the hill starts from its very doors. It has a good bar with food and a bunkhouse. One mile away in Torridon village is a Youth Hostel with a campsite and there are many cottages for rent or B&Bs. There is also a good campsite at Shieldaig in a most

stunning position. Beinn Alligin sits on the north shore of
Upper Loch Torridon and there are numerous self-catering
cottages in the small villages of Inveralligin, Alligin Shuas and
Diabaig from which a short drive leads to the car-park at the
bridge over the Abhainn Coire Mhic Nobuil which is the
starting point for the ascent. A post-bus covers the area
between Diabaig and Torridon. Contact the Gairloch TIC for
accommodation details, tel. 01445 712 130 or the Inverness TIC,
tel. 01463 234 353.

Beinn Eighe rises to the west of Kinlochewe and may be
ascended by a path that turns off left from the road beyond the
village. There is a campsite. The Kinlochewe Hotel offers the
usual accommodation and also a bunkhouse. Midway on the
road between Torridon and Kinlochewe, near the head of Glen
Torridon itself, a path leads north through Coire Dubh Mor
round the west side of the hill and into the spectacular Coire
Mhic Fhearchair. Ling Hut, a Scottish Club Hut, is near the car-
park.

Slioch lies north-west of Kinlochewe and is approached from
there.

An Teallach can be conveniently approached only from
Dundonnell to its north. The peak is best reached by a stalkers'
path that starts near the Dundonnell Hotel which offers the
only bar and food for miles. There is also a bunkhouse nearby
which is excellent.

Ben Mór Coigach, Stac Pollaidh, Cul Beag and Cul Mor are
all fairly close together, 5–10 miles/8–16 km north of Ullapool.
Ullapool is a sizeable 'town' for the north-west and as it is the
sailing point for the ferry to Stornoway on the Outer Hebrides,
it is well served by coaches from Inverness. There are hotels
and many B&Bs, a campsite in the centre of the town and a
Youth Hostel. There is also a good campsite at Ardmair just
north of Ullapool from which Ben Mór Coigach is within
walking distance. This peak can also be approached from
Achiltibuie to the north-west. A long drive along single-track

roads leads to this, the longest village in Scotland, which also has a small inn which looks like a regular house. There are a few cottages for rent. Stac Pollaidh, Cul Beag and Cul Mor all require transport to reach the starts of the routes although the last can be reached on foot easily from the village of Elphin. There is also a privately run hut here. The Inverness TIC will supply other accommodation options, tel. 01463 234 353. This is also true of the north-west areas described below.

Suilven can most easily be reached from Lochinver on the west coast. The usual hotel, guest house and self-catering accommodation exists. The nearest Youth Hostel is at Achmelvich, 4 miles/6.4 km west of Lochinver.

Quinag is too far away from any of the centres of accommodation to be reached on foot so a car is a necessity. The hotel at Inchnadamph is the closest, or accommodation in Lochinver.

Foinaven rises to the east of Rhiconich where the hotel offers accommodation and bar food. Other forms of accommodation are few and far between although there are good campsites at Scourie, Shiegra and Durness. There is also a Youth Hostel at Durness next to the famous Smoo Caves.

Ben Hope may be reached by a wild moorland single-track road from Altnahara, which has a surprisingly good hotel.

Ben Loyal rises to the south of Tongue. There is hotel accommodation and a campsite from which the peak can be reached on foot.

Lochnagar may be most conveniently reached from Ballater where there are several hotels, guest houses and a Youth Hostel. But since it is some 13 miles/21 km distant the return walk would be an extremely long and tiring day with most of the walking along the road up Glen Muick. With transport, a car can be left at the Spittal of Glenmuick thus saving 9 miles/14.5 km. It should be noted, however, that on a summer weekend this dead-end single-track road can become gridlocked. Braemar is a possible alternative, which has two hotels and a bunkhouse and a Youth Hostel. The walk from the car-park, however, is longer than from Glen Muick. Braemar TIC can be contacted on tel. 013397 41600.

Ben Macdui may also be reached from Braemar or from Inverey. The peak stands within the Mar Lodge estate which has recently been acquired by the National Trust for Scotland. Mar Lodge itself used to offer bedroom accommodation to walkers many years ago and there are intentions to do so again in the future. If so then this would be the closest option. Another approach is from the chair-lift on Cairn Gorm to the north, reached by car from Aviemore. Accommodation on the way to Cairn Gorm, at Glenmore, includes a Forestry Commission campsite beside Loch Morlich, a Youth Hostel and B&B at Glenmore Lodge National Outdoor Training Centre (where there is also a bar).

The Lairig Ghru starts at Derry Lodge on the walk to Ben Macdui and finishes either near Glenmore or nearer Aviemore. The suggested accommodation for both Ben Macdui and Cairn Gorm are applicable for either end.

Cairn Gorm is easily reached along the Glenmore road from Aviemore by car to the ski area car-park. In winter there is a fairly regular bus service for skiers which can be taken advantage of. Accommodation in the Glenmore area is detailed above for Ben Macdui and there is also a Youth Hostel in Aviemore. For those with a car there are many other private bunkhouses in the vicinity of Kingussie and Newtonmore and Scottish Club Huts in the area as well. Aviemore TIC will give other options, tel. 01470 810 363.

The Storr and the Quiraing, Isle of Skye, lie in the north of the island on the Trotternish peninsula and are easily reached by road from Portree, which has ample accommodation from hotels to self-catering cottages and a campsite. The only Youth Hostel in the area, at Uig, is quite a distance away from the Storr but reasonably close to Quiraing. The Flodigarry Hotel is also close by and serves good bar food. A visit to the Storr would be best accomplished by car or from the campsite at

Staffin. The TIC at Portree will give information about local accommodation, tel. 01478 612 137.

The North Cuillin (Sgurr nan Gillian and Bruach na Frithe), Isle of Skye, can be reached from the north at the Kyle of Lochalsh by toll bridge or by ferry from Mallaig to the south. These particular peaks of the Cuillin may be most conveniently approached from the Sligachan Hotel which has been associated with walkers and climbers for many years and serves good food and offers great hospitality. It used to be possible to wild camp on the side of the road nearby but litter and pollution problems mean that this is no longer permitted and a formal campsite has been established. The Youth Hostel at Broadford is rather distant for these peaks without a car.

The South Cuillin (Sgurr Dearg and Sgurr Alasdair) is best ascended from a base at Glen Brittle. Accommodation here consists of a Youth Hostel and a formal campsite, which because of the great distance to the main towns of Portree and Broadford also offers a small shop for essentials. There is an MCofS/BMC Hut here also, which is wardened during the summer months. Sligachan is the nearest hotel.

The Scottish Peaks

74 Routes of ascent

The Arran Hills Map 1

Ben Arthur (The Cobbler) Map 2

The Crianlarich Hills Map 3

Ben Lui Map 4

Ben Cruachan Map 5

The Black Mount Hills Map 6

The Glen Coe Hills Map 7

Buachaille Etive Mor
20 Kingshouse and Stob Dearg

Bidean nam Bian
21 Aonach Dubh and Stob Coire nan Lochan
22 The Dinner Time Buttress
23 Coire nam Beith
24 An t'Sron and Stob Coire nam Beith
25 Allt Coire Gabhail
26 Beinn Fhada and Stob Coire Sgreamhach

Aonach Eagach
27 The Aonach Eagach Traverse

Beinn a'Bheithir Map 8
28 The Beinn a'Bheithir Horseshoe

Garbh Bheinn Map 9
29 By Sgor Mhic Eacharna
30 By Glen Iubhair
31 By Sron a'Gharbh Choire Bhig

The Mamores Map 10
32 Binnein Mor from Kinlochleven
33 Sgurr a'Mhaim from Polldubh
34 Stob Ban from Polldubh

Ben Nevis Map 11
35 By Carn Mor Dearg
36 By Carn Dearg
37 From Achintee

Creag Meagaidh Map 12
38 Creag Meagaidh by Coire Ardair

The Kintail Hills Map 13

The Saddle
39 By Sgurr na Forcan
40 By Sgurr na Creige
41 By Sgurr a'Gharg Gharaidh

The Five Sisters of Kintail
42 The Traverse of the Five Sisters

Beinn Bhan Map 14
43 Beinn Bhan from Bealach na Ba
44 The Corries of Beinn Bhan

Beinn Damh Map 15a
45 Beinn Damh from the Loch Torridon Hotel

Liathach Map 15b
46 The Traverse of Liathach

Beinn Alligin Map 16
47 The Traverse of Beinn Alligin

Beinn Eighe Map 17
48 The Traverse of Beinn Eighe

Slioch Map 18
49 Slioch from Kinlochewe

An Teallach Map 19
50 The Traverse of An Teallach

Ben Mór Coigach Map 20
51 From Drumrunie

Drumrunie and Inverpolly Peaks Map 21

Cul Beag
52 From Drumrunie
53 From Linneraineach

Quiraing Map 31
69 Quiraing from Staffin
70 Meall na Suiramach from Staffin

The Cuillin Map 32

NORTH

Sgurr nan Gillean
71 The Tourist Route from Sligachan

Bruach na Frithe
72 The Ascent from Sligachan

SOUTH

Sgurr Dearg
73 The Ascent from Glen Brittle

Sgurr Alasdair
74 The Ascent from Glen Brittle

MAPS
The Arran Hills

OS 1:50 000 Landranger map	No 69 Isle of Arran
OS 1:25 000 Outdoor Leisure map	No 37 Isle of Arran
Harveys 1:40 000 Walker's map	Arran North
Harveys 1:25 000 Superwalker	Arran North

Ben Arthur

OS 1:50 000 Landranger map	No 56 Inveraray & Loch Lomond
OS 1:25 000 Outdoor Leisure map	No 39 Loch Lomond
Harveys 1:40 000 Walker's map	Arrochar Alps
Harveys 1:25 000 Superwalker	Arrochar Alps

The Crianlarich Peaks

OS 1:50 000 Landranger maps	No 50 Glen Orchy
	No 51 Loch Tay &
	No 56 Inveraray & Loch Lomond

Ben Lui
OS 1:50 000 Landranger map   No 50 Glen Orchy
OS 1:25 000 Outdoor Leisure map   No 38 Ben Nevis & Glen Coe

Ben Cruachan
OS 1:50 000 Landranger map   No 50 Glen Orchy

The Black Mount Hills
OS 1:50 000 Landranger maps   No 50 Glen Orchy
                                    No 51 Ben Nevis & Fort William
OS 1:25 000 Outdoor Leisure map   No 38 Ben Nevis & Glen Coe
Harveys 1:40 000 Walker's map   Glen Coe
Harveys 1:25 000 Superwalker   Glen Coe

Buachaille Etive Mor
OS 1:50 000   No 41 Ben Nevis & Fort William
OS 1:25 000 Outdoor Leisure map   No 38 Ben Nevis & Glen Coe
Harveys 1:40 000 Walker's map   Glen Coe
Harveys 1:25 000 Superwalker   Glen Coe

The Bidean Nam Bian Range
OS 1:50 000 Landranger map   No 41 Ben Nevis & Glen Coe
OS 1:25 000 Outdoor Leisure map   No 38 Ben Nevis & Glen Coe
Harveys 1:40 000 Walker's map   Glen Coe
Harveys 1:25 000 Superwalker   Glen Coe

Aonach Eagach
OS 1:50 000 Landranger map   No 41 Ben Nevis & Glen Coe
OS 1:25 000 Outdoor Leisure map   No 38 Ben Nevis & Glen Coe
Harveys 1:40 000 Walker's map   Glen Coe
Harveys 1:25 000 Superwalker   Glen Coe

Beinn a'Bheithir
OS 1:50 000 Landranger map   No 41 Ben Nevis & No 47 Glen
                                       Coe

The Garbh Bheinn Group
OS 1:50 000 Landranger map   No 40 Mallaig & Loch Shiel

The Mamores
OS 1:50 000 Landranger map   No 41 Ben Nevis & Glen Coe
OS 1:25 000 Outdoor Leisure map   No 38 Ben Nevis & Glen Coe
Harveys 1:40 000 Walker's map   Ben Nevis
Harveys 1:25 000 Superwalker   Ben Nevis

Ben Nevis
OS 1:50 000 Landranger map   No 51 Ben Nevis & Glen Coe
OS 1:25 000 Outdoor Leisure map   No 32 Mountainmaster of Ben
                                             Nevis
OS 1:25 000 Outdoor Leisure map   No 38 Ben Nevis & Glen Coe
Harveys 1:40 000 Walker's map   Ben Nevis
Harveys 1:25 000 Superwalker   Ben Nevis

Creag Meagaidh
OS 1:50 000 Landranger maps   No 34 Fort Augustus & St Albyn
                                          No 35 Kingussie & Monadhliath
                                             Mountains

The Saddle
OS 1:50 000 Landranger map   No 33 Loch Alsh & Glen Shiel

The Five Sisters of Kintail
OS 1:50 000 Landranger map   No 33 Loch Alsh & Glen Shiel

Beinn Bhan
OS 1:50 000 Landranger map   No 24 Raasay, Applecross &
                                             Torridon

Beinn Damh
OS 1:50 000 Landranger map   No 24 Raasay, Applecross &
                                             Torridon
                                          No 25 Glen Carron

Liathach
OS 1:50 000 Landranger maps   No 19 Gairloch & Ullapool
                                     No 24 Raasay, Applecross &
                                         Torridon
                                     No 25 Glen Carron
OS 1:25 000 Outdoor Leisure map   No 8 The Cuillin & Torridon Hills

Beinn Alligin
OS 1:50 000 Landranger map   No 24 Raasay, Applecross &
                                         Torridon
OS 1:25 000 Outdoor Leisure map   No 8 The Cuillin & Torridon Hills

Beinn Eighe
OS 1:50 000 Landranger maps   No 19 Gairloch & Ullapool
                                     No 25 Glen Carron
OS 1:25 000 Outdoor Leisure map   No 8 The Cuillin & Torridon Hills

Slioch
OS 1:50 000 Landranger map   No 19 Gairloch & Ullapool
OS 1:25 000 Outdoor Leisure map   No 8 The Cuillin & Torridon Hills

An Teallach
OS 1:50 000 Landranger map   No 19 Gairloch & Ullapool

Ben Mór Coigach
OS 1:50 000 Landranger map   No 15 Loch Assynt

Cul Beag
OS 1:50 000 Landranger map   No 15 Loch Assynt

Cul Mor
OS 1:50 000 Landranger map   No 15 Loch Assynt

Stac Pollaidh
OS 1:50 000 Landranger map   No 15 Loch Assynt

Suilven
OS 1:50 000 Landranger map   No 15 Loch Assynt

Quinag
OS 1:50 000 Landranger map   No 15 Loch Assynt

Fionaven
OS 1:50 000 Landranger map   No 9 Cape Wrath

Ben Hope
OS 1:50 000 Landranger map   No 9 Cape Wrath

Ben Loyal
OS 1:50 000 Landranger map   No 10 Strathnaver

Lochnagar
OS 1:50 000 Landranger maps   No 43 Braemar to Blair Atholl
                                    No 44 Ballater & Glen Clover
Harveys 1:25 000 Superwalker   Lochnagar

Ben Macdui
OS 1:50 000 Landranger maps   No 36 Grantown, Aviemore &
                                        Cairngorm
                                    No 43 Braemar to Blair Atholl
OS 1:25 000 Outdoor Leisure map   No 3 Aviemore & the Cairngorms
Harveys 1:40 000 Walker's map   Cairn Gorm
Harveys 1:25 000 Superwalker   Cairn Gorm

The Lairig Ghru
OS 1:50 000 Landranger maps   No 36 Grantown, Aviemore &
                                        Cairngorm
                                    No 43 Braemar to Blair Atholl
OS 1:25 000 Outdoor Leisure map   No 3 Aviemore & the Cairngorms
Harveys 1:40 000 Walker's map   Cairn Gorm
Harveys 1:25 000 Superwalker   Cairn Gorm

Cairn Gorm

OS 1:50 000 Landranger map	No 36 Grantown, Aviemore & Cairngorm
OS 1:25 000 Outdoor Leisure map	No 3 Aviemore & the Cairngorms
Harveys 1:40 000 Walker's map	Cairn Gorm
Harveys 1:25 000 Superwalker	Cairn Gorm

The Storr

OS 1:50 000 Landranger map	No 23 North Skye

Quiraing

OS 1:50 000 Landranger map	No 23 North Skye

The Peaks of the North Cuillin

OS 1:50 000 Landranger map	No 32 South Skye
OS 1:25 000 Outdoor Leisure map	No 8 The Cuillin & Torridon Hills
Harveys 1:25 000 Superwalker	Skye: The Cuillin

The Peaks of the South Cuillin

OS 1:50 000 Landranger map	No 32 South Skye
OS 1:25 000 Outdoor Leisure map	No 8 The Cuillin & Torridon Hills
Harveys 1:25 000 Superwalker	Skye: The Cuillin

Mountain photography

I have already written and lectured extensively on this fascinating branch of photography, and in four of my works devoted to Scotland I included copious notes on the problems involved in securing good camera studies of many of the Bens and Glens. But since these books have been out of print for many years, it may be useful to deal more fully with the subject herein, as I have already done in companion volumes on the Lakeland and Welsh Peaks. These notes are written largely for the benefit of keen photographers with an interest in both black and white and in colour photography.

1 **The ideal camera for the mountaineer** is undoubtedly the modern miniature owing to its compact form, quick manipulation, great depth of focus, variable zoom lenses and lightness in weight. While these instruments are represented in their very best and most expensive type by the Leica, Pentax and Nikon series, it does not follow that other less costly makes will not give good photographs. Many of these cheaper cameras will give perfectly good results for those who require their camera to provide them with pictures of the most poignant moments of their holiday. The great joy of such equipment is that it is foolproof in use and so long as you remember to keep your finger away from the lens you will have good pictures. For the more discerning photographers, those who require greater flexibility in choosing aperture and shutter speed, an SLR camera with a zoom lens or a variety of fixed focus lenses is essential. Here too it is possible to obtain fully automated cameras that require little more than a point and click technique – even the winding on of the film frame is done for you. Such cameras are heavily reliant on battery power and in the event of battery failure may not work at all.

2 **The lens** is the most important feature and the best of them naturally facilitate the perfect rendering of the subject. A wide aperture is not essential, because it is seldom necessary to work out of doors at anything greater than F/4.5. It is advisable to use the objective at infinity in mountain photography because overall sharpness is then obtained, and to stop down where required to bring the foreground into focus. It is in this connection that the cheaper camera, which of course is fitted with an inexpensive lens, falls short of its more costly competitors; for the latter are corrected for every known fault and the resulting photographs are then not only more acceptable for enlarged reproduction but also yield exhibition prints of superlative quality. Three lenses are desirable in this branch of photography: 1. a 28mm or 35mm wide angle; 2. a standard 50mm which is usually supplied with most cameras; and 3. a long focus lens such as a 135mm or even a 200mm. These cover every likely requirement: the wide angle is most useful when on a mountain or lofty ridge; the 50mm encompasses the average scene, such as hill and valley; and the long focus is an advantage when the subject is very distant. An analysis of their use in the photographs in this book is as follows:

> Wide angle 50 per cent
> Standard 45 per cent
> Long focus 5 per cent.

It is possible to obtain extremely high quality zoom lenses that incorporate all of the above focal lengths. This is quite obviously an advantage in that it not only means carrying less weight and bulk but also facilitates the accurate framing of the picture without having to change lenses.

3 **A lens hood** is an indispensable accessory, because it cuts out adventitious light and increases the brilliance and clarity of the picture. Many people have the illusion that this gadget

is only required when the sun is shining and that it is used to keep the direct rays out of the lens when facing the light source. While its use is then imperative, they often overlook the fact that light is reflected from many points of the hemisphere around the optical axis, and it is the interception of this incidental light that is important.

4 **A filter** is desirable, especially for the good rendering of skyscapes. For black and white photography a pale orange yields the most dramatic results, providing there are not vast areas of trees in the landscape in which all detail would be lost. It is safer to use a yellow filter, which does not suffer from this defect, and with autumn colours a green filter is very effective. The exposure factors do not differ materially, and in view of the wide latitude of modern black and white film the resulting slight differences in density can be corrected when printing.

For colour work a skylight filter is essential for reducing the intensity of the blues and for eliminating haze. Many people also like to use a polarising filter which can enhance a picture by making light waves vibrate in a single plane. This is particularly useful when there is light from many directions such as reflections off water or, more obviously, from snow.

5 **The choice of film** is wide. For straightforward colour print photography a film with an ASA rating of 100 will be sufficient for almost everything you need. For more dreary light faster speeds up to 400 ASA may be useful. Transparency, or slide, film yields excellent results and there is again a wide choice. Some films such as Kodachrome or Fujichrome include processing in the price whereas there are others that do not. Processing for such films is by the E6 process and if this is your chosen medium you should try to find a company that produces excellent results, for they do vary.

Black and white film is available in similar ratings and those that work with this medium will appreciate the subtleties that it offers both in the latitude of the film and in the creation of pictures in the dark-room.

A basic point to remember about any film is that the faster the ASA rating the more 'grainy' a picture becomes. Though this factor will not be noticeable on a small scale, it will become all too apparent the more the picture is enlarged.

6 **Exposure** is important when taking a picture but is not relevant to those cameras where the photographer has no control over the aperture and shutter speed.

A slow shutter speed will necessitate holding the camera very steady. If you are using a long or heavy lens it may be preferable to put it on a tripod. A fast shutter speed will capture images and freeze them even though the object may be moving. A minimum shutter speed of 1/125th of a second is a yardstick from which to work.

The aperture determines how much of the scene will be in focus. The smaller the aperture used, the larger the area of the picture that will be in focus. If you are taking pictures of faraway scenes it is not so important to consider the aperture. If, however, you would like to take a picture that includes some close foreground detail, such as your companion, you will require a greater depth of focus and a smaller aperture will be necessary (in photographic terms this is called Depth of Field). An aperture of F/8 is a versatile minimum with which to work.

The more successful pictures are the result of a carefully considered combination of shutter speed and aperture.

7 **The best time of year** for photography among the Scottish Peaks is during the months of April and May. A limpid atmosphere and fine cumulus are then a common occurrence and less time is wasted in waiting for favourable lighting. Moreover, during April many of the higher mountains are dressed in snowy raiment which adds sparkle and glamour

and transforms them into peaks of Alpine splendour. Colour work at these times is also satisfactory because the landscape still reveals the reds of the dead bracken, which, however, disappear in June with the rapid growth of the new fresh green fronds. Nevertheless, the most dramatic colour pictures are to be obtained during the last week of October because the newly dead bracken is then a fiery red, the grass has turned to golden yellow, and the longer shadows increase the contrast between ben and glen.

8 **Lack of sharpness** is a problem that causes disappointment and although one is often apt to blame the lens, this defect is generally caused by camera shake. It is one thing to hold the instrument steady at ground level with a good stance and no strong wind to disturb the balance, while it is quite another problem in the boisterous breezes on the lofty ridges of Scotland. When these conditions prevail, it is risky to use a slow shutter speed, and maximum stability may be achieved by leaning against a slab of rock or in a terrific gale of wind by even lying down and jamming the elbows into the space between the crags; but foreground should never be sacrificed on this account. In calm weather a light tripod may be used, but in all other conditions it is too risky to erect one and have it blown over a precipice!

9 **Lighting** is the key to fine mountain photography, and the sun at an angle of 45 degrees, over the left or right shoulder, will yield the required contrasts. These conditions usually appertain in the early morning or late evening. If possible avoid exposures at midday with the sun overhead when the lighting is flat and uninteresting. Before starting on any outing, study the topography of your mountain so that full advantage can be taken of the lighting. Moreover, never be persuaded to discard your camera when setting out in bad weather, because the atmosphere in the hills is subject to the most sudden and

unexpected changes, and sometimes wet mornings develop into fine afternoons, with magnificent clouds and limpid lighting. If your camera is then away back in your lodgings, you may live to regret the omission!

10 **The sky** is often the saving feature in mountain photographs, since cloudless conditions or a sunless landscape seldom yield a pleasing picture. But to capture a fine cloud formation as well as the subject in the same frame often means sacrificing the foreground. For example the picture of the Storr as seen in Plate 2 is typical and should be comparred with Plate 213 which includes Loch Fada and so misses the drama of the scene.

11 **Haze** is one of the bugbears in this branch of photography, and these conditions are especially prevelent among the Scottish Peaks during July and August. If an opalescent effect is desired, this is the time of year to secure it, but while such camera studies may be favoured by the purist, they seldom appeal to mountaineers who prefer to see the detail they know exists in their subjects.

12 **Design or composition** is the most outstanding feature of a good camera study; that is, one that not only immediately appeals to the eye, but can also be lived with afterwards. Everything I have so far written herein on this subject comes within the scope of technique, and anyone who is prepared to give it adequate study and practice should be able to produce a satisfying picture.

But to create a picture that far transcends even the best snapshot requires more than this and might well be described as a flair or, if you like, a seeing eye that immediately appreciates the artistic merit of a particular mountain scene. And strangely enough those who possess this rare gift usually produce a certain type of picture which is indelibly stamped

Plate 2 Skyscape taken with a 90 mm lens

with their personality; so much so that it is often possible to name the photographer as soon as his work is displayed. And, moreover, while this especial artistic trait may be developed after long application of the basic principles of composition, the fact remains that it is not the camera that really matters, for it is merely a tool, but the person behind the viewfinder, who, when satisfied with the design of his or her subject, ultimately and quite happily releases the shutter.

To painters, composition is relatively easy, because they can make it conform to the basic principles of art by moving a tree to one side of the picture, or by completely removing a house from the foreground, or by inducing a stream to flow in another direction, or by accentuating the real subject, if it happens to be a mountain, by moving it or by increasing or decreasing its angles to suit their tastes. Photographers on the other hand have to move themselves and their camera here and there in order to get these objects in the right position in their viewfinder. When you move to one side to improve the position of one of them, another is thrown out of place, or perhaps the lighting is altered. In many cases, therefore, a compromise is the only solution, because if too much time is spent in solving this problem the mood may change, and the opportunity could be lost. It is just this element in mountain photography that brings it into line with sport, and, like golf, it can be both interesting and exasperating. Of course, critics can sit in a comfortable chair by a warm fire at home and pull a photograph to pieces. They probably do not realise that the person taking the picture may have been wandering about knee-deep in a slimy bog, or that a bitterly cold wind was sweeping across a lofty ridge and making his teeth chatter, or that the light was failing, or that he had crawled out on a rocky spur with a hundred-foot drop on either side to get the subject properly composed.

Assuming, therefore, both lighting and cloudscape are favourable, what are the essential features of good composition? In the first place, you must select a pleasing object that is accentuated by tonal contrast as the centre of interest; in the second you must place this object in the most attractive position in the frame or picture space; and in the third you must choose a strong and appropriate foreground. Or, in other words, when the weather is favourable the success or failure of your photograph will depend entirely upon the viewpoint.

Thus, if your subject happens to be Ben Nevis I may be able to help you with a few hints about four of the illustrations in this book. It is generally agreed that the northern aspect of this mountain is the finest because its savage cliffs enclosing Coire na Ciste can be seen from this point of the compass, and they are only illuminated on a sunny afternoon or evening. But you must first decide whether you wish to make a picture of the range, including its satellite Carn Mor Dearg; or a similar scene with special emphasis on its precipices overhanging the Allt a'Mhuillin; or of its immense bulk as seen by the average observer. If the first two aspects are preferred, the available viewpoints are lacking in foreground interest other than trees, whereas the third aspect has several viewpoints with pictur- esque foregrounds of water and buildings. Moreover, good camera studies of this aspect can be made by contra jour lighting early in the day, as well as by direct illumination in the late afternoon.

All the best viewpoints for this subject are to be found on the Gairlochy road to the north-east of Banavie, and on the Glenfinnan road to the west of Corpach as far as Locheilside Station. Moreover, the former has the advantage of greater height, by only about 60 metres it is true, but this imparts an enhanced elevation to the peak and at the same time opens up views of its precipitous cliffs.

Let us begin with the range itself, whose tonal contrast is improved by side lighting in the late afternoon or evening; whose strongest placing is in a horizontal frame, and com- pletely fills the upper part of the picture space; and whose foreground is confined to trees, heather or gorse, although an

Plate 2. Carn Mor Dearg and the precipitous front of Ben Nevis.

Plate 4 Carn Mor Dearg, the Allt a'Mhuilinn and Ben Nevis

Plate 5 Carn Mor Dearg, Ben Nevis and Sgurr a'Mhaim from Corpach

Plate 6 Morning haze and still water at Corpach

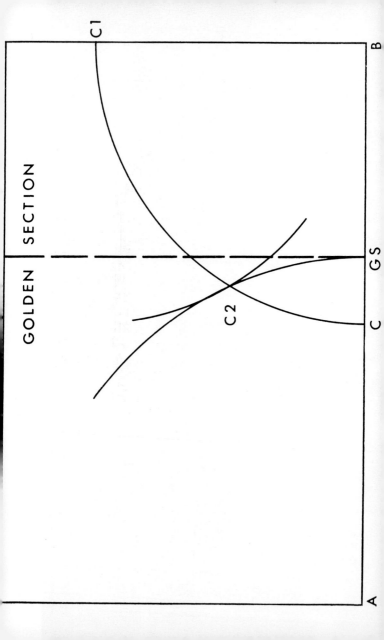

Plate 7 Stac Pollaidh and Loch Lurgainn

isolated cottage nearby can be used but its tangle of enclosing trees rather mars the subject. Plate 3 was taken about 8 km from Banavie and Plate 4 some 3 km distant. The former yields a better conception of the range as a whole, and the latter of the cliffs characterising the Ben. However, its immensity is revealed to greater advantage from the shore of Loch Eil and the most attractive foreground is at Corpach where the buildings at the entrance to the Caledonian Canal provide a strong and interesting foreground. Still water in the loch is to be preferred, as the buildings are then reflected on its surface as shown in Plate 5, but the same subject shown in Plate 6, taken on a hazy morning, better captures the picturesque qualities of the scene.

Finally, whenever you take a photograph of any of the Scottish Peaks, remember that it will be improved not only by placing a loch, a burn, a figure or a group of walkers in the foreground, but also on occasion by introducing a tree or cottage or some object whose size if known will impart both interest and scale to your picture.

Before leaving this interesting question of Design or Composition, it might be helpful to mention two systems that are used for arriving at the strongest placing of the subject in the frame. The favoured picture space measures 2 x 3, 4 x 6, 20 x 30 and so on, or as in the miniature camera 24 x 36, and when it is divided into thirds the horizontal lines cut the verticals at four points. To obtain a balance that satisfies the eye, the subject, such as a mountain peak, should be placed with its summit on one of the upper points, and an object such as a cairn, a cottage, a tree or a figure on the lower opposite point. This raises a problem when the subject is not well defined, as when a peak does not stand alone but is confused by other adjacent mountains which cannot be excluded from the picture space. In such instances the Design must be left to the photographer who will do his best to strike a balance that pleases the eye. And while it is a simple matter for anyone to guess at the thirds when looking through the viewfinder, the other system favoured by such great artists as El Greco, Leonardo, Raphael and Tintoretto is much more difficult to position precisely, although, as shown by the accompanying *Golden Section* drawing and the study of Stac Polladih (Plate 7), it can be acquired approximately by practice and is acknowledged as the ideal in Design. In fact, placing the subject on the *Golden Section* gives a perfect visual satisfaction to the observer. There is a feeling of balance and order, even excitement in dramatic conditions – the interest is demanded.

The method of finding the approximate *Golden Section* is as follows: draw a frame measureing 4 x 6 inches and bisect the base line AB at C. With B as the centre and radius BC, draw an arc that intersects the vertical edge at C1. With C1 as the centre and the same radius BC intersect C-C1 at C2. From A with A-C2 as the radius, find the *Golden Section* where it reaches the base line at GS. This vertical line rising from GS was called the 'Divine Proportion' by no less an artist than Leonardo, who considered the frame should be so divided in order to communicate most successfully through the eye an arrangement of shapes, dimensions and directions, mass and counter mass, that would solicit, hold and move the attention and interest.

The subject in the example is shown on the right, but is of course equally applicable on the left, and moreover, the same system can be applied to vertical frames, or to the more common whole plate, 8 x 6 inches, or to exhibition prints measuring 15 x 12 inches or 20 x 16 inches.

(It should be noted that in order to adapt the 24 x 36 negatives to the sizes required in this volume, it has sometimes been necesssary to reduce, or even omit, the foreground appearing in the original photographs.)

NOTES

1. In case readers are interested in the photographic equipment used by my father, I can disclose that on the many occasions he was asked this question, his reply was, 'Since the availability of 35mm film I have always used Leica cameras, replacing them as new models appeared.' In his last years he used an M2 with 35, 50 and 90mm lenses for monochrome with Kodak Plus X film; for colour work he used a Leicaflex with 28, 50, 90 and 135mm lenses, plus a 45/90mm zoom, in conjunction with his favourite Kodachrome 25.

2. Some years before my father died he presented the collection of black and white negatives he had amassed over a period of more than half a century to the Royal Photographic Society and they now form part of their archive. They wish it to be known that prints from these can be supplied for an appropriate fee.

Photography in the different hills

I have often been asked 'What is the best view *of* such and such a mountain?' or 'What is the most striking view *from* so and so?' These are difficult questions, because the answers depend so much upon one's personal tastes, which are influenced in no small degree by atmospheric conditions on any particular occasion. The present volume seems to be a convenient medium for an attempt to offer some guidance on this very debatable question, and while there are doubtless many who will disagree with my opinions, I shall give them for what they are worth. Where possible I have appended references to appropriate examples already portrayed in one or other of my works, as follows:

SL: *Scotland through the Lens*
HH: *Highland Holiday*
NH: *The North Western Highlands*
CC: *A Camera in the Cairngorms*
MS: *The Magic of Skye*
EH: *Escape to the Hills*
SP: *The Scottish Peaks* (the present work)

The number indicates the plate in the particular volume, to which I have added the most suitable time of day (G.M.T.). It should be noted that the examples given were not necessarily taken at the best time or season.

The suggestions are arranged according to the grouping system adopted throughout this work and under two headings: (1) The best pictorial views *of* the range, their dominating peaks or their separate tops; (2) The most striking views *from* the range. After what I have already written herein it will be obvious that foreground interest is of paramount importance since it bears a direct relationship to the pictorial rendering of the subject.

The best pictorial views of each range

The Arran Hills
From the Clauchland Hills to the south of Brodick before noon. HH 3; EH 80; SP 8

Ben Arthur
From the lower corrie before 11 a.m. HH 34; EH 95; SP 21.

Ben More
From Strath Fillan or Glen Dochart at any time of day. SP 25;

Ben Lui
From Coninish before noon. HH 55; EH 99; SP 26.

Ben Cruachan
From the road on the south side of Loch Awe at any time of day. HH 69; SP 30.

The Black Mount
(*a*) Stob Ghabhar from Loch Tulla before noon. SL 4; SP 38.
(*b*) The range to Meall a'Bhuiridh from Lochan na h'Achlaise before noon. SP 40.
(*c*) Sron na Creise from Kingshouse before 10 a.m. SL 7; EH 106; SP 41.

Buachaille Etive Mor
From Kinghouse in the early morning. EH 107; SP 42.

Bidean nam Bian
(*a*) The range from Aonach Eagach before noon. EH 118; SP 48.
(*b*) Aonach Dubh from Clachaig in the afternoon. SL 13; EH 111; SP 49.

Aonach Eagach
(a) From the River Coe opposite Clachaig up to 4 p.m. SL 10 &
     11; EH 117; SP 56.
(b) From the summit of Aonach Dubh up to 4 p.m. EH 112;
     SP 57.

Beinn a'Bheithir
From North Ballachulish morning or evening. SL 30; EH; 122 &
124; SP 66.

Garbh Bheinn
From Druim an Iubhair before noon. SP 71.

The Mamores
From Glen Nevis in the evening. SL 48, 53, 54 & 56; EH 133;
SP 73.

Ben Nevis
(a) From Corpach in the evening. SP 5.
(b) Coire na Ciste from Carn Mor Dearg before noon. SL 60,
     61, 62, 63; EH 136 & 137; SP 81.

The Saddle
From Glen Shiel in the morning. NH 20; SP 85.

The Five Sisters of Kintail
(a) From Mam Ratagain in the afternoon. NH 25; SP 87.
(b) From Loch Duich in the afternoon. NH 24.

Beinn Bhan
(a) From Loch Carron at any time of day. NH 49.
(b) From Loch Kishorn in the morning. NH 43; SP 91.
(c) The Corries from Kishorn Lodge in the morning. NH 45;
     SP 93.

Beinn Damh
(a) From the head of Loch Damh at any time of day. SP 98.
(b) From the Diabaig Road in the early evening. SP 99.

Liathach
(a) From Loch Clair in the morning. NH 51, 54; SP 1 & 104.
(b) From Beinn Alligin in the afternoon. NH 66; SP 115.
(c) From the Shieldaig road at any time of day.

Beinn Alligin
From the southern side of Upper Loch Torridon in the
morning. NH 64; SP 111.

Beinn Eighe
(a) From Kinlochewe up to noon. NH 52; SP 117.
(b) From Loch Coulin at any time of day. NH 53; SP 118.

Slioch
From Loch Maree at any time of day. NH 69; SP 123.

An Teallach
From the Road of Destitution up to noon. NH 72; SP 124.

Ben Mór Coigach
(a) From Ardmair Bay up to 4 p.m. NH 81; SP 129.
(b) Sgurr an Fhidhleir from Lochan Tuath in the morning.
NH 86; SP 130.

Cul Beag
From Loch Lurgainn in the afternoon. NH 84; SP 135.

Cul Mor
(a) From Stac Pollaidh at any time of day. NH 90; SP 137
(b) From Ledmore in the morning. SP 138.

Stac Pollaidh
(*a*) From the eastern end of Loch Lurgainn in the morning. SP 7
(*b*) From the lower southern slopes of the peak in the late afternoon. NH 85; SP 144.

Suilven
(*a*) From Elphin at any time of day. NH 97; SP 152.
(*b*) From the northern shore of Loch Inver in the late afternoon. NH 105; SP 153.

Quinag
(*a*) From the head of Loch Assynt up to noon. NH 102; SP 163.
(*b*) From the foot of Loch Assynt in the afternoon. NH 103; SP 164.
(*c*) From Loch a'Chairn Bhain, opposite Kylesku, in the late afternoon. NH 117; SP 166.

Foinaven
(*a*) From a small lochan near Rhiconich at any time of day.
(*b*) From above Loch Laxford at any time of day. SP 174.

Ben Hope
From near Hope Lodge in the late afternoon. SP 180.

Ben Loyal
From Lochan Hakel in the afternoon. NH 127; SP 181.

Lochnagar
(*a*) From the Spittal of Glen Muick at any time of day. CC 4; SP 183.
(*b*) From the Old Bridge of Dee at Invercauld in the afternoon. CC 21; SP 184.
(*c*) The Corrie from Meikle Pap before noon. CC 8.

Ben Macdui
From Black Bridge at any time of day. CC 30; SP 189.

The Lairig Ghru
From opposite the Devil's Point at any time of day. CC 54; SP 202.

Cairn Gorm
From the northern shore of Loch Morlich in the late afternoon. CC 74; SP 207

The Storr
From Loch Fada in the morning. MS 8; SP 213.

Quiraing
From the Prison up to noon. MS 37; SP 218.

Sgurr nan Gillean
(*a*) From Sligachan up to 11 a.m. MS 116 & 134; SP 224.
(*b*) From the South East Ridge up to 4 p.m. MS 118 & 119; SP 226.
(*c*) The Pinnacle Ridge from Sgurr a'Bhasteir between 3 and 4 p.m. MS 126 & 127; SP 233.

Bruach na Frithe
From Sgurr na Bhairnich in the afternoon. MS 109; SP 230.

Sgurr Dearg
(*a*) From Eas Mor in the morning. MS 88; SP 237.
(*b*) From Sgurr Sgumain or Sgurr Alasdair in the afternoon. MS 87.

Sgurr Alasdair
(*a*) From Sgurr nan Eag up to 2 p.m. MS 81; SP 241.
(*b*) From Sgurr Dearg in the late afternoon. MS 91; SP 240.

The most striking views from each range

The Arran Hills

Cir Mhor, the Peak of the Castles and the Witch's Step from North Goat Fell up to 3 p.m. HH 16; EH 84; SP 20.

Ben Arthur

The Last Overhang from the ridge in the afternoon. HH 35; EH 94; SP 22.

Ben Cruachan

(*a*) The Panorama to the North at any time of day.

(*b*) The Summit Ridge from Drochaid Glas at any time of day. HH 96 & 97; SP 37.

Buachaille Etive Mor

The vast expanse of Rannoch Moor and Schiehallion in the afternoon.

Bidean nam Bian

(*a*) Stob Coire nan Lochan from Aonach Dubh before 11 a.m. SL 14; SP 50.

(*b*) Lochaber from Stob Coire nan Lochan at any time of day. SL 21; SP 51.

(*c*) Aonach Eagach from Aonach Dubh up to 4 p.m. EH 112; SP 57.

Aonach Eagach

(*a*) Bidean nam Bian before noon. EH 118; SP 48.

(*b*) Glen Coe and Loch Achtriochtan from Am Bodach before 11 a.m. SL 25; SP 59.

Beinn a'Bheithir

Sgorr Dhearg from Sgorr Bhan before noon. SL 33; EH 125 & 126; SP 67.

The Mamores
(*a*) Am Bodach from Sgurr a'Mhaim before noon. SL 41; SP 75.
(*b*) The Devil's Ridge from Sgurr a'Mhaim before noon. SL 42;
       SP 74.
(*c*) Stob Ban from Sgurr a'Mhaim before noon. SL 47; SP 76.
(*d*) Stob Ban from the Devil's Ridge before noon. EH 128.

Ben Nevis
(*a*) The vast panorama in all directions.
(*b*) The Tower Ridge from the plateau in the afternoon. SL 73;
       EH 143; SP 83.

The Five Sisters of Kintail
(*a*) Sgurr na Ciste Duibhe from Sgurr nan Spainteach before
       11 a.m. NH 34; SP 88.
(*b*) Ben Nevis and the intervening ridges from Sgurr Fhuaran
       in the afternoon. SP 89.

Beinn Bhan
(*a*) Skye from the Bealach na Ba in the morning.
(*b*) Torridon, Ben Damph and Coulin forests from Beinn Bhan
       in the afternoon.
(*c*) Coire na Poite from the Ridge. SP 95.

Beinn Damh
(*a*) the sea and Torridon Peaks at any time of day.
(*b*) The peaks of Ben Damph and Coulin forests.

Liathach
The summit ridge from Spidean a'Choire Leith at any time of
day. NH 62 & 63; SP 107 & 108.

Beinn Alligin
The Peaks from Coire an Laoigh. SP 112.

Beinn Eighe
(*a*) The summit ridge from Sgurr nan Fhir Duibhe up to 3
  p.m. NH 59; SP 121.
(*b*) Coire Mhic Fhearchair after 7 p.m. NH 60; SP 122.

Slioch
The northern panorama at any time of day.

An Teallach
(*a*) The pinnacle ridge from Bidean a'Ghlas Thuill up to noon.
  NH 71; SP 125.
(*b*) Beinn Dearg Mhor from Corrag Bhuidhe up to noon.
  SP 127.
(*c*) Toll an Lochain up to 11 a.m. NH 74; SP 128.

Ben Mór Coigach
Stac Pollaidh from Sgurr an Fhidhleir at any time of day.
NH 87; SP 131.

Cul Beag
Stac Pollaidh up to noon. SP 136.

Cul Mor
Suilven at any time of day. NH 94; SP 141.

Stac Pollaidh
(*a*) Suilven at any time of day. NH 89; SP 149.
(*b*) Cul Mor at any time of day. NH 90; SP 137.
(*c*) Cul Beag, Loch Lurgainn and the Pinnacles in the
  afternoon. NH 91.
(*d*) Ben Mór Coigach and Beinn an Eoin in the late afternoon.
  NH 77.

Suilven
Meall Mheadhonach from Caisteal Liath at any time of day.
NH 109; SP 161.

Quinag
The head of Loch Assynt from Spidean Coinich in the
afternoon. NH 111; SP 168.

Foinaven
The eroded central spur of A'Ch'eir Ghorm, backed by Ben
Hope after 2 p.m. SP 177.

Lochnagar
(*a*) The vast panorama of the Cairngorms beyond Deeside at
    any time of day.
(*b*) The Corrie from Meikle Pap up to noon.

Ben Macdui
(*a*) Cairn Toul from Sron Riach before noon. CC 34; SP 198.
(*b*) The ridge and corries from Cairn Toul to Braeriach before
    noon. CC 39 & 40; SP 194 & 195.

Cairn Gorm
The view of Loch Morlich and Glenmore Forest at any time of
day.

The Storr
The mainland peaks and the Old Man from the summit ridge
up to 4 p.m. MS 22; SP 215.

Quiraing
The sea and Trotternish ridges from the Table in the afternoon.
MS 38, 43 & 44; SP 220.

Sgurr nan Gillean

(a) Bla Bheinn and Glen Sligachan in the afternoon. MS 121.

(b) Looking down the Western Ridge in the afternoon. MS 122;
     SP 228.

Bruach na Frithe

The Three Bends in the Main Ridge in the late afternoon.
MS 114; SP 231.

Sgurr Dearg

Sgurr Alasdair in the late afternoon. MS 91; SP 240.

Sgurr Alasdair

(a) The Dubhs in the late afternoon. MS 71.

(b) The Main ridge from Sgurr Dearg to Sgurr nan Gillean at
     any time of day. MS 70.

(c) The Thearlaich-Dubh Gap from Sgumain in the afternoon.
     MS 85.

Notes on the routes

I have arranged the Scottish Peaks from south to north for the sake of convenience and easy reference. They commence with the Arran Hills, and then continue from the Cobbler to Ben Loyal in the far north of the mainland. The Cairngorms follow and the work terminates with Trotternish and the Cuillin in the Isle of Skye.

Ascents. When there is more than one route to the dominating peak in a group of hills, I have described the most popular one first, followed by the alternatives, in which case the reversal of one of them could be used for the *Descent*.

The Panorama from the reigning peak in each group is always noted at the termination of its first ascent. But many of the routes involve the traverse of subsidiary tops and the conspicuous features revealed from them are mentioned in passing, despite the fact that there may be a similarity in the views when they are near together. Walkers will notice that in many parts of Scotland the panoramas do not clearly disclose any individual peaks, save those near at hand, and this is accounted for by the peculiar geological origin of the Highlands. For although this part of the mainland is usually considered to be a mountainous country, it is in fact the remnant of a dissected plateau having a general fall to the east. This strange feature can be observed from the summits of Ben Nevis and Bidean nam Bian, and is well illustrated by plate 89 taken from the summit of Sgurr Fhuaran, when it will be noticed that the panorama spread out at one's feet consists of ridge upon ridge and peak after peak, all of which rise to a general level above the intervening straths and glens, dominated however in the far distance by the bold summit of Ben Nevis. In general such a panorama is best appreciated in clear weather, but if the mountaineer is fortunate enough to stand by the summit cairn of one of these hills when the valleys are hidden by mist and the tops of the ridges and peaks only protrude from the protecting shroud, then the origin of the Highlands is more clearly revealed; for if the valleys were filled in, a large tableland would appear sloping gently from west to east.

Traverses. Several of the ranges in Scotland are so immense that in some of them it is an advantage to traverse all the peaks in one expedition; as in that of the Five Sisters of Kintail where the ascent is made at one end of the chain and the descent at the other, even though it is possible but more arduous to climb Sgurr Fhuaran direct from Glen Shiel.

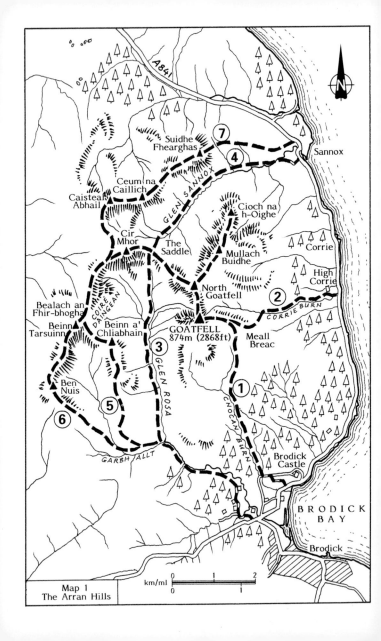

A84l

N

Sannox

Suidhe
Fhearghas

7

4

Glen Sannox

Ceum na
Caillich

Caisteal
Abhail

Cioch na
h-Oighe

Corrie

Cir
Mhor

The
Saddle

Mullach
Buidhe

High
Corrie

North
Goatfell

Bealach an
Fhir-bhogha

Coire Daingean

2

Corrie Burn

Beinn
Tarsuinn

Beinn a'
Chliabhain

GOATFELL
874m (2868ft)

Meall
Breac

3

1

Glen Rosa

Ben
Nuis

5

Cnocan Burn

6

Garbh Allt

Brodick
Castle

BRODICK
BAY

Brodick

km/ml
0   1   2
0   1

Map 1
The Arran Hills

The Arran Hills

Goat Fell	2866 feet	874 metres
Caisteal Abhail	2779 feet	847 metres
Beinn Tarsuinn	2706 feet	826 metres
Mullach Buidhe (Goat Fell)	2687 feet	819 metres
North Goat Fell	2683 feet	818 metres
Cir Mhor	2621 feet	799 metres
Beinn Nuis	2597 feet	792 metres
A'Chir	2444 feet	745 metres
Ceum na Caillich (the Witch's Step)	2300 feet	701 metres
Beinn a'Chliabhain	2217 feet	676 metres
Am Binnein	2178 feet	664 metres
Cioch na h'Oighe	2174 feet	663 metres
Suidhe Fhearghas	2165 feet	660 metres
Bealach an Fhir-Bhogha	2080 feet	634 metres
Meall Breac	1883 feet	574 metres
The Saddle	1456 feet	444 metres

The island of Arran lies in the Firth of Clyde and is almost kidney-shaped; its longer north-south axis covers some 20 miles/32 km, while it is 10 miles/16 km across from east to west. A road follows the coast round the island and is about 56 miles/90 km in length. The magnetic charm of Arran is concentrated in its splendid hills which occupy the northern half of the island and are easily accessible from the roads in the vicinity of Brodick and Corrie, a village lying about 6 miles/ 9.7 km to the north. Large expanses of heather-clad moorland occupy the main part of the southern half of the island, with here and there farmlands at the lower levels. The coast-line is charming and Brodick Bay, with its lovely sweep of sands backed by forests of Larch and Spruce and dominated by the peak of Goat Fell, provides a picture of exquisite beauty.

Nevertheless, the finest profile of the peaks clustered about Goat Fell is obtained from the Clauchland Hills which rise to the south of Brodick. The graceful lines of their grey granite, joined by the serrated intervening ridges, make an attractive skyline at any time of day, but when they are silhouetted against the sunset glow of evening, these magical lights impart a mysterious quality of atmosphere and purple majesty which is only equalled by the Cuillin Hills in Skye. These enchanting hills present a picture of inaccessibility when seen from afar, but with the exception of A'Chir and the Witch's Step they have no great difficulties for the walker. In fact, any fit person can walk over them with ease, but if the crests of the ridges are strictly adhered to, there are places where the granite pinnacles require the use of the hands to pass them in safety. Possibly their finest asset is the proximity of the sea, which can be observed from them in almost all directions.

The Arran Hills are composed mainly of granite which has been forced upwards through beds of sandstone and slate. Great whin dykes are a notable feature and are conspicuous on A'Chir, where they form the gullies and chimneys splitting the face of the granite masses. The fantastic pinnacles crowning the ridges and the amazing Cyclopean walls supporting them are also a remarkable feature. Perhaps the most striking example of erosion is to be seen on the pinnacled ridge rising from the Saddle to North Goat Fell, where disintegration is so far advanced that the granite forms vast areas of rough golden sand, much of which is washed down the burns descending from each side into the valleys beneath.

The topography of the Arran Hills is very simple. There are roughly three ridges, each running approximately north-south and separated by well-defined glens. The most westerly is the Beinn Bharrain–Meall nan Damh group, with Beinn Bhàrrain reaching an altitude of 2368 feet/722 m. Then comes Glen Iorsa between these hills and the Central Ridge, which stretches from Beinn Nuis to Suidhe Fhearghas, with Caisteal Abhail, as

Plate 8 The Arran Hills seen from above Brodick Bay

the highest summit, rising to 2779 feet/847 m above sea level. Glens Rosa and Sannox separate this group from the Goat Fell Massif, which dominates the island at 2866 feet/874 m.

Route 1. Brodick and Goat Fell. Leave by the Corrie road which skirts the bay and golf course. Take the path on R just past the golf course, which crosses the lower part of the Rosa Burn by a bridge and gives access to the beach, and rejoins the road at Cladach, a small distance before the entrance to Brodick Castle. A track signposted to Goat Fell, near the saw mill on the opposite side of the road, passes through the castle grounds and winds up through the woodlands and on to open moorland. Where it bears R follow a signposted path beside the Cnocan Burn, rising across the boulder-strewn ground to Meall Breac, the eastern shoulder of Goat Fell. On attaining the ridge bear west and keep to the path which leads to the summit of the island's reigning peak. If you are thirsty after the ascent, you will find pools of water in the hollows of the rock.

On a clear day the panorama from Goat Fell is one of the most entrancing in all Scotland. It is a marvellous combination of fantastic mountain scenery so near, sunlit seas far below, and the Isles away to the west that makes this prospect so unique. To the east lie the glimmering waters of the Firth of Clyde in which seemingly float the Cumbraes near the mainland, backed by the low hills of Renfrew. To the south-east the eye skims across the surface of Brodick Bay to rest finally upon Holy Island in Lamlash Bay. To the south the rocky cone of Ailsa Craig is a conspicuous object some 26 miles/42 km distant. To the south-west rise the Beinn Nuis-Beinn Tarsuinn ridges with the lower summit of Beinn a'Chliabhain intervening and the floor of Glen Rosa over 2000 feet/600 m below. To the west stands the ridge of A'Chir and to the north-west the colossal obelisk of Cir Mhor with the Saddle at its feet. Swinging round to the north are the Peak of the Castles, the Witch's Step and Suidhe Fhearghas which enclose Glen

Plate 9—**Route 1**—Holy Island, Lamlash and Brodick Bays from Goat Fell

Sannox, while nearer at hand runs the ridge of the Goat Fell Massif.

Now walk due north along the crest of the ridge and if you do not wish to traverse the pinnacles take the sheep tracks round them. On reaching North Goat Fell note the magnificent prospect of the Caisteal Abhail group on the L, and just before attaining Mullach Buidhe examine the gigantic Cyclopean buttress on the west, perhaps the most remarkable on the island. The ridge continues by descending to Cioch na h'Oighe and becomes very narrow and exposed and requires some scrambling. The cliffs on the east flank drop precipitously into the famous Punch Bowl 1000 feet/300 m below and contain some of the finest and most demanding rock climbing on the island. Descent into Glen Sannox can be made down the north-west edge of Cioch na h'Oighe but it is difficult in execution and route finding, and involves scrambling down steep smooth slabs; unless you are an experienced mountaineer it is best to retrace your steps back to North Goat Fell. From here a good path descends the north-west ridge, initially steep, leading to the Saddle, thus reversing Route 3 down Glen Rosa and back to Brodick.

Cir Mhor

Caisteal Abhail

Plate 10 **Route 1**—A pinnacle on the Goat Fell Ridge

Plate 11 **Route 1**—Cyclopean Buttress overhanging Glen Sannox

Plate 12 **Route 1**—Cioch na h'Oighe and the Punch Bowl on the right

Route 2. Corrie and Goat Fell. Walk south from the village of Corrie along the road towards Brodick to where a small road ascends to High Corrie and is signposted to Goat Fell. From here follow the track up the north bank of Corrie Burn before bearing south-west up the slopes of Meall Breac and joining Route 1 to the summit of Goat Fell.

Route 3. Glen Rosa, the Saddle and Goat Fell. Leave the B880 road just after its junction with the A840 ring road and follow a small lane past charming cottages ending at the farm and campsite standing at the entrance to Glen Rosa. Follow a track beside the Rosa Burn with the sharp peak of Beinn Nuis ahead, the ridge of Beinn a'Chliabhain on the skyline, and a glimpse of A'Chir over its R shoulder. A grass-covered terminal moraine is soon encountered, above which on the R appears the well-known Pinnacle which has been climbed and is about 40 feet/12 m high. A little further along Glen Rosa turns sharply to the north and is dominated by Cir Mhor which stands in splendid isolation at its head. Now cross a wooden bridge over the turbulent Garbh Allt, a torrential stream followed by the path to the Beinn Nuis Ridge. Continue on a good path beside the Glen Rosa Burn. On reaching the last tree in the glen, which overhangs a pretty cascade, pause for a moment to admire the fine prospect of Cir Mhor with the Witch's Step visible on R beyond the Saddle. Thence the barren glen is a scene of sombre desolation, but you must plod on bravely until you attain the Saddle, whence bear east and climb the shattered and pinnacled ridge to North Goat Fell. Here you turn south and follow the ridge to the reigning peak.

Plate 13 **Route 3**—Looking up Glen Rosa to Cir Mhor and Ceum na Caillich

Route 4. Glen Sannox, the Saddle and Goat Fell. Leave the coast road at Sannox Bay and walk along the cart track from Glen Cottage, passing the cemetery, until you reach a ford and stepping stones across the burn near the old barytes mine. Alternatively there is a small bridge hidden slightly downstream. The glen above is a wilderness of bog and tangled heather through which a path finds a way as best it can, following the west bank of the burn almost to its source. Ahead rises the magnificent pyramid of Cir Mhor, flanked by 1200 feet/360 m of precipitous cliffs that are riven by gullies, ridges, caves and pinnacles, all of which are the treasured playground of the climber. To the east of them reposes the Saddle, and the path crosses the burn and climbs steeply to reach a conspicuous whin dyke which is the key to your route, terminating on its crest. Now turn east and follow Route 3 to Goat Fell.

Route 5. Beinn a'Chliabhain and Caisteal Abhail. Follow Route 3 to the wooden bridge over the Garbh Allt. Follow the path up the north side of the burn to where the ground levels out. A faint path branches off north over Cnoc Breac which gives access to the south ridge of your first peak. Its ascent is easy and the steep gradient continuous, but on attaining its narrow, wall-like crest you will find it paved with immense flat slabs, akin to a lofty flagstone pavement, which is flanked here and there with granite pinnacles between which on the east you will obtain a dynamic prospect of North Goat Fell. On the west there are revealing views across Coire Bhradain of both Beinn Nuis and Beinn Tarsuinn. Now walk down to the col, with close views ahead across Coire Daingean of the great whin dykes splitting the eastern flanks of A'Chir. From the col follow the ridge north-west to the Bealach an Fhir-Bhogha to the start of the south ridge of the A'Chir ridge. Then keep to a good path that passes below the west side of the crags of the ridge on the Glen Iorsa side and bypasses any difficulties but presents a formidable appearance of the great overlapping

Plate 14 **Route 4**—A hazy morning in Glen Sannox

Cioch na h'Oighe

Cir Mhor

Caisteal Abhail

Suidhe
Fhearghas

granite slabs overhead. Continue ahead until you reach the col below Cir Mhor.

A party of more experienced walkers with some rock climbing ability may prefer to traverse the sharp crest of the ridge of A'Chir which is the most entertaining scramble on the Arran Hills and is often compared to the Cuillin Ridge on Skye. Its south ridge emanating from the Bealach an Fhir-Bhogha consists of an easy scramble over unbroken towers above massive walls of granite. Beyond its summit there is a sharp and difficult descent to the famous *mauvais pas* which displays a definite hiatus in the ridge. Its traverse requires a steady head owing to the precipices on each side, and in ascent (in reverse) would be given a 'Very Difficult' grade in rock climbing. From here the going is easier all the way to the aforementioned col below Cir Mhor.

Now walk up the easy slopes to the summit of Cir Mhor, noting on the south-east the Rosa Pinnacle with its superb granite slabs. Pause for a moment to admire the vistas along both Glen Rosa and Glen Sannx, and then retrace your steps and turn north for the summit of the Peak of the Castles, passing *en route* a cairn that marks a spring of ice-cold water.

The splendour of the panorama from Caisteal Abhail has to be seen on a clear day to be believed. The first object to catch the eye is the tapering peak of Cir Mhor which is one of the most impressive spectacles on the island. To the south-east there is a grand prospect of the Goat Fell Massif terminating with Cioch na h'Oighe; to the south you look back to A'Chir with the Beinn Tarsuinn group; to the west across Glen Iorsa and its western ridges the eye skims across the glimmering sea to its islands; while to the north-east your gaze is held by the ridge to Suidhe Fhearghas and the gloomy stretches of Glen Sannox, to rest finally upon the familiar Firth of Clyde and the more distant mainland.

Plate 15 **Route 5**—North Goat Fell from Beinn a'Chliabhain

Beinn Tarsuinn

Beinn a'Chliabhain

Beinn Nuis

Plate 16 **Routes 5** and **6** seen from the summit of Goat Fell

Plate 17 **Route 5**—Beinn Nuis from Beinn a'Chliabhain

Plate 18 **Route 5**—Beinn Tarsuinn from Beinn a'Chliabhain

Plate 19 **Route 5**—The granite walls and Whin Dykes of A'Chir

Route 6. Beinn Nuis and Caisteal Abhail. Follow Route 5 up the north bank of the Carbh Allt. Cross the moor directly ahead to the south-east shoulder of Beinn Nuis and continue the tramp to its summit. Observe on the east the 500 feet/150 m of precipices, split by gullies, all of which are the resort of the keen rock climber. Then, after delighting in the spacious views, skirt the cliffs and stroll along the grassy, moss-covered ridge to Beinn Tarsuinn, which unfolds grand prospects of hill and sea. Thereafter descend to the Bealach an Fhir-Bhogha and bear east to pick up Route 5 to Caisteal Abhail.

Route 7. Suidhe Fhearghas and Caisteal Abhail. Your first peak is a prominent landmark when seen from Sannox Bay, and to attain it you must make your way across the moor in a westerly direction from the road north of Mid Sannox. Flanked with crags, its crest presents no difficulties and you continue south-westwards along the lofty ridge for Ceum na Caillich (the Witch's Step), a conspicuous deep gash in the ridge. The direct descent of its 150 feet/46 m of granite chimney and slab to the saddle at the base is difficult. This can be avoided by descending slightly on the north-west side of the ridge before the gash and traversing round ledges of rock and turf to each the saddle. Thence, leaving behind the Witch's Step, climb steadily up the broadening ridge to the Peak of the Castles.

Walkers will observe that some of the above Routes may be combined to make a long and invigorating tramp. Route 6 and Route 7 afford the finest traverse in Arran, and photographers should walk from south to north, to take full advantage of the lighting. Interested readers will find further details and photographs in the author's *Highland Holiday*.

Cir Mhor

Ceum na Caillich

Plate 20 Terminal sections of **Routes 5, 6** and **7** seen across the Saddle from North Goat Fell

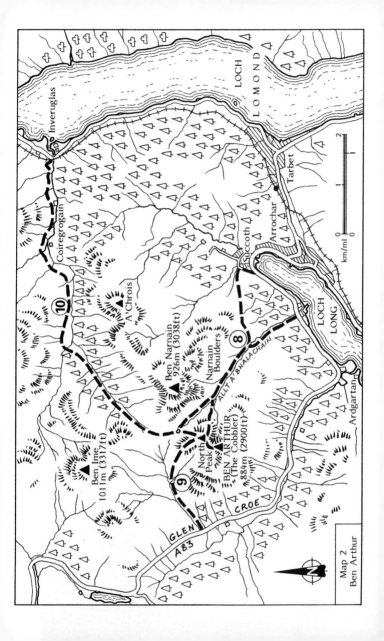

Map 2
Ben Arthur

Ben Arthur

Ben Arthur (The Cobbler)   2900 feet   884 metres

This conspicuous mountain rises to the north-west of Loch Long, from the head of which the well-known road over Rest and Be Thankful passes below it and through Glen Croe to Loch Fyne. It is inferior in height to its neighbour, Ben Ime, but its weird, serrated profile at once stamps it as the most striking peak in the Southern Highlands. Known familiarly as the Cobbler it is well seen from the railway in the vicinity of Arrochar, from which station it is readily accessible. And while this mountain has a great attraction for the hill walker, it is chiefly of interest as a rock climbing venue within easy reach of Glasgow. It displays three separate and well-defined summits, of which the central peak only is properly called the Cobbler. That to the south of it is affectionately known as Jean or the Cobbler's Wife, while that to the north, with its spectacular overhangs, is the Cobbler's Last. And strange as it may seem, the latter is the only summit that can be easily attained by the pedestrian; for the other two require some experience in rock climbing if their summits are to be reached in safety.

Route 8. From Arrochar. Leave the station by the road round the head of Loch Long, and after crossing the bridge spanning the turbulent waters of the river flowing down Glen Loin, take the road on the R for Succoth. From the south side of the bridge over the Allt Sugach follow a path up the hillside to attain a forestry track. Turn L and follow it to meet up with a path which follows a line of concrete slabs from an old cable railway; this leads uphill to a level track that gives direct access southwards to the Allt a'Bhalachain, or Buttermilk Burn. Now keep to the path on the north bank until you reach a collection of large boulders on the slopes of Beinn Narnain, whence cross the main stream and follow its tributary on the L that descends from the main corrie, whence a rough path leads steeply to the immense depression between the north and centre peaks.

There are several variations to this route, two at the start and another at the finish. The former begins on the west side of the Buttermilk Burn at the point where it enters Loch Long, but the path is seldom used nowadays. Alternatively, from a lay-by on the shore of the loch, just after the turn-off to Succoth, a short track runs into the trees. From this a path runs directly up the hill through afforested ground (felled and replanted in 1996) to join the concrete slabs. The latter follows the main stream from the Narnain Boulders as far as its source in a small lochan, whence the path turns sharp south and climbs to the north peak, from which the ridge may be followed to the summit tower.

On a clear day the panorama from the Cobbler is very fine and includes all the surrounding hills, but the most striking landmark is Ben Lomond whose shapely lines appeal to the eye and dominate the intervening blue of Loch Lomond.

South Peak

The Cobbler

North Peak

Plate 21 **Route 8**—The Cobbler seen from the approach to the upper corrie

Route 9. From Glen Croe. Leave the road at a small lay-by beyond the plantations and follow a small path beside the burn, the Allt a'Chothruim, and eventually its southern tributary which has its source beneath the crest of Ben Arthur. This ascent is steep but not difficult, and since it is lacking in interest it is seldom used.

Route 10. From Upper Inveruglas. This is the longest and most picturesque approach to the Cobbler. From Inveruglas follow the road towards the dam on Loch Sloy to a point beyond Coiregrogain. Take the track which branches left and follows the burn of the same name into the back of the corrie. Climb beside the burn to its source on the col between Ben Ime and Narnain, whence make for the North Peak by joining Route 8 near the lochan.

Plate 22 Spectacular overhangs of the North Peak

Plate 23 Centre Peak of the Cobbler

Plate 24 The South Peak

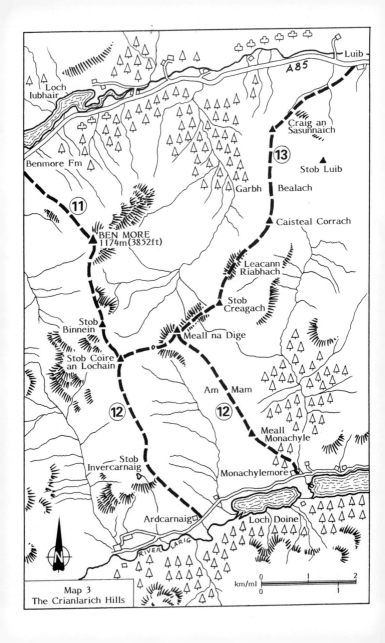

Map 3
The Crianlarich Hills

The Crianlarich Hills

Ben More	3852 feet	1174 metres
Stob Binnein	3822 feet	1165 metres
Stob Coire an Lochain	3504 feet	1068 metres
Meall na Dige	3169 feet	966 metres
Stob Creagach	2966 feet	904 metres
Meall Monachyle	2123 feet	647 metres
Caisteal Corrach	1998 feet	609 metres

Ben More is a beautifully shaped mountain and a conspicuous landmark throughout the length of Glen Dochart and Strath Fillan, and together with its equally graceful neighbour, Stob Binnein, affords one of the easiest ascents in Perthshire, providing always the atmosphere is clear and it is not snowbound. It is the highest peak in Britain south of Loch Tay and in consequence discloses a stupendous panorama on a clear day.

Route 11. Ben More from Benmore Farm. This is the most favoured starting point for the ascent as it is only 2 miles/3.2 km from Crianlarich. From the farm follow the path leftwards to the flanks of Sron nam Forsairean which leads to the top. The 3,300 feet/1000 m of steep, grassy slopes have a foreshorted aspect and as a result the climb seems endless. Aside from the shallow corrie, which is passed on the west, there are no features to rivet the eye until the summit cairns are attained, when the rewarding panorama bursts upon the view. Owing to the dominating altitude of Ben More the prospect is extensive, and on a clear day the Cairngorms can be seen far away to the north-east. The southern arc is impressive, as both Edinburgh and Glasgow can be picked out, while to the west Rhum and Jura can be distinguished on the glistening sea.

Strong walkers may wish to continue along the summit ridge

to Stob Binnein, but it should be borne in mind that it falls about 1,000 feet/300 m to the Bealach-eadar-dha Beinn and rises again almost as much to the second peak, so making a long and strenuous expedition before the walker reaches his lodgings in the evening.

Route 12. Stob Binnein from Balquhidder. This approach is subject to two variations: the first starts from Monachyle and the second from the head of Glen Carnaig. Both open up splendid views of the adjacent tops and ridges, and are more interesting than Route 11. To reach the starting points drive to the end of Loch Voil for the former and continue to Loch Doine for the latter, a distance of about 5 miles/8 km. If desired both may be combined for the ascent and subsequent descent.

Park at the Monachyle Mhor Hotel (please ask permission), follow the road a short distance west to beyond the plantation and climb the steep slopes of Meall Monachyle to gain the ridge. Walk along it past Am Mam to Meall na Dige where observe the fine prospect of Stob Binnein and the corrie to its south. Now descend sharply to the tiny lochan on the col to the west and ascend Stob Coire an Lochain, whence it is only a short step to Stob Binnein. From Glen Carnaig skirt Stob Invercarnaig and then cut up steeply to gain the ridge which leads to Stob Coire an Lochain, thence to Stob Binnein. A popular route also ascends the west side of this ridge from Inverlochlarig beyond Loch Doine.

Plate 25 **Routes 11** to **13**—Ben More and Stob Binnein from Strath Fillan

Route 13. Stob Binnein from Glen Dochart. Park opposite Glen Dochart Caravan Site on the A85 and walk back along the road towards Crianlarich. Leave the road on the L where it is crossed by the disused railway, pass beneath an old bridge and gain the hillside on the left. Gain the ridge, passing Creag Sasunnaich on the R. Make for the first summit above it, descend to Garhb Bhealach and then climb steeply to Caisteal Corrach. Now continue along the crest of Leacann Riabhach to the rocky top of Stob Creagach, whence make your way over the shattered rocky ridge to Meall na Dige where you join Route 12 for Stob Binnein. Passing over Ben More, then descending easily into the corrie on the east and returning to the A85 via the good tracks through the forest, sometimes alongside the Allt Coire Chaorachan, gives a long but satisfying route.

Ben Lui

Ben Lui (Beinn Laoigh)	3707 feet	1130 metres
Beinn a'Chleibh	3005 feet	916 metres

When garbed in white and seen from the railway between Crianlarich and Tyndrum on a sunny winter or spring morning, the Alpine splendour of Ben Lui's twin-topped peak commands the attention of all passengers and affords an unforgettable picture to all mountaineers. Its great north-eastern Coire Gaothach, guarded to the north by the satellite peak of Stob Garbh, will be noticed as the chief topographical feature of the mountain. The western aspect of Ben Lui is of less interest, but is a conspicuous landmark in all the eastern prospects from Loch Awe. It is most famous for the snow climbs in its great Coire Gaothach, and under good winter conditions it is no unusual sight to observe a party of enthusiasts forcing their way to the summit ridge through the massive snow cornices that overhang the precipices to the north-east of its crest. In favourable conditions the ascent of this peak has no great difficulties, and there are three routes described. Of these the first described herein is the most interesting and revealing.

The finest walk is to ascend Route 14 and descend by Route 16, returning to Tyndrum from Dalmally by road or rail.

Route 14. Tyndrum and Ben Lui. Leave the A82 north of Crianlarich at the signpost to Dalrigh and park near the old schoolhouse, now used as a barn. Follow the track to Coninish, with magnificent views ahead of your mountain. Continue along the track in a south-westerly direction with the River Coninish on your L to the old mine workings, but desert it L when facing the corrie. Drop down to the Allt an Rund and, after crossing the burn, make for the south ridge of Coire

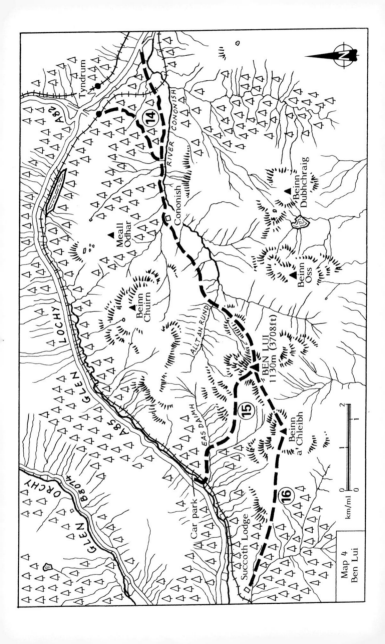

Tyndrum

RIVER CONONISH

Cononish

Beinn
Dubhchraig

Meall
Odhar

Beinn
Oss

Beinn
Chùirn

GLEN LOCHY

A82

A85

14

ALLT AN RUND

BEN LUI
1130m (3708ft)

15

EAS DAIMH

Beinn
a'Chlèibh

GLEN ORCHY

B8074

Car park

Succoth Lodge

16

km/ml

2

1

0
0

Map 4
Ben Lui

Gaothach. Climb it steadily and be careful in its higher reaches because the rock is often loose and much shattered. You will soon attain the short, flattish summit ridge where there are two cairns; that to the south is the higher. The panorama is extensive and the first object to catch the eye on a clear day is the massive range of Ben Cruachan that frowns upon the glittering surface of Loch Awe to the west. In the opposite direction Ben More and Stob Binnein are prominent, while to the north Ben Nevis tops the skyline of peak after peak.

Since Coninish is the key to this route, it can also be reached from Tyndrum Station. Beyond the locked gate on the railway a forestry road follows the line of the original path, now planted with conifers, and contours the flanks of Sron nan Colan Odhar. After about 1 mile/1.6 km it emerges from the plantations and bends to the R to reveal Ben Lui and Coninish ahead, whence it descends in long curves to merge with the track from Dalrigh.

Plate 26 **Route 14**—Ben Lui from above Coninish

Plate 27 **Route 14**—The summit ridge of Ben Lui

Route 15. Glen Lochy and Ben Lui. This route involves fording the River Lochy, an exercise that at various times of the year may be either uncomfortable or dangerous. Although bridge access is possible from Glenlochy Crossing to the north, it involves following the railway where British Rail notices warn walkers they are trespassing. Ford the river with great care and follow the north bank of the Eas Daimh to the beautiful fall of Eas Morag. Thence, bear R and exit from the plantation into the Fionn Choirean. Cut across to the L to the fine north ridge of Ben Lui with splendid views ahead of the summit of your mountain.

Route 16. Dalmally and Beinn a'Chleibh. West of Glen Lochy on the road to Dalmally, just before Corryghoil a turning on the left leads up to Succoth Lodge. There is no parking available at the lodge, so it is best to leave the car at GR 205265, where the left turning in the track is followed over the Eas a'Ghaill and leads under the railway to Succoth Lodge. Continue on the track from the lodge and then south-east following electricity pylons alongside the Allt a'Chaorainn to emerge at open hillside. Head north-east to the summit of Beinn a'Chleibh, whence drop down to the col and scale the rocky ridge to the summit of Ben Lui. Unfortunately recent tree planting makes this a less pleasant walk than in the past.

Plate 28 Ben Lui and the new plantations in Glenorchy Forest, in 1982, since when the plantations have grown considerably

Plate 29 Cloud over Ben Lui and Beinn a'Chleibh

Ben Cruachan

Ben Cruachan	3694 feet	1126 metres
Stob Dearg (Taynuilt Peak)	3622 feet	1104 metres
Drochaid Glas	3310 feet	1009 metres
Stob Diamh	3274 feet	998 metres
Stob Garbh	3215 feet	980 metres
Sron an Isean	3169 feet	966 metres
Meall Cuanail	3012 feet	918 metres
Beinn a'Bhuiridh	2940 feet	896 metres
Monadh Driseig	2103 feet	641 metres

Ben Cruachan is the highest of the eight peaks in this great range of peaks, bounded on the north by the deep rift of Glen Noe and on the south by the Pass of Brander and Loch Awe. It covers an area of about 20 sq. miles/ 52 sq. km and forms a horsehoe stretching some 4 miles/6.4 km from east to west. The lower slopes of its two southern spurs are shagged with woods, but the higher parts are bare, and great smooth slabs of granite characterise the ridges. To obtain any real conception of its fine topography it is necessary to walk over the low hills between Cladich and Portsonachan, some 6 miles/9.7 km to the south on the shores of Loch Awe, where many of its salient features can be clearly discerned. Stob Dearg is the peak on the extreme L and is also known as the Taynuilt Peak. A narrow ridge about 0.5 mile/0.8 km long connects it with Ben Cruachan, the dominating peak on the R. A long rounded hill known as Meall Cuanail rises in front of it and forms the western wall of the vast Coire Cruachan on the R. From Ben Cruachan a narrow shattered ridge sweeps across the skyline for about a mile/1.6 km to the east and terminates with Drochaid Glas. It then falls to a windy col and rises again to Stob Diamh, immediately to the south of which stands Stob Garbh.

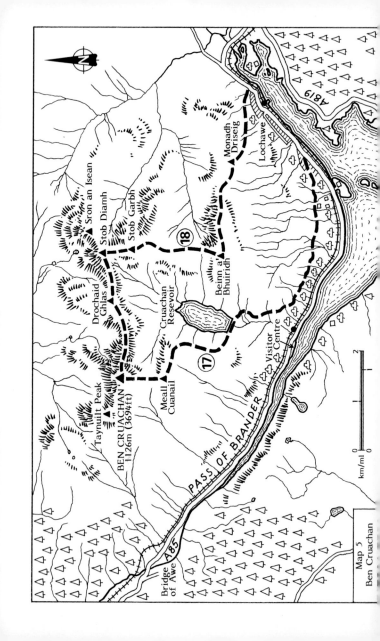

Map 5
Ben Cruachan

In Plate 30 this top is seen behind the L shoulder of the massive Beinn a'Bhuiridh. To the north-east of Stob Diamh there is another subsidiary peak called Sron an Isean, which stands at the head of Glen Noe. This latter group is well seen from the east, and particularly so from Ben Lui on a clear day. There are no difficulties encountered in the climb to any point on the ridge, but the finest expedition is to traverse the whole of it from east to west, which in favourable conditions is a rewarding experience for the mountain photographer.

Route 17. Coire Cruachan and Ben Cruachan. This vast gloomy hollow cradles a reservoir and forms the first step in the direct ascent of the reigning peak. It may be reached by a road which ends at the dam, completed in 1965. The road turns west off the highway just south of St Conan's Kirk, south of Lochawe, and rises gradually for 3 miles/4.8 km round the flanks of Beinn a'Bhuiridh to reach the dam at a height of 1315 feet/401 m. During the day there are splendid views of the Pass of Brander far below on the L. Here you are surrounded on three sides by lofty ridges, whence head north-west and make for the broad ridge ahead which rises to Meall Cuanail. The ascent is continuously steep until you attain the cairn, then walk down to the col and ascend the easy final slopes of your peak. On reaching the lofty cairn you should walk along the ridge to the L, keeping to the edge of the precipices until you attain Stob Dearg.

The panorama from both these peaks is of the first order, but the view round Ben Cruachan's northern arc will hold your gaze because it reveals the full length of Loch Etive, bounded on the east by the graceful peak of Ben Starav. On a clear day you can pick out many of the familiar Glen Coe hills beyond the head of the loch, some of the mountains of the Mamore Forest still further away, and your eye will rest finally upon the great dome of Ben Nevis in the far north. To the south, east and west rise a perfect galaxy of peaks, with here and there the

Plate 30 The Cruachan Range and Loch Awe from Cladich

glint of light on the many lochs and lochans that add charm to this delectable landscape. Immediately to the east of Ben Cruachan there is a magnificent prospect of the ridge which slants down to the two peaks and falls precipitously on the L into the depths of Glen Noe.

Plate 21 The Pass of Brander, from the finder station of Ben Cruachan

Meall Cuanail

Ben Cruachan

Plate 32 The dam in Coire Cruachan is the key to **Route 17**

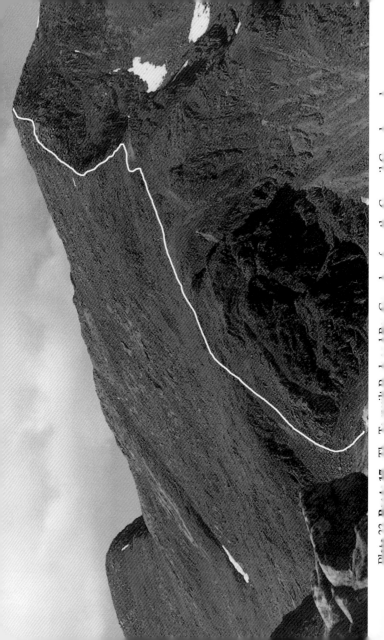

Plate 22

Route 18. The Traverse of the Cruachan Ridge. Park the car on the back road to Dalmally at a track south of the bridge over the Allt Mhoille. Follow the track until the east ridge of Monadh Driseig can be gained. From the summit continue along the crest of the rising edge to Beinn a'Bhuiridh, from whose crags you will obtain a fine view of Ben Cruachan across the depths of the intervening corrie. Now turn R and descend sharply to the col from which a steep climb will place you on the summit of Stob Garbh. Thence after a slight ascent you step on to the summit of Stob Diamh, which is a commanding viewpoint for the main ridge stretching westwards, and as it is only a short walk to Sron an Isean you may wish to make this diversion for the splendid vista along Glen Noe. Returning to Stob Diamh, you descend to the col and then climb to Drochaid Glas, also known as the Grey Bridge, which opens up a superb prospect to the final section of the ridge, crowned by both Ben Cruachan and Stob Dearg. Since the next mile is very narrow in places you must advance with care, eventually to stand beside the summit cairn of the reigning peak. When you have rested from the ardours of the ascent and admired the splendour of the panorama, walk over to Stob Dearg and then retrace your steps to join Route 17 for the descent, visiting the cairn on Meall Cuanail *en route*.

Other routes to the main ridge from Taynuilt can be worked out from the map, but they are just hard grinds and lacking in interest compared with the two routes described.

Plate 34 **Route 18**—Ben Cruachan from beinn a'Bhuiridh

Plate 35 **Route 18**—Ben Cruachan and Drochaid Glas from Stob Diamh

Stob Garbh

Stob Diamh

Sron an Isean

Plate 37 **Route 18**—Looking down the summit ridge

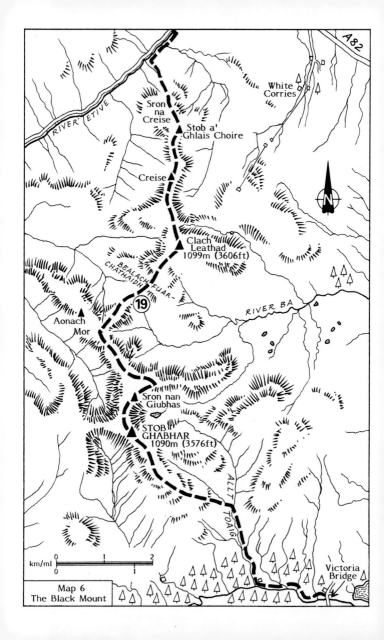

A82

White
Corries

RIVER ETIVE

Sron na
Creise

Stob a'
Ghlais Choire

Creise

N

Clach
Leathad
1099m (3606ft)

BEALACH FUAR-
CHATHAIDH

RIVER BA

19

Aonach
Mor

Sron nan
Giubhas

STOB
GHABHAR
1090m (3576ft)

ALLT TOAIG

Victoria
Bridge

km/ml   0   1   2

Map 6
The Black Mount

The Black Mount Hills

Meall a'Bhuiridh	3635 feet	1108 metres
Creise	3609 feet	1100 metres
Clach Leathad	3605 feet	1099 metres
Stob Ghabhar	3576 feet	1090 metres
Mam Coire Easain	3504 feet	1068 metres
Aonach Eagach	3271 feet	997 metres
Stob a'Ghlais Choire	3268 feet	996 metres
Sron a'Ghearrain	3248 feet	990 metres
Sron nan Giubhas	3195 feet	974 metres
Stob a'Choire Odhair	3100 feet	945 metres
Stob a'Bhruaich Leith	3087 feet	941 metres
Sron na Creise	2953 feet	900 metres
Aonach Mor	2844 feet	867 metres
Bealach Fuar-chathaidh	2319 feet	707 metres

Any mountaineer who has driven north over the road to Glen Coe will have been impressed by the magnificent array of peaks that come into view on the L after passing the foot of Loch Tulla and extend in an unbroken line all the way to Kingshouse. The old road wound its way across their flanks, but was too near to open up such grand prospects of them as are now revealed across the many glittering blue lochans that deck the wayside across Rannoch Moor. The range is known as the Black Mount, which, however, strictly speaking includes Ben Starav, referred to in Route 17. The Black Mount includes thirteen other separate peaks, but in the course of their traverse from Inveroran to Kingshouse, which is usually regarded as a classic among the many expeditions in the Central Highlands, it is customary to visit only seven or eight of them. The first peak to be climbed is Stob Ghabhar in the south, and the last Sron na Creise in the north; the map distance between them is about 5 miles/ 8 km and the lowest point the Bealach Fuar-chathaidh. Given favourable weather in summer, when no snow should be encountered, the walk from start to finish, allowing for halts for food and to view the scenery, and also for photography, will occupy a whole day. Its total length is 11 map miles/17.7 km. However, when walkers make this traverse from south to north in mist the only difficulty is to locate with certainty the exact spot on Aonach Mor, at 2844 feet/867 m approx., where the spur on the R descends to the Bealach Fuar-chathaidh. It should be noted that Route 19 may be shortened by turning R at Mam Coire Easain for Meall a'Bhuiridh, whose lower slopes may be descended from 2090 feet/637 m by the White Corries chairlift. The chairlift station is only just over a mile/1.6 km from the Kingshouse Hotel in Glen Coe.

Route 19. From Inveroran to Kingshouse. Leave the car at the end of the A8005, beyond the Inveroran Hotel, at Victoria Bridge, beyond which motor traffic is impossible. Turn L along the private road that follows the course of the river, and in about 1 mile/1.6 km turn R up the path beside the Allt Toaig. On reaching the 1000 feet contour cross the burn and bear L to ascend the Aonach Eagach, the south-east ridge of Stob Ghabhar. On attaining the summit cairn note the rock-bound corrie to the north-east which cradles the shining Coirein Lochain and beyond it the vast prospect of Rannoch Moor, dappled with innumerable lochans as far as the eye can see. Keeping to the edge of the precipices, walk downhill to Sron nan Giubhas and continue along the ridge of Aonach Mor. This rises gently in a north-westerly direction and discloses Coireach a'Ba on the R, with a glimpse of Ba Bridge on the old Glen Coe road some 3 miles/4.8 km to the east. Less than 1 mile/1.6 km ahead bear R and descend the spur that leads down some 500 feet/150 m to the Bealach Fuar-chathaidh, the lowest point on the ridge. Then tackle the steep declivities of

Plate 38 **Route 19**—Stob Ghabhar from Loch Tulla

Plate 20 **Route 19** Clach Leathad and Meall a'Bhuiridh from Ba Bridge

Plate 40 **Route 19**—Clach Leathad and Meall a'Bhuiridh from Rannoch Moor

Creise →   Stob a'Ghlais →   Sron na Creise
Choire

Stob a'Ghlais
Choire →

Plate 41 **Route 10** The terminal peaks of the Black Mount seen from Kingshouse

some 1200 feet/365 m rising to Clach Leathad, and on reaching the cairn pause for a moment to admire the wild prospect in which Meall a'Bhuiridh is prominent to the north-east and the long crest of Buachaille Etive Mor to the north-west. Now walk due north for nearly 2 miles/3.2 km over the almost level ridge, passing Mam Coire Easain and Creise to attain Stob a'Ghlais Choire, which suddenly discloses the Kingshouse Hotel on the moor far below. Now make your way through the crags to Sron na Creise, the terminal point on the ridge, and descend to the L of its long shoulder to pass the buttress in safety. Scree and heather lead across the Allt Cam Ghlinne falling from the Cam Ghleann to the car-park at the White Corries chairlift.

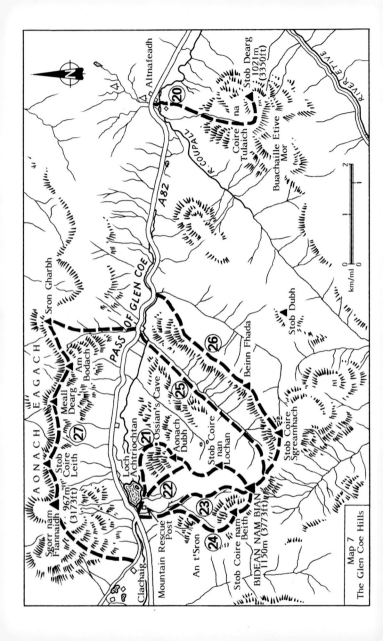

Map 7
The Glen Coe Hills

Buachaille Etive Mor

Stob Dearg	3350 feet	1021 metres
Stob na Doire	3316 feet	1011 metres
Stob na Broige	3136 feet	956 metres
Stob Coire Altrium	3087 feet	941 metres

On passing the watershed on the road over Rannoch Moor, above the Kingshouse Hotel, the whole of this mountain comes into view and reveals three of its four tops, as follows: Stob na Broige on the L; Stob na Doire in the centre hides Stob Coire Altruim; and Stob Dearg on the R. However, the beautiful elevation of the latter peak is not disclosed until the Kingshouse Hotel is reached, when it becomes clear that Stob Dearg is the most attractive of all the mountains frowning upon the vast wilderness of the moor. It presents the appearance of a broken, reddish-black symmetrical rock cone and in one sweep rises from the level moor, its lines converging on the Crowberry Ridge and North Buttress immediately below the summit. The view of it is most arresting when seen by early morning sunlight, because it throws into sharp relief all its main topographical features. It will be noticed that its northern and eastern flanks are split up into numerous buttresses and gullies which have become famous as a treasured playground for the rock climber. The first recorded ascent was in 1894, but today the whole facade is festooned with climbs (summer and winter) of varied difficulty, all of which are described in detail in the excellent Scottish Mountaineering Club guide *Glen Coe Rock and Ice Climbs*. On the Glen Etive side, the Buachaille, as it is familiarly called, contains a wild rift, known as the Chasm, which for many years had the distinction of being the longest gully climb on the mainland; its only rival at the time being the Water Pipe Gully in the Cuillins of Skye. However, the

Plate 42 Bunchr...lle Fhinn Mor from Kinochouse as it was in former years.

Plate 43 Buttresses and gullies flank the northern front of Stob Dearg

Clachaig Gully on Aonach Eagach is now acknowledged as the longest gully climb in Scotland. Buachaille Etive Mor is almost surrounded by the River Coupall which rises in the adjacent Lairig Gartain, swings round to the east beside the road and then turns south in Glen Etive to fall into the sea at Loch Etive. Bounded on the east by the Black Mount, this glen is 13 miles/ 21 km in length and one of the loveliest in Scotland. Both climber and tourist will be charmed by the artificial lochan and its rhododendrons, about half-way down on the L, whereas the former will make for the Slabs of Beinn Trilleachan on the R, above the derelict pier at the head of Loch Etive, to experience some of the most unique climbing in Scotland.

Route 20. Kingshouse and Stob Dearg. In view of the precipitous nature of the peak it does not offer the ordinary pedestrian a choice of routes to its summit. The most interesting is to start from the road at Altnafeadh, cross the River Coupall by a footbridge passing Lagangarbh hut, and follow a well-worn path into the mouth of Coire na Tulaich opposite. Follow the path alongside the burn and continue by a rough scramble over steep scree and boulders to attain the lip of the corrie, whence turn L and walk up the remaining 0.5 mile/0.8 km of slopes to the summit cairn. The panorama is disappointing owing to the lack of any interesting features on the nearer peaks. The only compensation is the view of Schiehallion which dominates the vast solitudes of Rannoch Moor to the northeast. A less interesting ascent can be made from a point about 2 miles/3.2 km down Glen Etive by way of Coire Cloiche Finne, between Stob Dearg and Stob na Doire.

Providing an early ascent of this route has been made, there is a most interesting and revealing addition that can be completed in the afternoon. Retrace your steps to the top of Coire na Tulaich and follow the ridge on its west. About halfway down the ridge turn L, descend into the Lairig Gartain and cross the River Coupall. Thence turn L again and follow the stream to its main tributary on the R and then climb up on to the ridge of Buachaille Etive Beag. Follow the ridge to its highest point, Stob Dubh, for the splendid vista of Glen Etive and its beautiful loch.

Plate 44 **Route 20**—Stob Dearg and Coire na Tulaich from Altnafeadh

Plate 45 Lochan Creag na Caillaich in Glen Etive

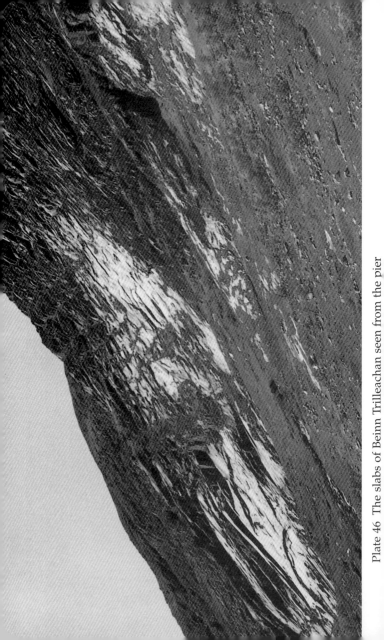

Plate 46 The slabs of Beinn Trilleachan seen from the pier

Bidean nam Bian

Bidean nam Bian	3773 feet	1150 metres
Stob Coire nan Lochan	3657 feet	1115 metres
Stob Coire nam Beith	3631 feet	1107 metres
Stob Coire Sgreamhach	3517 feet	1072 metres
Beinn Fhada	3123 feet	952 metres
An t'Sron	2951 feet	900 metres
Aonach Dubh	2920 feet	890 metres
Gearr Aonach	2267 feet	691 metres

Bidean nam Bian is the dominating peak in the great range of hills bearing its name, and the crowning glory of Argyll. It hems in the south side of Glen Coe and from the highest point on the old road, near the Study, its three northern spurs, well known as the Three Sisters, exhibit a remarkable pendent profile, but the real grandeur of the whole group is not seen to advantage from such a close viewpoint. While it assumes a striking elevation when seen from the adjacent ridge of Aonach Eagach, its real dominance of the landscape is best observed from some of the peaks in the Mamore Forest and on a clear day even from the distant summit of Ben Nevis. In the vicinity of the Clachaig Hotel, the actual summit of Bidean is hidden by its satellite, An t'Sron which encloses, with Stob Coire nan Lochan, the deep rift of Coire nam Beith.

From the bridge over the River Coe at the junction of the main road and the old road to the Clachaig Inn, the Diamond and Church Door Buttresses can be seen through the entrance to this corrie but they again hide the summit itself. Furthermore, owing to the close proximity of the eight tops which rise from the ridges of this massive group, none of them assumes any individual beauty when seen from afar, but when viewed from closer range the graceful lines of Stob Coire nan Lochan

Benn Fhada

Stob Coire
nan Lochan

Gearr Aonach

Aonach Dubh

Plate 47 The Three Sisters of Glen Coe and Stob Coire nan Lochan from the Old Road

immediately attract the eye and stamp it as the Queen of this mountain range.

Bidean nam Bian may be ascended without difficulty from several points within easy reach of the Clachaig Inn, but the usual approach is via Coire nam Beith or by way of An t'Sron when the ridge may be followed over Stob Coire nam Beith to the summit. The finest ridge walk, however, is to climb one of the Three Sisters of Glen Coe, take in Bidean on the way, and descend from An t'Sron. This means a longer expedition which can be accomplished in an easy day and is more than repaid by the variety of views obtained *en route*.

Route 21. Aonach Dubh and Stob Coire nan Lochan. The finest prospect of Aonach Dubh is obtained from the Clachaig Inn by afternoon sunlight which throws into sharp relief the innumerable buttresses and gullies that split its western front. Here, the Dinner Time Buttress is the most conspicuous feature and rises in an unbroken line in the centre of its immense facade. To the L, on the extreme northern end of Aonach Dubh, is a great gash known as Ossian's Cave. It looks like a dark keyhole just below the summit when seen from the road and immediately below it a deep gorge rises in an almost straight line from the glen. This gives access to the sloping ledge below the cave and is the key to our route which is only for the experienced walker with some scrambling experience and should be severely left alone by the ordinary pedestrian. Cross the bridge that gives access to Achnambeithach beside Loch Achtriochtan, skirt the loch's southern shore and continue below the cliffs until you reach the mouth of the gorge. Follow an indistinct path immediately to the L of the gorge until a large sloping trough appears on the R, a little below the level of the cave. The ledge runs parallel to this trough and just above it. It is reached by crossing the gorge and carefully scaling the rocks on the far side. This is loose and often wet. Once on the ledge, the path is again visible. Any deviations

Stob Coire Sgreamhach   Bidean nam Bian   Stob Coire nan Lochan   Aonach Dubh

Aonach Dubh

Dinner Time
Buttress

Plate 49 **Routes 21, 22, 23** and **24**—The slopes of An t'Sron are on the right and hide Coire nam Beith

from this route will lead on to precipitous ground. In particular, do not follow the faint track in the trough itself.

Now skirt the Porphyry Buttress on the L and beyond it climb the first short gully on the L to attain the rocky summit of Aonach Dubh. From the cairn note the dynamic prospect of Aonach Eagach on the other side of Glen Coe and then turn your steps to ascend the broad ridge rising to Stob Coire nan Lochan, noting on the L the four fine rock buttresses that support the ridge and peak. On attaining the cairn, pause for a moment to admire the superb northern panorama, where the eye skims over Aonach Eagach and then the Mamores, to rest finally upon the dominating peak of Ben Nevis. Now continue your climb by traversing the narrow but easy ridge that rises to the cairn on the summit of Bidean nam Bian, noting on the R the Diamond and Church Door Buttresses with Collie's Pinnacle at their feet.

The panorama is stupendous and the first section of note lies to the south where Loch Etive leads the eye past Ben Starav on the L to the Cruachan Range, then to the R to the western seas, Mull and the hills of Ardgour. The northern section is not so good as that from Stob Coire nan Lochan, but to the east it is possible on a clear day to pick out the tapering cone of Schiehallion immediately above Buachaille Etive. The cairn stands at the junction of three supporting ridges, all of which look easy, but unless the walker is familiar with their topography it is best to leave them alone and descend by Route 24.

Plate 51, Route 21 — Ben Nevis, the Mamores and Aonach Eagach from Stob Coire nan Lochan

Plate 52 **Route 21**—Bidean nam Bian from Stob Coire nan Lochan

Route 22. The Dinner Time Buttress. This rib is such a prominent feature of Aonach Dubh's west face that after crossing the bridge to Achnambeithach you make direct for its base. Alternatively a good path follows the west bank of the burn issuing from Coire nam Beith which can be crossed below the obvious waterfalls. Ascend the grassy centre of the buttress until you reach the crags and then climb them by the easiest variation until you emerge on the skyline. Here bear L for the cairn and join Route 21 for Bidean. This route involves some scrambling.

Route 23. Coire nam Beith. Start by Route 22, up the good path on the west bank of the burn passing the mouth of the corrie where the burn cascades down through its narrow opening. The path crosses the burn above here and follows the left tributary up the scree towards the Church Door Buttress. Pass to the R of this and climb to the Saddle where one turns L for Bidean.

Route 24. An t'Sron and Stob Coire nam Beith. Follow Route 23 to the mouth of the corrie and climb through the scanty trees on the R. Then make for the long gully splitting the north face of An t'Sron and ascend its west side to the cairn. Now contour round to the R and follow the well-marked path rising to the summit of Stob Coire nam Beith, whence keep to the lip of the corrie all the way to Bidean.

Route 25. Allt Coire Gabhail. Leave the Glen Coe road car-parks opposite Gearr Aonach, the prominent rocky central buttress of The Three Sisters, and descend the path to the upper foot-bridge over the River Coe. Pass the pools and then climb steeply beside the burn making your way through the maze of boulders piled one on top of another in its higher reaches, with the hidden stream gurgling away out of sight beneath them. When you step on to the grassy floor of the

Plate 53 **Routes 23** and **24**—Bidean, the Diamond and Church Door Buttresses from Stob Coire nam Beith

Plate 55 **Route 24**—Stob Coire nam Beith

corrie, which is littered with gigantic boulders, go straight ahead and climb the grassy tongue on the R of the scree to the saddle at the head of the glen and to the L of Bidean. Then turn R and walk up the ridge to its summit.

Route 26. Beinn Fhada and Stob Coire Sgreamhach. Leave the Glen Coe road near the waterfall at its head, and follow the path through the Lairig Eilde for a short distance to where it crosses the burn. Then bear R and make your way up the north-eastern slopes of Beinn Fhada. Continue along its lofty ridge with splendied views on the R of Bidean and Stob Coire nan Lochan, and after passing its two tops climb some 400 feet/120 m to reach the summit of Stob Coire Sgreamhach. Here turn R and ascend the narrow ridge to the cairn on the reigning peak.

Aonach Eagach

Sgorr nam Fiannaidh	3172 feet	967 metres
Meall Dearg	3127 feet	953 metres
Am Bodach	3094 feet	943 metres
Stob Coire Leith	3084 feet	940 metres
A'Chailleach	2936 feet	895 metres
Sron Charbh	2864 feet	873 metres
Pap of Glen Coe (Sgor na Ciche)	2431 feet	741 metres

This is the name given to the Notched Ridge surmounting the north wall of Glen Coe and stretching for over 5 miles/8 km from the Devil's Staircase in the east, to the Pap of Glen Coe in the west. Although it comprises eight peaks in its entirety, the narrowest part of the ridge from which its innumerable pinnacles project is under 2 miles/3.2 km in length and lies between Am Bodach in the east and Stob Coire Leith in the west. The south side of Aonach Eagach is most spectacular and stretches in one unbroken line along the north of Glen Coe, but a more realistic view of its amazing structure is obtained from the cairn on Aonach Dubh on the south side of the glen. To mountaineers it is famous for its ghostly pinnacles, all of which have to be climbed in the traverse of the ridge which is the narrowest and most sensational on the mainland. The best route is to ascend Am Bodach from the car-park on the north side of Glen Coe, just below the cottage at Alt-na-ruigh opposite Gearr Aonach, from where a well-worn path leads to the summit of Am Bodach. The highest peak to be traversed is Meall Dearg which is about half-way along. The section of the ridge between Am Bodach and Meall Dearg is often referred to as the Chancellor, while the complete ridge is known to local keepers as the Ptarmigan Ridge as these beautiful birds are often encountered on its lofty crest. Much of the ridge is steep

Stone Shoot

Am Bodach

Plate 57 **Route 27**—Aonach Eagach from the summit of Aonach Dubh

and exposed and the rock well-worn, so considerable care should be taken in wet weather or poor visibility, especially on the pinnacles and the descents. In winter the ridge is a Grade II snow and ice climb and should only be attempted by experienced climbers.

Route 27. The Aonach Eagach Traverse. Park your car in a lay-by below Alt-na-ruigh in Glen Coe and ascend the path, later alongside the Allt Ruigh, into Coire an Ruigh and the east flank of Am Bodach. There are several rocky outcrops on the higher slopes of this peak which are best avoided on the R. The ascent is steep all the way and on reaching the cairn you must linger for a while to admire the views of the glen far below, the

Plate 58 **Route 27**—Warning sign

Plate 59 **Route 27**—Loch Achtriochtan from Am Bodach

great yawning gullies that split the face of the cliffs which are a characteristic feature of this sentinel when seen from the glen, and the dynamic prospect of Bidean nam Bian and its supporting ridges which are revealed to greater advantage from this lofty coign of vantage. You will also note the central peak of Meall Dearg to the north-west, and to reach it you must exercise care in descending to its connecting ridge from Am Bodach, where you will find ample hand and footholds on its precipitous northern face. On attaining Meall Dearg you get a splendid conception of the line of pinnacles stretching away to the west, and to reach the first of them you descend the track that meanders in and out of the rocks on its south side. About half-way along you will encounter the Crazy Pinnacles, three of which stand at the top of gullies falling down both sides of the mountain. On a wild day the wind shrieks through the narrow gap in the ridge, but with a steady head you should have no difficulty in passing them, whence you climb a steep little chimney to set foot on the next pinnacle. Here you should pause to admire the retrospect, which reveals your last pinnacle standing boldly between Meall Dearg on the L and Am Bodach on the R, with immense precipices sweeping down on either side. On and on you go with no way of escape until eventually you reach the last two pinnacles which are the narrowest and most sensational of them all. You must again exercise the utmost care and balance to traverse them in safety. Thence the wider ridge is grassy all the way to Sgorr nam Fiannaidh and ultimately to the Pap of Glen Coe at its terminus. But not all walkers take in these two summits as they are less interesting after the delights of the narrower ridge. Various descents are now possible. The first descends from the col just short of Sgorr nam Fiannaidh and down the easier slopes beside the burn to the bridge over the River Coe at the west end of Loch Achtriochtan. Further on it is also possible to descend a steep, stony path following the west side of Clachaig gully to the Clachaig Inn. In wet weather or poor visibility this descent is quite unpleasant and exposed in places and considerable care should be taken. Either descent soon ends one of the most entertaining traverses in the Highlands.

Sgor nam Fiannaidh   Stob Coire Leith

Plate 60 **Route 27**—Looking west along the narrowest section of the ridge

Stob Dearg

Am Bodach

Meall Dearg

Plate 61 **Route 27**—Looking east along the crest of Aonach Eagach

Plate 27 **Route 62** The last pinnacle but one in the Western Traverse

Sgor nam Fiannaidh

Leith

Plate 63 Descent of **Route 27** seen from the last pinnacle on the ridge

Plate 64 **Route 27** Retrospect of the last pinnacle on Aonach Eagach

Plate 65 **Route 27**—Eastern prospect of the ridge from Stob Coire Leith

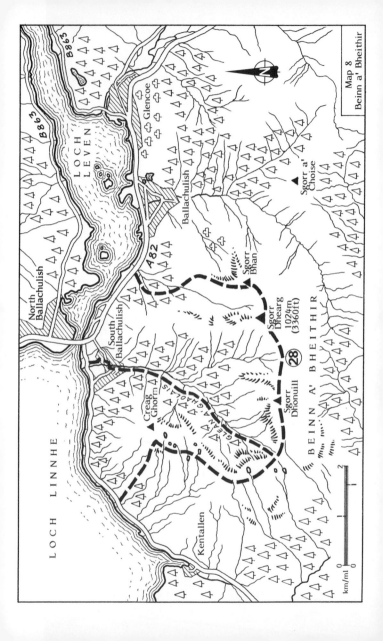

Map 8
Beinn a' Bheithir

LOCH LINNHE

LOCH LEVEN

B863

B863

Glencoe

North Ballachulish

Ballachulish

South Ballachulish

482

Kentallen

Sgorr a' Choise

Sgorr Bhan

Sgorr Dhearg
1024m
(3360ft)

28

Sgorr Dhonuill

Creag Ghorm

BEINN A' BHEITHIR

GLEAS A' CHAOLAIS

km/ml
0   1   2

Beinn a'Bheithir

Sgorr Dhearg	3359 feet	1024 metres
Sgorr Dhonuill	3284 feet	1001 metres
Sgorr Bhan	3107 feet	947 metres
Sgorr a'Chaolais	2700 feet	823 metres
Creag Ghorm	2372 feet	723 metres

This beautiful group of peaks rises to the south of Loch Leven and forms a great horseshoe which extends from above the village of Balluchulish and ends above the wooded slopes, 1 mile/1.6 km west of the Balluchulish Bridge. it exhibits three well-defined peaks: Sgorr Bhan, Sgorr Dhearg and Sgorr Dhonuill. A rocky spur known as Sgorr a'Chaolais extends to the north from the latter and forms a horn-shaped peak which is a prominent feature when seen from the bridge. The western ridge is broad and dappled with a collection of small lochans; it terminates in the summit of Creag Ghorm, and its lower slopes, together with those of the more easterly ridges, are surrounded by dense plantations. The fine topography of this magnificent range is well seen from the hills to the north of Loch Leven, and even better from the westerly peaks of the Mamore Forest. No problems will be encountered during the traverse where the going is easy and the views attractive. But it might be as well to warn walkers that the direct descent to the road through the plantations from Creag Ghorm is fraught with difficulties. It is advisable, therefore, to descend a grassy gully beyond Sgorr Dhonuill into the corrie and follow a path and forestry track back to South Ballachulish, or to descend from Creag Ghorm in a south-westerly direction to Kentallen and so avoid the plantations.

Sgorr Bhan   Sgorr Dhearg   Sgorr Dhonuill

Plate 66 Beinn a'Bheithir seen across Loch Leven, since this photograph was taken there has been much felling and regrowth of trees on the sides of the hill.

Route 28. The Beinn a'Bheithir Horseshoe. Turn R off the A82 about 0.25 mile/0.4 km to the west of Ballachulish just beyond the church beside a disused railway signal, and follow the forestry road through the trees enclosing the Allt Giubhsachain. On emerging from the leafy canopy bear L and climb the steep path leading to the ridge of Sgorr Bhan, which is followed in a southerly direction until you attain the cairn, noting on the L the impressive subsidiary spur of slate that falls to the east. The view of the adjacent peak of Sgorr Dhearg is always attractive, but especially so under snow when the graceful curves of its ridge delight the eye. It swings round to the R for about 0.5 mile/0.8 km to end by the cairn on this dominating peak, which unfolds a fine panorama. A pleasant feature is the prospect to the north-east of the whole of the Mamores beyond the blue of Loch Leven, while to the west across the intervening bealach, Sgorr Dhonuill assumes a magnificent profile; to reach it from the col involves a steep ascent of 800 feet/245 m. When you attain its cairn, pause for a moment to scan the retrospect which discloses the zigzag pattern of the ridge you have just descended, with the sharp little peak of Sgorr a'Choise peeping over its R shoulder. To the north you look over the craggy top of Sgorr a'Chaolais to the narrow entrance of Loch Leven below, but to the west Creag Ghorm obscures the broad stretches of Loch Linnhe, above which Garbh Bheinn rises into the sky above Ardgour. Now walk down the stony slopes of Sgorr Dhonuill, along the broad plateau with its tiny lochans to a small flat-topped undulation and a dip in the ridge at about 2625 feet/800 m, which gives access to a grassy gully leading to the corrie below. From here a path leads to a forestry track through the woods in Gleann a'Chaolais and to South Ballachulish. Otherwise one may continue along the ridge which sweeps round to the north of Creag Ghorm, whence turn L and go down its slopes to Kentallen with spacious views ahead of Loch Linnhe.

Plate 67 **Route 28.** The graceful curve of Sgor Dhonuill seen from Sgorr Bhan

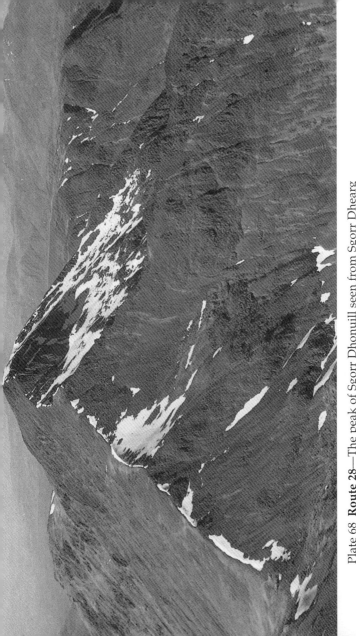

Plate 68 **Route 28**—The peak of Sgorr Dhonuill seen from Sgorr Dhearg

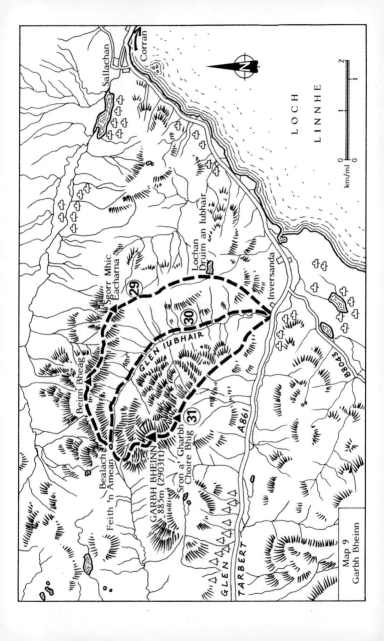

SALLACHAN

Corran

N

km/ml 0   1   2

L O C H

L I N N H E

Sgorr Mhic
Eacharna

(29)

Lochan
Druim an Iubhair

(30)

Inversanda

GLEN IUBHAIR

Beinn
Bheag

B8043

Bealach
Feith 'n Amean

GARBH BHEINN
885m (2903ft)

(31)

Sron a' Gharbh
Choire Bhig

A861

GLEN TARBERT

Map 9
Garbh Bheinn

Garbh Bheinn

Garbh Bheinn	2903 feet	885 metres
Sron a'Gharbh Choire Bhig	2671 feet	814 metres
Beinn Bheag	2387 feet	728 metres
Meall a'Chuillin	2254 feet	687 metres
Sgor Mhic Eacharna	2130 feet	649 metres
Bealach Feith'n Amean	1772 feet	540 metres
Druim an Iubhair	1600 feet	488 metres

When seen from Corran Ferry, the magnificent rock peak of Garbh Bheinn is a conspicuous feature in the western prospect of Ardgour, and may be reached by following the narrow road skirting Loch Linnhe to Inversanda, whence the R fork leads to a bridge over the river flowing down from Coire an Iubhair. This is the starting point of the three following routes, all of which are interesting but longer than they seem, and cars may be parked in the lay-by immediately to the east of the bridge. The mountain flanks the northern side of Glen Tarbert, along which the road continues to Loch Sunart. Looking back from the vicinity of Strontian discloses a splendid view of its immense rocky declivities dominating the head of the loch. On closer acquaintance Garbh Bheinn is revealed as a superb rock peak whose eastern front is riven by ridges, buttresses and gullies, of which the Great Gully is a prominent feature cleaving the face of the mountain. It is hemmed in on the L by the Great Ridge, and further to the R by the Pinnacle Ridge, beyond which the North-East Buttress falls steeply to the Bealach Feith'n Amean and its lonely Lochan Coire an Iubhair.

To the L of the peak a bealach separates it from Sron a'Gharbh Choire Bhig, and its lofty ridge falls to the bridge, flanked by immense slabs of rock which are well seen from the other side

Garbh Bheinn

Plate 60 Garbh Bheinn from Camas Fearna

of the glen. The best way to see the topographical features of
this great peak is to combine Routes 29 and 31, which keep to
the skyline of Glen Iubhair, ascending by the former and
descending by the latter. But even under favourable conditions
this is a long and arduous expedition, totalling over 7 map
miles/11.3 km, with 4300 feet/1300 m of ascent, and should
only be undertaken by walkers in very fit condition.

Route 29. By Sgor Mhic Eacharna. Pass by the large boulder
lying beside the road and make your way through bog, tangled
heather and crags in a north-easterly direction. After climbing
about 1300 feet/400 m you set foot on the gradually rising
Druim an Iubhair, where a small lochan can be seen on the R.
Continue along the flattish ridge and note the great slabs of
rock flanking the glen on the L, and when just short of the first
top observe the fine elevation of Garbh Bheinn on the L. After
passing Sgor Mhic Eacharna descend to the col and thence
climb to the narrow crest of Beinn Bheag. This opens up a view
of the Bealach Feith'n Amean and its blue lochan, above which
rise abruptly the precipitous northern slopes of your peak.

Descend sharply to the lochan and note the great rock
buttresses ahead which seemingly halt your progress, but do
not attempt to climb them or their adjacent gullies. Go further
to the R until you encounter a long talus slope which terminates
in a narrow stone shoot high above. Scramble up this to enter
the little north-west corrie and so gain the main ridge near the
top of the Pinnacle Ridge on the L. Then walk up to the summit
cairn which is perched almost on the rim of the Great Ridge.
The stupendous panorama from Garbh Bheinn is breath-taking
in its magnificence, with the crags dropping away at your feet
to Glen Iubhair far below. Its eastern arc will hold your gaze as
it unfolds the splendour of Ben Nevis, the Mamores, the Glen
Coe Hills and Beinn a'Bheithir across the glimmering stretches
of Loch Linnhe. To the west Ben Resipol is a prominent
landmark, and to its L your eye will skim over the shining

Sgor Mhic Eacharna

Beinn Bheag

Plate 70 **Route 79** Seen from Druim an Iubhair

surface of Loch Sunart to Ardnamurchan and the sea, with, in the south-west, vistas over Morvern to the hills of Mull.

Route 30. By Glen Iubhair. Follow the boggy path beside the burn descending the glen, which peters out after about 1 mile/ 1.6 km. Then continue over boggy ground along its north bank and eventually climb the rough heathery slopes to its source on the bealach, observing the fine views of the immense crags on the L. There join Route 29 for the summit of Garbh Bheinn.

Route 31. Sron a'Gharbh Choire Bhig. Cross the bridge over the river and make your way through a maze of tangled heather and grass to the foot of the ridge that rises on the L of the glen. Keep the precipitous crags on your R as you climb and make your way in and out of the many slabby outcrops. The going is steep and strenuous, but on reaching the top of your first objective you will be rewarded by a close view of the magnificent Great Ridge that falls in one unbroken sweep from the summit of Garbh Bheinn, on the other side of the intervening bealach. Now descend to it and climb the 500 feet/150 m of steep ground to the cairn on the reigning peak of the group.

From Glen Tarbert there is a wild prospect of the steep rock walls enclosing Coire a'Chothruim, which is the source of the Carnoch River. Its ascent looks tempting, but is best left alone by all save the experienced rock climber.

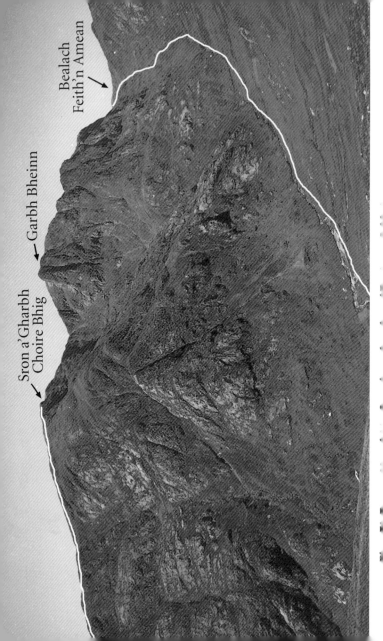

Sron a'Gharbh Choire Bhig — Garbh Bheinn — Bealach Feith'n Amean

The Mamores

Binnein Mor	3707 feet	1130 metres
Sgurr a'Mhaim	3605 feet	1099 metres
Na Gruagaichean	3464 feet	1056 metres
Am Bodach	3386 feet	1032 metres
Sgurr Eilde Mor	3313 feet	1010 metres
Sgor an Iubhair	3284 feet	1001 metres
Stob Ban	3277 feet	999 metres
An Gearanach	3222 feet	982 metres
Stob Coire a'Chairn	3218 feet	981 metres
Sgor Eilde Beag	3135 feet	956 metres
Binnein Beag	3094 feet	943 metres
Mullach nan Coirean	3081 feet	939 metres

This delightful range of hills stretches from east to west for nearly 10 miles/16 km and is bounded on the north by Glen Nevis and on the south by Loch Leven. On a clear day the whole of it can be seen from Beinn a'Bheithir and Aonach Eagach in the south, and although the views of it are against the light when observed from the north, Ben Nevis and Aonach Beag have the advantage of proximity and superior height as coigns of vantage for its appraisal. The group comprises a main ridge about 7 miles/11.3 km in length, with three well-defined northern spurs, and includes several shapely conical tops; it is therefore ideal terrain for the ridge wanderer. White quartzite is well distributed on the ridges, but is most noticeable on the summits of Sgurr a'Mhaim and Stob Ban. Both these peaks are a conspicuous feature of the views looking up Glen Nevis. Some of the peaks can be reached from Glen Nevis in the vicinity of Polldubh, or from its remote stretches between Steall and Tom an Eite, and on the south side the Old Military Road through Kinlochleven gives easy access throughout its entire length.

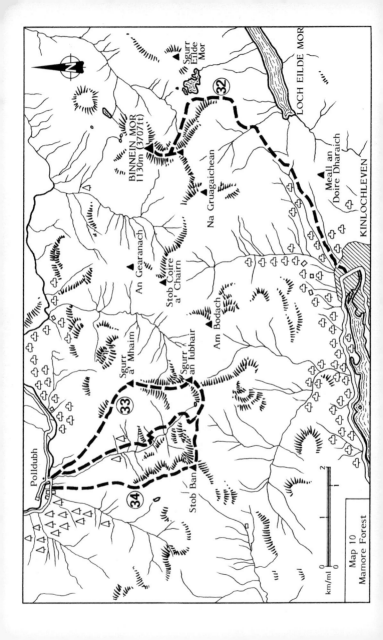

Map 10
Mamore Forest

Plate 72 An Gearanach and the gorge of Glen Nevis

The more westerly tops are usually climbed from the former and the more easterly from the latter. Strangely enough the most picturesque peaks are clustered round Sgurr a'Mhaim, and include the superb elevations of Stob Ban, Am Bodach and the Devil's Ridge.

Glen Nevis is one of the most beautiful in Scotland and should be seen by all climbers as well as walkers. The finest section begins at Polldubh and increases in splendour as you walk east, but its most spectacular feature is only revealed where the path turns to the right beyond the cataract. Here you are confronted by a scene of wild grandeur, with the An Steall waterfall coming into view beyond the narrow gorge where it descends the steep and rugged slopes of An Gearanach. With favourable lighting it makes a superb subject for your camera.

Route 32. Binnein Mor from Kinlochleven. Depart by the path that leaves Kinlochleven just to its west and walk through woodland alongside the burn until the path rises and skirts Meall an Doire Dharaich to its north. After crossing the Old Military Road the path continues rising towards Coire nan Laogh below Na Gruagaichean, with views on the R down to Loch Eilde Mor, and then traverses round the steep craggy spur of Sgor Eilde Beag until Coire an Lochain is reached. From here it is possible to traverse L again to ascend the rough scree in upper Coire a'Bhinnein to the saddle due south of your peak, or to ascend the north spur of Sgor Eilde Beag and continue north along the ridge to the saddle. Since Binnein Mor is the highest peak in the Mamores the panorama is extensive and to the west reveals most of the range in which the wall-like ridge of An Gearanach is prominent. Ben Nevis and its easterly satellites stretch across the skyline to the north and disclose their extremely steep declivities to advantage. Aonach Eagach does not look so formidable from this viewpoint and is crowned by the indented skyline of Bidean nam Bian in the south. To the south-west glimpses of Loch Leven lead the eye to Loch Linnhe, backed by the hills of Ardgour.

Route 33. Sgurr a'Mhaim from Polldubh. While this peak can be climbed direct by its north-west ridge rising straight to the summit, it is more interesting to start from Achribhach near Polldubh in Glen Nevis and follow the Allt Coire a'Mhusgain into Coire nam Miseach and the saddle east of Stob Ban, and then turn east to attain Sgor an Iubhair. Now turn north and traverse the Devil's Ridge which leads to the summit, passing *en route* the little peak of Stob a'Choire Mhail. The views from the cairn are magnificent and include the three features already noted.

Route 34. Stob Ban from Polldubh. This peak is usually ascended without difficulty by its north ridge, but again it is more interesting to follow Route 33 to the saddle as it opens up grand prospects of the precipitous buttress supporting Stob Ban's summit. Turn west at the saddle and scramble up the rough quartzite scree to the cairn.

Sgurr a'Mhaim

Allt Coire a'Mhusgain

Stob Ban

Plate 74 **Route 33**—Sgor an Iubhair and the Devil's Ridge from Sgurr a'Mhaim

Plate 75. **Route 33.** Am Bodach from Sgurr a'Mhaim

Plate 76 **Route 34**—Stob Ban and Mullach nan Coirean from Sgurr a'Mhaim

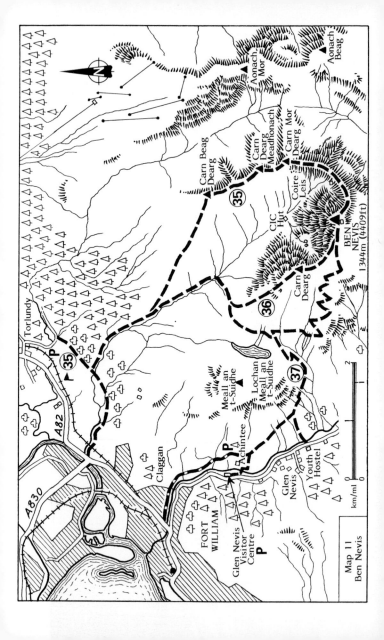

Map 11
Ben Nevis

Ben Nevis

Ben Nevis	4409 feet	1344 metres
Carn Dearg	4006 feet	1221 metres
Carn Mor Dearg	4002 feet	1220 metres
Carn Dearg Meadhonach	3868 feet	1179 metres
Carn Mor Dearg Arête	3750 feet	1143 metres
Carn Beag Dearg	3300 feet	1006 metres
Meall an Suidhe	2333 feet	711 metres

Ben Nevis is the highest mountain in Scotland and also the Monarch of our British Hills. It frowns upon the busy town of Fort William, but is obscured by its satellite Meall an Suidhe to the west. Its smooth and steep western flanks completely belie its hidden grandeur, but its rugged southern slopes, crowned by Carn Dearg and well seen from Polldubh in Glen Nevis, are an indication of its real magnificence. When viewed from Corpach across the glittering blue of Loch Linnhe, Ben Nevis reveals some of these features, but the main impression is that of its immense bulk, whereas the more easterly coign of vantage of Banavie opens up a glimpse of its towering cliffs that enclose the precipices of Coire na Ciste, a secret that is hidden from the average tourist but well known to the legions of rock and ice climbers who visit this delectable playground. Facing the north-east, this superb display of buttress, ridge, gully and couloir is hemmed in by the lofty ridge crowned by Carn Mor Dearg, whose altitude is only about 400 feet/120 m less than its peer, and to which it is joined by the famous Arête. Between these two peaks lies the glen of the Allt a'Mhuilinn, which is the usual line of approach for the rock and ice climber, and at its head stands the remote CIC Hut of the Scottish Mountaineering Club, protected from the gales that sweep across the nearby summits.

Owing to its dominating altitude, Ben Nevis is often snow-bound during both winter and spring, when great cornices overhang the lip of the corrie to an unknown depth, and in whose north-eastern gullies it usually lingers on into the summer. This great mountain, therefore, has everything to offer the climber and in consequence is perhaps the most powerful magnet in the Highlands. But, since it has the reputation of being curtained by cloud for as much as 300 days each year, those who wish to enjoy to the full its glorious scenery must choose a day for the climb with discretion, savoured with luck, and the best opportunities for success are in April and May. Pedestrians who are content to gaze in wonder upon the towering precipices with as little effort as possible should stroll up the Allt a'Mhuilinn into Coire na Ciste, or if they are more energetic could walk up the less interesting Tourist Route from Achintee in Glen Nevis, whence in good weather they may wander at leisure along the rim of the summit plateau and see at their feet the splendours of the mountain.

All walkers should, however, bear in mind that in low cloud, hill fog or at night, navigation from the summit of Ben Nevis is very difficult. The gullies of the north face cut deeply into the plateau and the upper reaches of Five Finger Gully to the south are often mistaken for the way down. The margin for error on safely navigating back down the line of the path is very small despite the large size of the mountain and Five Finger Gully itself is precipitous and presents a formidable hazard for those less experienced. Do not rely on following cairns in such conditions as many 'tourists' build them all over the plateau in celebration of their ascent! In winter, indeed for much of the year and often into May, the path is obscured by snow and visibility is rarely good. Blizzards can develop extremely fast and temperatures and wind speeds on the summit can be formidable. The avalanche hazard in Five Finger Gully is often high and there have been deaths here. It is vital that walkers can navigate competently; that they plan their route in advance (even if just going up the Tourist Route) in case they get caught out in deteriorating weather – which can happen very quickly; and that they are prepared for the worst weather and conditions likely.

But the experienced walker will select the only route that displays the mountain's charms to perfection; by first ascending Carn Mor Dearg, then crossing the sensational Arête, and finally wending his way along the plateau, and if the weather is calm and sunny he will see Ben Nevis in one of its most gentle moods.

Route 35. By Carn Mor Dearg. Start at the Ben Nevis Distillery on the A82, just beyond the junction with the A830 to Corpach to the north of Fort William. Skirt the distillery to the north and cross the railway to the south side of the Allt Coire an Lochain/Allt a'Mhuilinn. Continue to a bridge and follow a boggy path which contours north towards the Allt a'Mhuilinn, east of the golf course. Continue on the steep path alongside the Allt a'Mhuilinn and then a section of track to a dam.

Alternatively the steep path alongside the Allt a'Mhuilinn can be reached more easily from Torlundy. Drive north on the A82 for 2 km and turn right at Torlundy, cross the railway bridge, then turn immediately right on to a forest track. This leads to a car park. A path branches off the track from the left-hand bend beyond and joins an old dismantled tramway. Follow this south to join the Allt a'Mhuillin path and so on to the dam.

From here strike up to the L in the direction of Carn Beag Dearg, the first peak on the Carn Mor Dearg ridge. The going is very arduous until it is attained, whence the walk along the lofty ridge is a revelation; as it gradually unveils Coire na Ciste on the R and the massive Aonachs on the L. Pass Carn Dearg Meadhonach to reach the shapely top of Carn Mor Dearg, which is a viewpoint without compare in this region, since it

Plate 77. **Route 25.** The summit of Camp Dome Meadbrough

Plate 78 **Route 35**—Carn Mor Dearg

Plate 80 **Route 35**–The twin ridges of Ben Nevis from Carn Mor Dearg

reveals the whole of Coire na Ciste from the North-East Buttress on the L to Carn Dearg on the R. Ahead the ridge falls to the Arête, with beyond its graceful sweep splendid prospects of the Mamores, among which Sgurr a'Mhaim and its little corrie are conspicuous.

Then begin the traverse of the Arête, moving along its rocky crest with care until you come to the last section where the steepest rise is some 700 feet/210 m to the top of the North-East Buttress. Should this last section be under snow and ice, exercise the utmost alertness and make use of your ice axe and crampons to ensure stability of each step, as a slip and slide backwards would precipitate you into the depths of Coire Leis and certain death. Having safely passed this lofty sentinel, the rest of the route is straightforward in good weather, with first a close view of the derelict observatory, and then the many attractive topographical features of Coire na Ciste, in which Gardyloo Gully, Tower Ridge and the Trident Buttress are prominent. On a clear day the summit panorama from Ben Nevis is stupendous, with the distant sea and its islands to the west, and in all other directions peaks and ridges, enlivened by the glint of light on lochs and lochans, as far as the eye can see. In an atmosphere of exceptional clarity you may be able to pick out such well-known landmarks as Ben Wyvis to the north; the Cairngorms to the north-east; Ben Lawers and Schiehallion to the east; Ben Lomond and the Cobbler to the south-east; Ben Cruachan, the Paps of Jura and the sea to the south; Mull beyond Loch Linnhe to the south-west; the Cuillin of Skye to the west with Beinn Fhada and Mam Sodhail to the north-west. And beyond the summit plateau you look into the wide green valley where the River Lochy leads your eye to the R into the Great Glen which ends at Inverness. Having now gained many varied impressions of and from this peak, you will turn your steps homewards, descending by one of the following routes according to your destination.

Plate 81 **Route 36**—Coire na Ciste and Carn Dearg from Carn Mor Dearg

Route 36. By Carn Dearg. Follow Route 35 to the dam which can be crossed to the south side of the Allt a'Mhuilinn. Climb the rather indistinct track over a deer fence and then alongside the L bank of the Allt Coire an Lochain, with occasional wooden posts, to gain Lochan Meall an t-Suidhe, the Halfway Lochan. Turn L and pick your way over rough scree and through the crags that deck the slopes to the summit of Carn Dearg. On passing the main summit, descend to the col at the top of Coire na h-Urchaire and then follow the rising rim of the plateau to pick up the main track and arrive at the cairn on Ben Nevis. This route is not recommended in winter or in weather with poor visibility.

Route 37. From Achintee. Just beyond the turning to Glen Nevis on the A82 north of Fort William is a signpost on the right to Achintee. Leave the car before the farm and follow the well-worn pony track, now known as the Tourist Route, that rises diagonally round the steep flanks of Meall an Suidhe, to the lochan hidden in the corrie to the north. Climb the seemingly endless stony zigzags until the lip of Coire na Ciste is reached, whence turn R for the summit of the mountain. This route is also easily reached from the visitor centre below Achintee in Glen Nevis and by the path from the Youth Hostel in Glen Nevis. Although somewhat tedious this route is the most popular line of ascent and in winter or in changeable weather is the only recommended route of ascent to and descent from the summit of Britain's highest and most dangerous mountain.

Plate 82 **Routes 36** and **37**—Snow cornices overhang the precipices of Ben Nevis

Plate 83. **Routes 26 and 27.** The Tower and the final section of its ridge

Creag Meagaidh

Creag Meagaidh	3701 feet	1128 metres
Creag Mhor	3494 feet	1065 metres
Stob Poite Coire Ardair	3458 feet	1054 metres
Beinn a'Chaorainn	3441 feet	1049 metres
Meall Coire Choille-Rais	3369 feet	1027 metres
Carn Liath	3301 feet	1006 metres
An Cearcallach	3259 feet	993 metres
Sron Garbh Choire	3248 feet	990 metres
The Window	3200 feet	975 metres
Meal an-t-Snaim	3180 feet	969 metres
A'Bhuidheanach	3169 feet	966 metres
Stob Coire Dhuibh	3006 feet	916 metres
Carn Dearg	2913 feet	888 metres
Lochan a'Choire	2046 feet	624 metres

Creag Meagaidh dominates the massive group of rounded hills that extend for some 12 miles/19.3 km along the entire north-western border of Loch Laggan. When seen from the lochside road they display little of interest to the climber, other than an invigorating traverse of the ups and downs of the lofty connecting ridges. But, hidden away in the deep fastnesses of the range, lies a wild corrie that is hemmed in on the south and west by immense cliffs that drop precipitously for about 1500 feet/450 m to Lochan a'Choire in Coire Ardair. This is the most spectacular prize of the group and may be reached by a stalkers' path which starts at the farm of Aberarder; it is some 4 miles/6.4 km in length and takes about two hours of easy going to attain the lochan.

The path rises sharply from the moorland as far as the first group of scattered trees, at a height of about 1800 feet/550 m, whence it levels out and contours round the northern slopes of

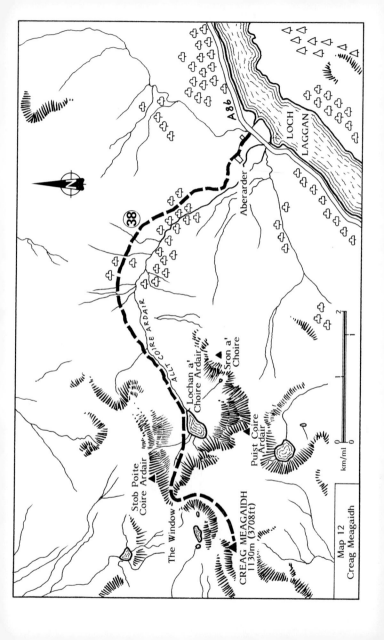

LOCH LAGGAN

A86

Aberarder

38

ALLT COIRE ARDAIR

Lochan a'
Choire Ardair

Sron a'
Choire

Stob Poite
Coire Ardair

Puist Coire
Ardair

The Window

CREAG MEAGAIDH
1130m (3708ft)

km/ml

0   1   2

Map 12
Creag Meagaidh

the vast corrie. But then about 1 mile/1.6 km from the cliffs it descends slightly to the burn and follows its L bank to the shore of the lochan. Photographers should note that even during the summer months, the light goes off the cliffs about 1 p.m. so that it is essential to get there by midday if satisfactory shots are to be secured.

The cliffs were first explored by rock climbers as long ago as April 1896, but in recent years they have received more attention in winter and are now one of the major ice climbing venues in the area. The most popular ascents are the three buttresses and the three 'Posts' or gullies that cleave them. To the north the cliffs diminish in height and finally merge with the rising ground leading to the lofty narrow pass, known as the Window.

Route 38. Creag Meagaidh via Coire Ardair. Turn off the A86 on the shore of Loch Laggan and park at Aberarder farm. After changing into walking boots, follow a good path behind the farm across the lower moorland. Beyond the trees the rough track levels out and swings round to the L along the contours of the lower corrie. Hereabouts the cliffs at the head of Coire Ardair come into view and reveal the sharp dip on their right, already referred to as the Window. The last mile of the ascent seems endless until finally the lochan suddenly appears at your feet. The scene is magnificent and the epitome of sombre desolation, with only the music of the burn to break the profound silence, save on occasion the sudden flight of a brace of Ptarmigan with their chicks fluttering away to seek cover. Should you wish to scale Creag 'Meggie', as it is familiarly known to climbers, walk up to the Window and turn L to ascend the final slopes to its summit cairn.

It should be noted that the summit plateau of Creag Meagaidh is very flat and featureless and in poor visibility particularly accurate navigation will be required to locate the Window back into Coire Ardair.

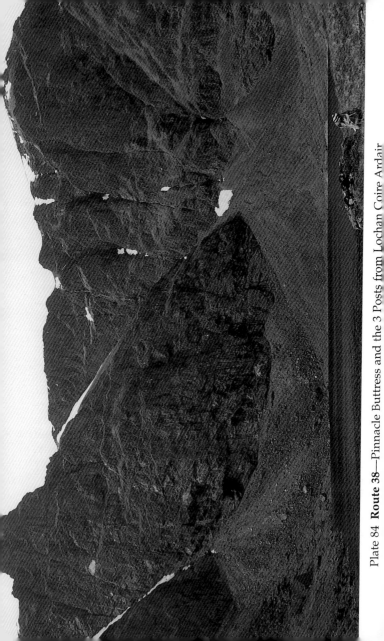

Plate 84 **Route 38**—Pinnacle Buttress and the 3 Posts from Lochan Coire Ardair

The Saddle

The Saddle	3314 feet	1010 metres
Sgurr na Forcan	3159 feet	963 metres
Sgurr na Sgine	3103 feet	946 metres
Spidean Dhomhuill Bhric	3081 feet	939 metres
Sgurr Leac nan Each	3015 feet	919 metres
Faochag	3008 feet	917 metres
Sgurr na Creige	2851 feet	869 metres
Bealach Coire Mhalagain	2290 feet	698 metres
Sgurr a'Gharg Gharaidh	2251 feet	686 metres

The finest elevation of this graceful, tapering peak comes into view during the long descent of Glen Shiel, and for about 2 miles/3.2 km it dominates the scene, framed by the rugged enclosing slopes of the narrowest part of the glen. It only disappears from view on reaching Shiel Bridge, whence the road skirts its flanks almost to the head waters of Loch Duich. In this classic view of the mountain, Faochag appears on the left as a sharp, well-defined peak, and it is customary to portray the two together, when, in snowy raiment, the beauty of one is complementary to that of the other. Moreover, when seen from Sgurr na Carnach on the other side of the glen, the serrated eastern ridge of the Saddle charms the eye and is a prominent feature of the view.

The two peaks are separated by the lofty Bealach Coire Mhalagain, which is the starting point for the most sporting ascent of the Saddle. This is really the culminating point of a U-shaped group of hills, to the east of which extends the rocky spur of Sgurr na Forcan. It affords an interesting scramble of which about 1000 feet/300 m are very steep, but should not be scaled by inexperienced walkers as the knife-edge section is sensational and yields the summit only by way of a short

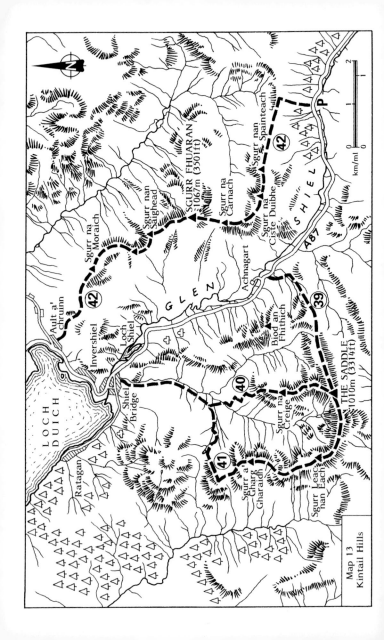

Map 13
Kintail Hills

narrow gully. The two northern ridges are in part narrow and characterised by precipitous rock faces, with, here and there, knife-edges and pinnacles. But the main ridge proper is about 1.5 mile/2.4 km in length and extends due east-west from Sgurr na Forcan to Spidean Dhomhuill Bhric. The ascent of the two northern ridges can be made without difficulty and the best route is to ascend via Sgurr na Creige and descend by Sgurr a'Gharg Gharaidh. Two wild corries flank the Sgurr na Creige ridge; Coire Uaine lies to the west and is the finer, with a small lochan at its head almost directly below the Saddle, whose face hereabouts is cleaved by a great gully. Coire Chaoil lies to the east and is of less interest.

Route 39. By Sgurr na Forcan. Start in Glen Shiel about 350 yards/320 m north of the bridge over the Allt Mhalagain, facing the Saddle and directly below Meallan Odhar. Follow the stalkers' path which winds its way uphill across the moor to the west and then skirts north below Meallan Odhar to the broad ridge between Biod an Fhithich and that peak. Pass over Meallan Odhar to the base of the Forcan Ridge which is supported by shattered, precipitous cliffs of menacing aspect. Climb to the R of the ridge crest, then cross the knife-edge and scale the gully that will place you at the foot of the rocky cone carrying the summit cairn. The panorama is extensive but shut in to the north-east by the Five Sisters of Kintail. To the south-east a veritable sea of peaks and ridges lead the eye on a clear day to Ben Nevis. To the west Beinn Sgritheall is prominent by reason of its proximity, with glimpses of Loch Hourn to its south, while beyond, the blue arms of the sea, backed by the distant Cuillin of Skye, make a beautiful vista.

Plate 86 **Route 39**—The saddle, Sgurr na Forcan and the connecting ridge

Route 40. By Sgurr na Creige. Leave Shiel Bridge, follow the path up the Allt Undalain to where it divides into the Allt a'Coire Uaine on the R and the Allt a'Choire Chaoil on the L, cross the burn and climb the slopes of Sgurr na Creige ahead. This ascent is steep and strenuous, and continues for about 1500 feet/450 m, but the going may be facilitated by taking a wide zigzag course. The sharp nose of the peak appears on the skyline, but after passing over it the angle eases off and good progress can be made along the ridge and over its narrow sections to the cairn on the Saddle.

Route 41. By Sgurr a'Gharg Gharaidh. Follow Route 40 but keep to the path all the way to the col between Sgurr Mhic Bharraich and Sgurr a'Gharg Gharaidh above Loch Coire nan Crogachan, with striking views on the L of Coire Uaine. Turn L at the col and traverse the crest of the ridge over Sgurr a'Gharg, Sgurr Leac nan Each and Spidean Dhomhuill Bhric all the way to the reigning peak, noting on the R glimpses of Loch Hourn far below.

The Five Sisters of Kintail

Sgurr Fhuaran	3500 feet	1067 metres
Sgurr na Ciste Duibhe	3369 feet	1027 metres
Sgurr na Carnach	3287 feet	1002 metres
Sgurr nan Spainteach	3247 feet	990 metres
Sgurr nan Saighead	3048 feet	929 metres
Sgurr na Moraich	2874 feet	876 metres
Bealach an Lapain	2372 feet	723 metres
Sgurr an t'Searriach	1890 feet	576 metres

This mighty range of hills dominates the head of Loch Duich and its conspicuous, well-defined tops can be picked out among its cluster of lofty neighbours from many points to the west. Its finest elevation is revealed from the viewpoint on the Bealach Ratagain on the minor road linking Shiel Bridge and Glenelg where the view includes the blue of Loch Duich below, but a good idea of its topography is also obtained from the Youth Hostel at Ratagan on the shore of Loch Duich north-west of Shiel Bridge. A reference to the map will show that there are actually six peaks in this range, but since Sgurr nan Spainteach is hidden behind Sgurr na Ciste Duibhe in the above prospect, the impression is gained of only five, hence the name. The complete traverse of the Five Sisters is a considerable undertaking, even with transport to a point in Glen Shiel immediately below Sgurr nan Spainteach.

But in the walk from east to west a saving can be made by omitting the last of the Five Sisters, Sgurr na Moraich, by descending into Coire Criche from the bealach after Sgurr nan Saighead and carefully following the Allt a'Chruinn to the road. And moreover, since the walk involves over 10,000 feet/ 3000 m of ascent and descent, an early start should be made if

Plate 87 The Five Sisters of Kintail and Loch Duich from Mam Ratagain, today the trees in the

the members of the party wish to be back at their lodgings in time for dinner.

Route 42. The Traverse of the Five Sisters. Park at Glenshiel Bridge and follow the ascending path alongside the burn at the plantation boundary, which leads to the ridge near Sgurr nan Spainteach. Approaching Sgurr nan Spainteach you should note the view ahead and to the R of Sgurr Fhuaran across the depths of Coire Dhomdain. One of the best views of the ridge is disclosed on reaching the cairn, with Sgurr na Ciste Duibhe ahead and a glimpse over its L shoulder of the Saddle on the opposite side of Glen Shiel. Continue along the rocky crest of the ridge to Sgurr na Ciste Duibhe, with a bird's-eye view of the glen below on the L, and then cross the next bealach to climb Sgurr na Carnach. This peak opens up a superb vista of Loch Duich below and of the fine eastern ridge of the Saddle, together with Sgurr na Forcan, and also unveils the real dominance of Sgurr Fhuaran to the R. Now cross the deep bealach and scale its slopes, resting awhile by the cairn to admire the magnificent panorama which is one of the most celebrated in all Scotland.

There is such a galaxy of peaks in this region that it is difficult to pick out any one of them for special mention, save perhaps that of Beinn Fhada to the north-east on the other side of Gleann Lichd. But far away to the south-east and above the long skyline of peaks and ridges appears the dome of Ben Nevis, which is mostly clearly perceived in a limpid atmosphere when carrying a mantle of snow.

Sgurr na Ciste Duibhe

The Saddle

Sgurr na Forcan

Plate 88. Route 43. The ridge on *one form* Sgurr na Ciste Duibhe.

Plate 89 **Route 42**—Ben Nevis and the intervening peaks and ridges from Sgurr Fhuaran

Now commence the descent to the next bealach, which is the longest and steepest in this range, noting on the approach to the triple-peaked Sgurr nan Saighead its fine supporting cliffs that drop away into the depths of Gleann Lichd on the ʀ. Walk round the rim of the corrie to attain its chief cairn, and then proceed over easier ground to Sgurr na Moraich, your last peak, whence descend its grassy slopes eventually to reach the shore of Loch Duich. As mentioned in the introduction to this route Moraich can be left out for a quicker descent.

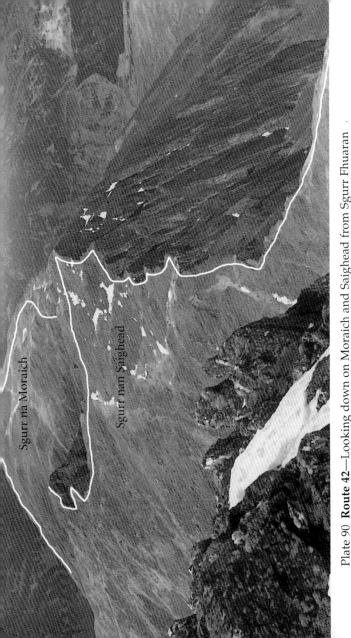

Sgurr na Moraich

Sgurr nam Saighead

Plate 90 **Route 42**—Looking down on Moraich and Saighead from Sgurr Fhuaran

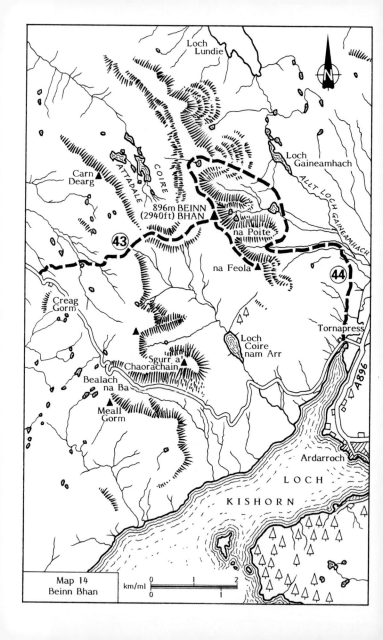

Loch
Lundie

Loch
Gaineamhach

ALLT LOCH GAINEAMHACH

Carn
Dearg ▲

ATTADALE

COIRE

896m BEINN
(2940ft) BHAN ▲

na Poite

43

na Feola ▲

44

Creag
Gorm

Tornapress

Loch
Coire
nam Arr

▲

Sgurr a'
Chaorachain ▲

A896

Bealach
na Ba

Meall
Gorm ▲

Ardarroch

LOCH

KISHORN

N

Map 14
Beinn Bhan

km/ml   0   1   2
         0   1

Beinn Bhan

Beinn Bhan	2940 feet	896 meters
Sgurr a'Chaorachain	2598 feet	792 metres
Meall Gorm	2329 feet	710 metres
Bealach na Ba	2053 feet	626 metres

Seen from Skye, the Applecross tableland presents an unattractive appearance as its western slopes of bare, broken sandstone fall gradually to the tree-fringed shore of the Inner Sound between Toscaig and Applecross Bay. But when observed from the wild hill road connecting Lochcarron with the charming fishing village of Shieldaig these hills assume an entirely different aspect, and on proceeding downhill to Loch Kishorn the scene unfolded is one of the most dramatic in Scotland. For ahead rises the dominating southern satellite of Sgurr a'Chaorachain whose precipitous front of purplish-red sandstone is stratified horizontally and flanked on the L by the deep glen that carries the road over to Applecross, and on the R by its dynamic outlier, the Cioch. At Tornapress there is a fork in the road which is the starting point for one of the most spectacular drives in Britain. In a distance of only 6 miles/9.7 km this L branch rises from sea level to a height of 2053 feet/626 m at the Bealach na Ba, where there is now a large car-park, ascending *en route* the wild glen of the Allt a'Chumhaing and ending with a series of zigzags at a gradient of 1 in 3. On a clear day it's cairn-littered crest reveals a splendid prospect of the peaks of Rhum and the Cuillin and Red Hills of Skye, with on their R a glimpse of the Storr and on their L the ranges that extend southwards from Loch Duich. Some 2 miles/3.2 km to the north of Tornapress on the Shieldaig road the four great corries of Beinn Bhan come into view on the L. They face northeast and their mural precipices fall vertically for about 1500

Meall Gorm →   Sgurr a Chaorachain →   The Cioch →   Beinn Bhan →

Photo 91 The Satellites of Beinn Bhan from Loch Kishorn

Plate 92 Looking down to Loch Kishorn from the zig-zags of the Bealach na Ba

Plate 92. The four corries of Beinn Bhan from Kishorn Lodge.

feet/450 m; each corrie is separated by a castellated spur and the whole provides a picture of mountain grandeur that completely belies the uninteresting western aspect of the plateau. From L to R the four corries are an Each, na Feola, na Poite and nan Fhamhair.

Motorists who have driven up to the Bealach na Ba should continue downhill to the village of Applecross, turn R and enjoy miles of sea and mountain scenery where the views unfolding in rapid succession are some of the finest in Scotland. The engineering of this road is marvellous; it goes up and down hill, sometimes beside the sea and often right up into the wild hills. By taking the drive in this direction, the light is most favourable for both colour and monochrome photography. Based on a start and finish at the Loch Torridon Hotel, the total distance of the drive is about 60 miles/97 km.

It should be noted that both walking routes are exceedingly rough, since they are decked with the thousands of red sandstone boulders through which the easiest way has to be found, meanwhile keeping an alert eye on the objective ahead. Both routes may be combined to make a most enjoyable round, but it is best to start from the Bealach na Ba and return to be picked up at Tornapress.

Route 43. Beinn Bhan from Bealach na Ba. To reach the dominating cairn of the group involves a very rough tramp of about 3 map miles/4.8 km but with a rise of less than 1000/ 300 m. On looking north-east from the Bealach na Ba, the configuration of the ground is obvious; for a horizontal ridge connects the northern slopes of Sgurr a'Chaorachain with the saddle which is in line with Beinn Bhan, whence gently rising ground leads to the cairn on the skyline. However, while this may seem the best line of approach, the broken character of the connecting ridge, supported on its north side by 1000 foot/300 m precipices, is not clearly revealed from this distance and on closer acquaintance will be found to consist of great inclined

Beinn Bhan

Plate 95 **Route 43**—Looking into Coire na Poite from the ridge

slabs of sandstone with considerable drops between them. It is therefore advisable to take a direct line for the saddle, first going downhill to the floor of the immense intervening Coire nan Cuileag and thereafter climbing to the summit by a sketchy cairned track over less broken ground, returning by the ridge and slopes of Sgurr a'Chaorachain. To view the corries it is best to turn R from the summit and to keep to the crest of the ridge as far as Coire na Feola, with sensational vertical drops on the L and splendid prospects on a clear day of the vast panorama round the eastern arc. Then, retrace your steps and continue to the end of Coire nan Fhamhair, noting in passing the awesome vertical buttress and deep gully that separate it from Coire na Poite. The latter, with its two gleaming green lochans far below, affords the most dramatic scene of all. The first peak to rivet the eye in the panorama to the north is Beinn Damh, whose undulating ridge stretches for some 3 miles/4.8 km and reveals the Stirrup Mark below its highest top, and below it a glimpse of Loch Damh. Beinn Alligin, Beinn Dearg and Lia-thach form the skyline, while further to the R rise the many peaks of the Ben Damph and Coulin Forests. To the south-east there is a perfect galaxy of peaks with Beinn Sgritheall promi-nent in the south, then to the L the Saddle and an end-on view of the Five Sisters of Kintail. Skye is disclosed to the west and, on a clear day, the Outer Hebrides in the far north-west.

Route 44. The Corries of Beinn Bhan. Leave Tornapress and cross the stone bridge over the River Kishorn. Turn R at the building and pick up the stalkers' path that skirts the south-eastern shoulder of Beinn Bhan. This rises gradually in the direction of Loch Gaineamhach, but should be deserted when in sight of Coire an Each which is reached over rough heather and steep boulder-strewn ground. In misty weather it is safer to keep to the stalkers' path as far as the bridge spanning the burn coming down from Coire na Feola. Here turn L and ascend the sketchy path which rises along the R bank of the burn and ends at the poised boulder shown in the foreground of Plate 96. Walk into each corrie in turn to admire the splendour of their perpendicular mural precipices, all of which look most impressive under snow and might well be courses of Cyclopean masonry, and note the spectacular spurs that remind one of titanic castles. Go as far as the lochans cradled in Coire na Poite and then continue over easy ground to the ridge on the R of Coire nan Fhamhair. Climb this with care and then bear L along the crest for the cairn on Beinn Bhan.

Plate 96 **Route 44**—The Mural Precipices of Coire na Feola

Plate 97 **Route 44**—The last of the Four Great Corries—Coire nan Fhamhair

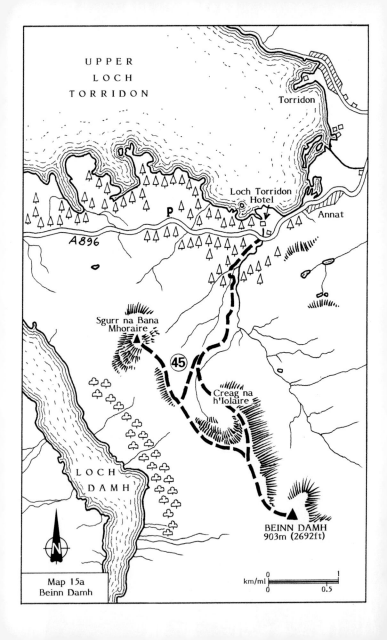

UPPER
LOCH
TORRIDON

Torridon

Loch Torridon
Hotel

Annat

P

A896

Sgurr na Bana
Mhoraire

45

Creag na
h'Iolaire

LOCH
DAMH

BEINN DAMH
903m (2692ft)

N

Map 15a
Beinn Damh

km/ml

0   1

0   0.5

Beinn Damh

Beinn Damh	2962 feet	903 metres
Sgurr na Bana Mhoraire	2254 feet	687 metres

Ben Damph House, now the Loch Torridon Hotel, is superlatively situated for the exploration of this mountain and its adjoining peaks, and may be reached conveniently from Lochcarron via Shieldaig on the south side of Upper Loch Torridon, or from Kinlochewe by the old, single-track road down Glen Torridon. The twin summits of Sgurr na Bana Mhoraire, also known as Creag Sgorach, stand at the northern extremity of the lofty ridge of Beinn Damh, and overhang the hotel to dominate the foreshortened view of the Ben Damph Forest. And while the whole mountain, together with its strange Stirrup Mark immediately beneath the highest summit, are seen at their best on a clear day from Beinn Bhan, or from the Shieldaig road near Loch an Loin, the many peaks of the forest, together with those of the adjacent Coulin Forest, are revealed at their finest from the Diabaig road on the north side of Loch Torridon late on a sunny afternoon. One of the great many charms of the Ben Damph Forest is that it is threaded by a maze of well-preserved stalkers' paths, which reveal more intimately its several peaks as they come into view and, moreover, are so easily graded that they can be ascended with equal facility by old and young.

Beinn Damh

Sgurr na Bana Mhoraire

Plate 98 The long ridge of Beinn Damh is well seen from the head of Loch Damh

Beinn Damh

Maol Chean-Dearg

Beinn na h-Eaglaise

Plate 99 The Coulin and Ben Damph forests are well seen from the Diabaig road

Plate 100 Beinn Damh from the same viewpoint with a telephoto lens.

Plate 101 The cottages of Diabaig

Route 45. Beinn Damh from the Loch Torridon Hotel. Follow the road to the bridge spanning the tumultuous Allt Coire Roill, and just below it on the L pass through a gate to gain the stalkers' path threading the forest. This rises at an easy gradient on the L bank of the burn, and on emerging from the leafy canopy note the fine waterfall in the deep gorge on the L. Continue along the path, with views of your mountain ahead. Above the trees the path forks. Continue on the path uphill over heather into the corrie and then more steeply through bog and boulders to the saddle between Sgurr na Bana Mhoraire and Beinn Damh. Notice on your L the vast stony corrie that deeply penetrates the mountain and is dominated on the L by Creag na h'Iolaire. On gaining the ridge turn R and ascend its broad crest to Sgurr na Bana Mhoraire, noting the precipitous crags on the L overhanging Loch Damh far below.

The twin summits of Sgurr na Bana Mhoraire unfold magnificent vistas round an arc from south to north, in which Beinn Bhan, Beinn Alligin and Liathach are prominent, but it is the blue sea with its islands and rocky coastline that will hold your gaze, backed by Skye and the Outer Hebrides. Now retrace your steps to the saddle and climb the steeper ridge to the top of Beinn Damh, observing on the L the remarkable bold elevation of the Maol Chean-dearg, the highest peak in Ben Damph Forest, and to the L of it the more distant Sgorr Ruadh, the crowning peak of the Coulin Forest. To the south-west observe the wonderful vista along Lochs Kishorn and Carron to Scalpay and the Red Hills of Skye, backed by the sharp peaks of the Cuillin. If time is not pressing, encircle the wild corrie of Toll nam Biast to the south, until you reach the strange flat-topped Stuc Toll nam Biast, which is a superlative viewpoint for the appraisal of the peaks of Ben Damph Forest, for the glittering lochans between them, and for the whole of the vast panorama round the southern arc.

Sgurr na Bana Mhoraire

Beinn Damh

Stuc Toll nam Biast

Loch Torridon
Hotel

Plate 102 **Route 45**—A distant view from Upper Loch Torridon

Sgurr na Bana Mhoraire

Plate 103. A view of **Route 45** from Beinn Damh

Liathach

Spidean a'Choire Leith	3461 feet	1055 metres
Mullach an Rathain	3356 feet	1023 metres
Bidean Toll a'Mhuic	3225 feet	983 metres
Meall Dearg	3133 feet	955 metres
Am Fasarinen	3041 feet	927 metres
Stuc a'Choire Dhuibh Bhig	3002 feet	915 metres

Walkers who know this great mountain will agree that it is the mightiest and most imposing in all Britain. On leaving Kinlochewe to drive down Glen Torridon, you first skirt the quartzite slopes of Beinn Eighe, but on reaching Loch Clair, Liathach suddenly bursts upon the view across the moor, its eastern ramparts falling almost vertically and its impending cliffs of red sandstone stretching as far as the eye can see. As you continue your drive beneath them you cannot fail to be impressed by their extreme steepness and horizontal bedding, as they hem in the north side of the glen for no less than 6 miles/9.7 km, to end suddenly above Torridon village. On a clear sunny morning you will also notice the glittering cap of white quartzite which has often been mistaken for snow and is the crowning feature of the lofty ridge. When driving eastwards from Shieldaig, Liathach appears to dominate the whole scene until the grim portals of Glen Torridon are entered. On the north side of this mountain it is even more precipitous, and the perpendicular cliffs enclosing Coire na Caime are some 2000 feet/600 m high. Such a mountain commands not only admiration but also respect, both of which are heightened as you walk along the narrow sections of its summit ridge. Liathach should be traversed from east to west on a favourable day, and it requires a good two-hour scramble to attain the eastern end of the ridge by one of two steep gullies that split the upper section of this face.

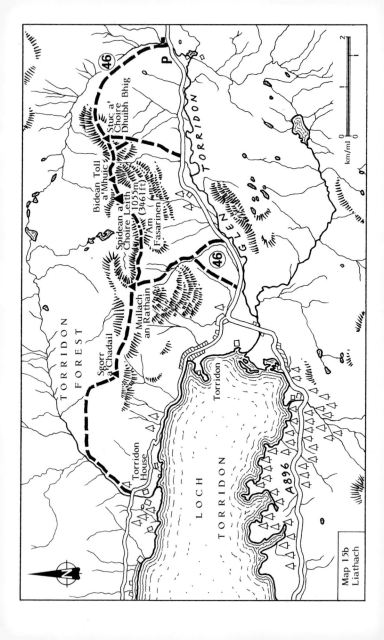

P

46

Stuc a'
Choire
Dhuibh Bhig

Bidean Toll
a'Mhuic

Spidean a'
Choire Leith
1055m
(3461ft)

Am
Fasarinen

46

Mullach
an Rathain

Sgorr
a'Chadail

TORRIDON   FOREST

Torridon
House

Torridon

LOCH

TORRIDON

A896

N

2

0

km/ml

GLEN   TORRIDON

Map 15b
Liathach

After visiting the nearby eastern top for the close view of Beinn Eighe, you retrace your steps and climb steadily over two subsidiary tops before setting foot on the reigning peak. The views throughout are spectacular and especially so of the corries on the north side of the mountain, but it is only on reaching Spidean a'Choire Leith that both sections of the ridge are revealed to your gaze. The absence of quartzite to the west will be noticed, but as compensation there is the bird's-eye view of Am Fasarinen and a fine prospect of Mullach an Rathain. This is the last top to be visited by most walkers, who on reaching the stone shoot on the L used to run down its 2000 feet/600 m of scree to quickly reach Fasag on Upper Loch Torridon. But in recent years there has been considerable deterioration in the scree and it is no longer a safe route of descent. Hence, it is better to leave the ridge to the south-east of Mullach an Rathain and to go due south down the grassy tongues into a wide grassy corrie. Thence follow the course of the Allt an Thuill Bhain, either directly to Glen Torridon or when the sandstone bands appear, descend westwards along the sloping terraces to the road near the campsite and Youth Hostel.

The standard time for the Liathach traverse by a fit and experienced walker is eight hours, split up as follows: two hours up to the ridge from the glen; four hours over the summit from Stuc a'Chiore Dhuibh Bhig to Mullach an Rathain, which allows time for lunch and photography; and two hours down to the road.

It should be noted that the traverse of Liathach is a considerable undertaking and is for the experienced walker rather than for the ordinary pedestrian, by whom it should be severely left alone. However, it is possible for the latter to reach Sgorr a'Chadial, the most westerly top on the ridge, by following the stalkers' path in Coire Mhic Nobuil for about 1 mile/1.6 km and then to take a diagonal course up the north-western slopes of the mountain. Thence, the summit ridge may be followed

Plate 104 A mountain scene

safely to Mullach an Rathain and the descent made as described above.

Since the road threading Glen Torridon runs along the actual base of the southern front of Liathach, the foreshortened aspect of its cliffs is misleading and gives no true conception of their angle or immensity. Walkers who are interested should make the easy ascent of Beinn na h-Eaglaise on the opposite side of the glen and in the late afternoon, when the westering sun clearly delineates every detail, they will obtain the most spectacular prospect of the mural precipices of this mighty peak.

Route 46. The Traverse of Liathach. Park your car a short distance west of the bridge carrying the Glen Torridon road over the Allt a'Choire Dhuibh Mhoir, between Beinn Eighe and Liathach, and commence the ascent by making a bee-line for the two gullies on the skyline, below Stuc a'Choire Dhuibh Bhig. You will encounter bands of sandstone, most of which can be turned or easily climbed, and do not fail to note the immense Coire Leith on your L which is almost symmetrically rimmed with sandstone. Select the gully that seems easiest and on attaining the ridge turn R for Stuc a'Choire Dhuibh Bhig. On a clear day the quartzite slopes of Beinn Eighe are most impressive and this coign of vantage discloses more clearly the true elevation of the ups and downs of its ridge.

Then retrace your steps and be careful while passing along the narrowest sections of the ridge, with absymal drops into the deep corries on your R. Proceed ahead by climbing Bidean Toll a'Mhuic and its satellite, beyond which you come to the large blocks of rough quartzite that deck the highest peak of Spidean a'Choire Leith. Rest awhile on this lofty perch to admire not only the entire summit ridge of your mountain which is 5 miles/8 km in length, but also its surrounding peaks. Strangely enough those to the north are not very beautiful, and Beinn Alligin in particular is most disappointing.

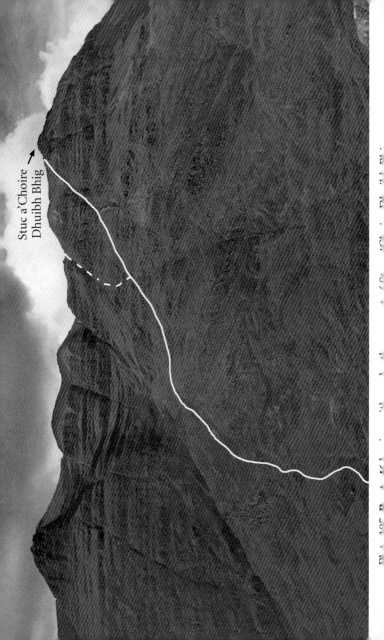

Stuc a'Choire
Dhuibh Bhig

Spidean a'Choire Leith →

← Bidean Toll a'Mhuic

Plate 106 **Route 46**—Looking west along the lofty ridge of Liathach

But those to the south will hold your gaze by reason of their distinctive elevations, and especially that of Beinn na h-Eaglaise whose remarkable curving bands of sandstone will attract your eye.

Now descend the western slopes of the reigning peak and make your way carefully over the sensational pinnacles of Am Fasarinen which fall vertically on your R into Coire na Caime. Hand and footholds are ample and safe, but if you wish to avoid the pinnacles follow the path below and to the south. Continue up the gradually rising grassy ridge to Mullach an Rathain and then descend slightly L to reach the top of the grassy tongues that are the key to the descent beside the Allt an Thuill Bhain.

Beinn Eighe

Plate 107 **Route 46**—Looking east from Spidean a'Choire Leith

Mullach an Rathain

Meall Dearg

Corrie below Mullach an Rathain

Plate 109 **Route 46**—A safe descent by Allt an Thuill Bhain

Mullach an Rathain

Am Fasarinen Spidean a'Choire Leith

Plate 110 The mural precipices of Liathach seen late in the day from a Bienn na h'Eaglise

Beinn Alligin

Sgurr Mhor	3235 feet	986 metres
Tom na Gruagaich	3025 feet	922 metres
Meall an Laoigh	2920 feet	890 metres
Horns of Alligin	2841 feet	866 metres

This is the most westerly of the Torridon peaks, and rises immediately to the north of Torridon House and Inveralligin. When seen from the Shieldaig road south of Upper Loch Torridon its fine elevation commands attention by reason of two unusual topographical features: first, the great gash splitting the central and highest peak, Sgurr Mhor; and second, the three Horns of Alligin that extend eastwards, eventually to fall steeply to the moor. The same characteristics may also be observed from the private road that runs along the south shore of Upper Loch Torridon, which was formerly the connecting link between Ben Damph House, now the Loch Torridon Hotel, the River Balgy famous for its salmon, and Loch Damh renowned for its trout. To photographers the viewpoints on this winding road, which is hemmed in by lofty rhododendrons, have much to commend them, due to several charming foregrounds where red sandstone cliffs enclose little bays that at low tide are rimmed with brilliant orange wrack.

The ascent and traverse of the summit ridge of Beinn Alligin is a sporting course much enjoyed by all keen walkers. There are no special problems to be encountered until the Horns are reached, where great care is needed in making the ascent. Thereafter the difficulties decrease and there is a final descent to the stalkers' path which leads back to the starting point of the climb – the fine old stone bridge spanning the deep gorge through which the turbulent waters of the Abhainn Coire Mhic Nobuil rush down to the sea. The panorama from the summit

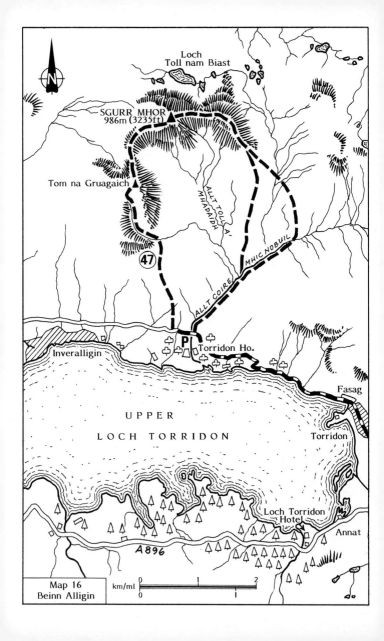

N

Loch
Toll nam Biast

SGURR MHOR
986m (3235ft)

Tom na Gruagaich

ALLT TOLL A'
MHADAIDH

47

ALLT COIRE MHIC NOBUIL

Inveralligin

P
Torridon Ho.

Fasag

UPPER

LOCH TORRIDON

Torridon

Loch Torridon
Hotel

Annat

A896

Map 16
Beinn Alligin

km/ml   0   1   2
         0   1

is one of the finest hereabouts as it not only opens up an uninterrupted prospect of hill and sea round the western arc, but also unfolds a superb view of its eastern neighbours where the horizontal sandstone bedding is seen at its best.

Route 47. The Traverse of Beinn Alligin. Turn R at the foot of Glen Torridon, and after passing the cottages of Fasag continue along the shore of the loch. Drive up the graceful sweeps of the single-track road, pass through a beautiful collection of trees and emerge at the stone bridge, immediately beyond which there is space to park several cars. Thence the track begins and goes uphill through heather straight to the southern shoulder of the mountain, and into the mouth of Coire an Laoigh. Follow the burn to its source on Meall an Laoigh which is the steepest section of the ascent; it ends on the skyline whence bear R for the cairn on Tom na Gruagaich. On the north side this summit is supported by vertical, terraced cliffs which are not completely disclosed until the next is attained, but its chief merit is that of opening up a matchless prospect of Sgurr Mhor with its 1800 feet/550 m gash, which plunges down with almost vertical sides into the depths of Toll a'Mhadaidh. Thence an easy walk will place you by the highest cairn from which the above mentioned features of the whole panorama are best observed. On a very clear day it is possible to pick out Cape Wrath in the far north and Ardnamurchan in the south. Now stroll downhill to the narrow neck of rock that joins the reigning peak to the first of the Horns. Climb it with care as the drops on the L into the depths of Toll nam Biast are sensational, then traverse the three peaks and go down through boulders and heather by a well-trodden path to pick up the stalkers' path beside the Allt a'Bhealaich, over two bridges, and so back by the Abhainn Coire Mhic Nobuil to your car. It will be noted that locally this route is often recommended in reverse. This may be an easier ascent, but for keen photographers the other takes greater advantage of the lighting.

Meall an Laoigh

Tom na Gruagach

Plate 111 Beinn Alligin and Upper Loch Torridon from the Shieldaig Road

Sgurr Mhor

Horns of Alligin

Plate 112 **Route 47**—A close view of the peaks from the mouth of Coire an Laoigh

Tom na Gruagagh

Plate 113 **Route 47** Looking back on the first section from Sgurr Mhor

Plate 114 **Route 47**—The great gash in Sgurr Mhor seen from Tom na Gruagaich

Liathach

Beinn Eighe

Beinn Dearg

Plate 116 The trickiest section of **Route 47** goes over the Horns of Alligin

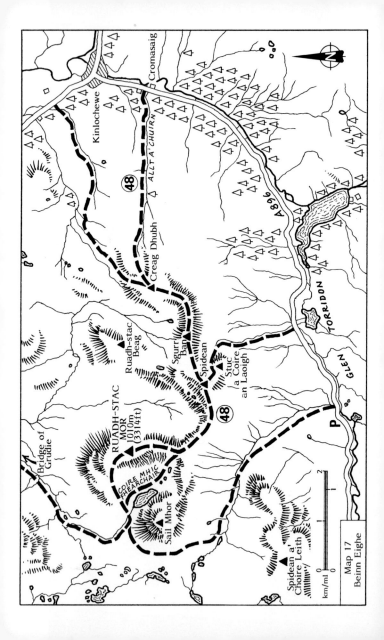

Map 17
Beinn Eighe

Kinlochewe

Cromasaig

A896

ALLT A' CHUIRN

Creag Dhubh

Ruadh-stac
Beag

Sgurr
Ban

Spidean

Stuc
a Coire
an Laoigh

RUADH-STAC
MOR
1010m
(3314ft)

COIRE MHIC
FHEARCHAIR

Sail Mhor

Bridge of
Grudie

TORRIDON

GLEN

P

Spidean a'
Choire Leith

48

48

km/ml 0   1   2

Beinn Eighe

Ruadh-stac Mor	3314 feet	1010 metres
Spidean Coire nan Clach	3258 feet	993 metres
Sail Mhor	3215 feet	980 metres
Coinneach Mhor	3202 feet	976 metres
Sgurr Ban	3182 feet	970 metres
Sgurr nan Fhir Duibhe	3159 feet	963 metres
Creag Dubh	3048 feet	929 metres
Ruadh-stac Beag	2940 feet	896 metres
Meall a'Ghiubhais	2907 feet	886 metres

This great mountain, by far the largest of the Torridon peaks, is a complete range in itself and when seen from Kinlochewe its north-eastern spur only is disclosed. If this were the whole mountain it would be impressive enough to draw the walker, as its crest is decked with a series of weird pinnacles, known as the Black Carls of Beinn Eighe. During the drive down Glen Torridon its southern front comes into view near Loch Clair, but as the road runs along its lower slopes the view of it is necessarily foreshortened. However, if the walker walks south to the adjacent Loch Coulin he will be rewarded by the best view of the range, which reveals not only its stupendous dimensions but also its tremendous covering of quartzite. The ridge then swings round to the north-west behind Liathach, and so the rest of it cannot be seen by the motorist. If the walker is prepared to walk from the roadside car-park through the deep glen of the Allt a'Choire Dhuibh Mhoir that separates the two peaks, he will be further rewarded by the superb prospect of Coire Mhic Fhearchair which is hidden away on the peak's north-western slopes and considered the finest in all Scotland.

The traverse of the ridge of Beinn Eighe is a considerable

Creag Dubh

Sgòrr an Fhir Duibhe

Plate 117 **Route 48**   The first section of the traverse seen from Creapoaig

Plate 118 Beinn Eighe from Loch Coulin

undertaking for the average pedestrian and without transport involves a walk of some 20 miles/32 km, the last 6 miles/9.7 km of which can be saved by a ride back to Kinlochewe from Bridge of Grudie on Loch Maree, or from the bridge over the Allt a'Choire Dhuibh Mhoir, between Beinn Eighe and Lia-thach. Moreover, the foreshortened view of the distances between the several summits is misleading and on closer acquaintance will be found to involve much more collar-work than expected. However, such an expedition is free of all technical difficulties, other than a sudden deterioration in the weather, and on a long summer day will afford the tough walker an experience he will long remember. The usual starting point is from Cromasaig just to the south of Kinlochewe and on attaining the first peak of Creag Dubh much of the hard grind is over. On reaching a point before Coinneach Mhor the ridge forks, with Coinneach Mhor and beyond it Sail Mhor on the L and Ruadh-stac Mor, the highest point, on the R. After visiting the latter peak there are two easy descents. The first is by way of the scree slopes to the north-west of the summit cairn, and the second is by returning to the junction whence a long stone shoot and easy rocks lead north down to the floor of the Coire Mhic Fhearchair with its lonely lochan. Thence, by following down the cascading burn, the stalkers' path can be picked up on the R and easy progress made northwards to Bridge of Grudie, or by turning L past Loch nan Cabar, a cairned track leads south to Coire Dubh Mor and Glen Torri-don. A conspicuous spot on the south side of the summit ridge, immediately above the bridge and car-park in the glen, encloses Coire an Laoigh down which a rapid descent could be made in bad weather.

Plate 119 **Route 48** passes over the eroded crest of Sgurr nan Fhir Duibhe

Route 48. The Traverse of Beinn Eighe. Leave Cromasaig and follow the south bank of the Allt a'Chuirn for some distance, then cross the burn to gain a steep grass slope that leads up to the ridge and Creag Dubh, the first peak on the ridge. All the eastern peaks of the range consist of Cambrian quartzite; on walking south along the ridge to Sgurr nan Fhir Duibhe the weird pinnacles or Black Carls are soon encountered and will be noticed to be in an advanced state or erosion. These are passed with care whence the ridge narrows on the approach to Sgurr nan Fhir Duibhe where the pinnacles afford no difficulty save that of a 30-foot/9 m pitch near the top which is more easily ascended than descended.

On attaining the cairn observe the views to the north in which Slioch is prominent and with a distant prospect on its L of An Teallach. To the south the peaks of the Coulin Forest are clearly defined, but the gaze will be held by the ridge trailing away to the west, to the L of which is a fine end-on view of Liathach. Now descend R for some 400 feet/120 m to the first col, with abysmal drops on the R, and climb the ridge to Sgurr Ban, whence the going is easier all the way to Coinneach Mhor. Continue the traverse, noting on the L the great rock walls and corries of Liathach, and at the junction keep to the R with an ascent of 450 feet/140 m to the reigning peak of Ruadh-stac Mor, whose panorama is not dissimilar to that already noted, save that of the view of Sail Mhor across the corrie on the L where a deep gully cleaves its bold and steep face. Do not attempt to descend on the north or east sides of Ruadh-stac Mor as its slopes consist of steep, terraced sandstone, but either retrace your steps to the junction on the ridge and go down the long scree shoot to the floor of Coire Mhic Fhearchair, or keep north-west from the summit cairn and go down the scree to the lochan. Now walk round the lochan and then view the rock wall opposite which is famous for its three immense buttresses, the lower halves of which consist of red sandstone and the upper halves of tapering quartzite.

Photographers should note that as this magnificent corrie faces the north-west, it is only illuminated satisfactorily on a summer evening; 8 p.m. is the ideal time of day which means a late return to your lodgings. Note also the flat floor of the corrie cradling the lochan at the base of the buttresses and then descend beside the cascading burn to the stalkers' path north to Bridge of Grudie or south for Glen Torridon.

Plate 120 The white quartzite ridge of Creag Dubh, seen from Scurr nan Fhir Duibhe

Plate 121 Looking west along **Route 48** from the summit of Sgurr nan Fhir Duibhe

Plate 122. Cairn Mhic Fhearchair in the terminal period of Route 48.

Slioch

Slioch	3218 feet	981 metres
Sgurr an Tuill Bhain	3064 feet	934 metres

This mountain stands in splendid isolation to the north of Loch Maree and frowns upon the head waters of this beautiful tree-fringed lake. It attracts attention not only by reason of its unopposed superiority but also by its bold, square, castellated summit. The ascent affords no difficulty, save that of the long tramp to its base round the head of the loch from Kinlochewe, a distance of some 5 miles/8 km, to reach Glen Bianasdail. The rather indistict track rises to the L, of the glen and eventually enters a hidden boulder-strewn corrie to the east of the peak. It is famous for its spring Alpines. The summit cairn is some little distance above and can be attained by an easy walk. If desired this may be continued by traversing the almost level ridge to Sgurr an Tuill Bhain.

Route 49. Slioch from Kinlochewe. 0.25 mile/0.4 km east of Kinlochewe a small road leads north to the tiny hamlet of Incheril. Cars can be parked at the end of the west branch of the road before the farm at Culaneilan. The path follows the north bank of the Kinlochewe River to enter the mouth of the deep U-shaped Glen Bianasdail. Cross the bridge over the burn issuing from it, the Abhainn an Fhasaigh, and ascend the path that rises to the west of the burn. After about 0.5 mile/0.8 km, leave it and follow the path leading to the ridge between Meall Each and Sgurr Dubh, and continue over heather to the top of Sgurr Dubh. From the small lochans beyond, a path leads up the final steepening to the summit cairn. The views of the loch below are enchanting and reveal the many islets at its foot. The Torridon Peaks to the south lack interest since their finest

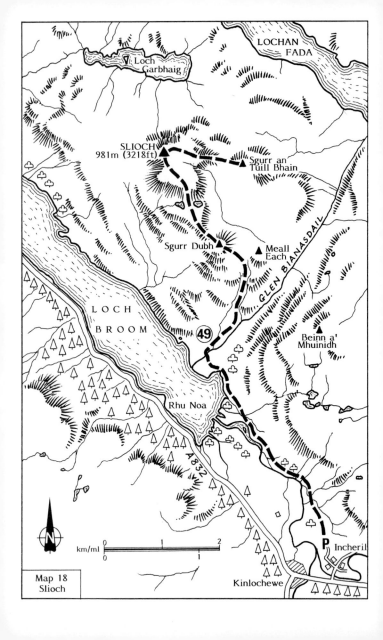

LOCHAN
FADA

Loch
Garbhaig

SLIOCH
981m (3218ft)

Sgurr an
Tuill Bhain

Sgurr Dubh

Meall
Each

GLEN BIANASDAIL

LOCH

BROOM

49

Beinn a'
Mhuinidh

Rhu Noa

A832

N

km/ml

0   1   2
          1

P Incheril

Map 18
Slioch

Kinlochewe

aspects are on the Glen Torridon side. But the panorama round the northern arc will hold the gaze by reason of the numerous blue lochans that stud the immense wilderness of peaks in which An Teallach and the Fannichs are prominent.

An alternative descent can be made from the top of Sgurr an Tuill Bhain, the eastern spur, by steep heather hillsides leading back down to the Gleann Bianasdail path.

Glen Bianasdail

Photo 123 **Route 40** Slioch from Loch Maree

An Teallach

Bidean a'Ghlas Thuill	3484 feet	1062 meters
Sgurr Fiona	3477 feet	1060 metres
Corrag Bhuidhe	3435 feet	1047 metres
Lord Berkely's Seat	3379 feet	1030 metres
Sgurr Creag an Eich	3337 feet	1017 metres
Glas Mheall Mor	3212 feet	979 metres
Stob Cadha Gobhlach	3150 feet	960 metres
Sail Liath	3130 feet	954 metres
Corrag Bhuidhe Buttress	3100 feet	945 metres

This complex mountain is one of the most spactacular in Scotland and vies in grandeur with the Torridon Peaks and the Cuillin of Skye. It rises due south of the head of Little Loch Broom and is usually climbed from Dundonnell. The 3 mile/ 4.8 km long main ridge is much indented and throws out three spurs which enclose two magnificent corries, one of which, Toll an Lochain, vies in splendour with Coire Mhic Fhearchair on the north-western flanks of Beinn Eighe. The best view of the range is obtained from the remote Road of Destitution to the east, and when seen on a bright sunny morning its superb sandstone architecture is revealed, including detail of the cluster of peaks surrounding Toll an Lochain. To climb the reigning peak, traverse the ups and downs of the main ridge as far as Sail Liath, descend the stone shoot to Toll an Lochain and return to Dundonnell, involves a long and strenuous day. Hence, unless the walker is experienced and in fit condition, An Teallach is best left alone.

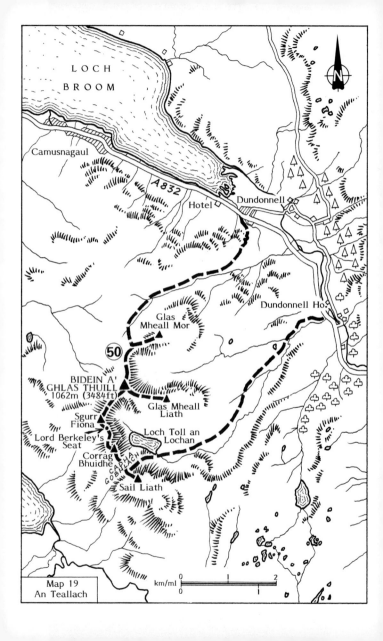

LOCH
BROOM

Camusnagaul

A832

Hotel

Dundonnell

Dundonnell Ho

Glas
Mheall Mor

50

BIDEIN A'
GHLAS THUILL
1062m (3484ft)

Glas Mheall
Liath

Sgurr
Fiona

Lord Berkeley's
Seat

Loch Toll an
Lochan

Corrag
Bhuidhe

CADHA
GOBHLACH

Sail Liath

N

km/ml   0   1   2
         0   1

Map 19
An Teallach

Plate 124 An Teallach from near the Road of Destitution

Route 50. The Traverse of An Teallach. Leave the road about 0.25 mile/0.4 km to the east of the Dundonnell Hotel and walk up the stalkers' path, whence follow the Allt a'Mhuilinn to its source. Turn L and ascend Glas Mheall Mor without difficulty and then wend your way round the rim of Coire a'Glas Thuill. From its lofty cairn the whole of the ridge is disclosed twisting away to the south and eventually to the south-east, in which the graceful peak of Sgurr Fiona is prominent, followed by Lord Berkeley's Seat which overhangs the corrie and is topped by the four peaks of Corrag Bhuidhe. But before commencing the traverse it is worthwhile to walk a short distance along the adjoining spur in the direction of Glas Mheall Liath, if only to gaze into the fantastic Hayfork Gully on the L, whose rectangular plan and perpendicular sandstone walls have a most sensational aspect. Now begin the traverse by tramping across the deep depression to Sgurr Fiona which unfolds a closer prospect of the ridge ahead; it narrows considerably and the going is longer and steeper. Proceed carefully and ascend the dizzy Lord Berkeley's Seat for the striking view of the immense void below, and then climb the Corrag Bhuidhe Pinnacles, the last of which opens up a grand view of the remaining section of the ridge and also of Beinn Dearg Mor on the other side of the wide Strath na Sealga. Descend the last pinnacle with the utmost care and go down the slabs that lead to the next col, whence scale Corrag Bhuidhe Buttress and continue thence to the end of the ridge at Sail Liath. Now retrace your steps to Cadha Gobhlach and descend the stone shoot which gives the easiest and quickest descent to Toll an Lochain. The simplest way back to Dundonnell is to first make for a large boulder that is poised conspicuously on a declining sandstone ridge, and then follow the ridge almost all the way down to the road near Dundonnell House. The changing panorama of shapely hill, black lochan and blue seas from the ridge of An Teallach is a great attraction, but it is the ridge itself that will hold the gaze.

Cadha Gobhlach

Corrag Bhuidhe

Lord Berkeley's Seat

Plate 125 **Route 50**—The ridge of An Teallach from Bidean a'Ghlas Thuill

Corrag Bhuidhe

Lord Berkeley's
Seat

Plate 126 **Route 50**—The ridge from Sgurr Fiona

Plate 127 Beinn Dearg Mhor seen from Corrag Bhuidhe

Corrag Bhuidhe
Buttress

Corrag Bhuidhe

Lord Berkeley's
Seat

Sgurr Fiona

Ben Mór Coigach

Ben Mór Coigach	2438 feet	743 metres
Sgurr an Fhidhleir	2313 feet	705 metres
Beinn an Eoin	2031 feet	619 metres

Walkers proceeding north from Ullapool get their first full view of this mountain from Ardmair Bay, whose graceful sweep of white shingle leads the eye across the water to its long summit ridge which is supported by a series of riven precipices. The peak comes into view again in the vicinity of Drumrunie when it is seen end-on, together with its spectacular satellite, Sgurr an Fhidhleir, which appears as a conspicuous sharp wedge on its R. While the ascent of the latter can provide difficult rock climbing, the ascent and traverse of the former from the north affords no difficulties whatsoever and culminates in a magnificent bird's-eye view of Isle Martin and the Summer Isles, together with glorious vistas of hill and sea round the western arc. To reach the mountain involves a long tramp over boggy moorland, and since it is not so accessible as its more attractive neighbour, Stac Pollaidh, it is less often visited.

However, those wishing to reach the summit by a shorter route may do so by driving through Achiltibuie to Culnacraig where the road terminates. Thence traverse to the western shoulder of the mountain, cross the Allt nan Coisiche and go straight up the steep grassy slopes to the cairn.

Route 51. From Drumrunie. Drive about 2 miles/3.2 km along the road from Drumrunie, almost to the head of Loch Lurgainn, and park the car at a convenient place off the road. Below the road, stepping stones lead across the river, just before it enters Loch Lurgainn. Set off across the moor and on reaching the

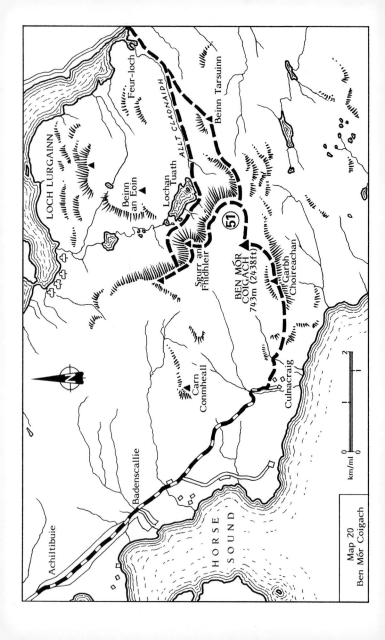

Feur-loch

Beinn Tarsuinn

ALLT CLAONAIDH

LOCH LURGAINN

Lochan Tuath

Beinn an Eoin

51

BEN MÓR
COIGACH
743m (2438ft)

Garbh
Choireachan

Sgurr an
Fhidhleir

Carn
Coinmheall

Culnacraig

N

Badenscallie

HORSE
SOUND

Achiltibuie

km/ml

0   1   2

Map 20
Ben Mór Coigach

Allt Claonaidh follow it to its source in Lochan Tuath at the foot of Sgurr an Fhidhleir. Skirting the lochan to the south, climb the steep hillside on the L of Sgurr an Fhidhleir. This route gives a close view of the peak's sandstone cliffs and is not difficult, and on emerging on the skyline turn north to admire the fine retrospect which reveals the true elevation of Stac Pollaidh to the L of the nearer Beinn an Eoin. Visit the nearby summit and afterwards walk southwards to attain the lofty ridge of Ben Mór Coigach, which is traversed to its terminus at Garbh Choireachan that overhangs the blue of Loch Broom. On a clear day all the above-mentioned features are disclosed to advantage, together with the Outer Hebrides across the sea to the west, while far away in the south the great range of An Teallach tops the extensive skyline of mainland peaks. If a descent is not made to Achiltibuie, it is worthwhile to take in Beinn Tarsuinn to the east on the return walk to the car.

Plate 120 Ben Mór Coigach - the summit ridge from Ardmair Bay

Plate 130 **Route 51**—Sgurr an Fhidhleir from Lochan Tuath

Plate 131 **Route 51**—Stac Pollaidh from the lip of the Corrie

Plate 132 **Route 51**—Ridge rising to the summit of Ben Mór Coigach

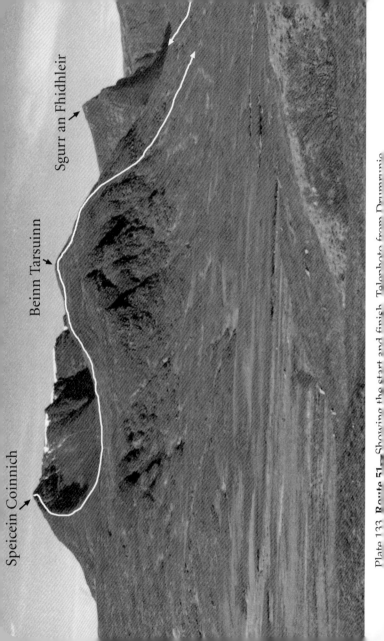

Speicein Coinnich

Beinn Tarsuinn

Sgurr an Fhidhleir

Plate 133 **Route 51.** Showing the start and finish. Telephoto from Drumrunie.

Cul Beag

Cul Beag   2523 feet   769 metres

The south-eastern slopes of this mountain are grassy and rise gradually from Drumrunie to terminate precipitously on both north and west. In consequence the finest prospect of the peak is from Loch Lurgainn, which reveals a gully slanting up to the R to split conspicuously the peak's triangular elevation of sandstone. The easiest ascent is from Drumrunie and the more difficult from Linneraineach. The panorama from the summit is disappointing, save that it opens up an end-on view of Stac Pollaidh to the west; a close prospect of Cul Mor to the north; and a rather complicated vista of Beinn an Eoin and Ben Mór Coigach to the south.

Route 52. From Drumrunie. Leave the road 2 miles/3.2 km to the west of Drumrunie, about opposite Lochan an Dubha, and climb steadily over steepish grass, interspersed here and there with sandstone boulders, until the cairn is attained almost on the edge of the cliffs.

Route 53. From Linneraineach. This route is only for experienced walkers who should make a bee-line for the V-shaped gullies splitting the western face of the peak. The going is rough and steep in places and some of the rock requires careful handling. Scramble up the gully on the R with care and on emerging on the skyline bear L for the summit cairn.

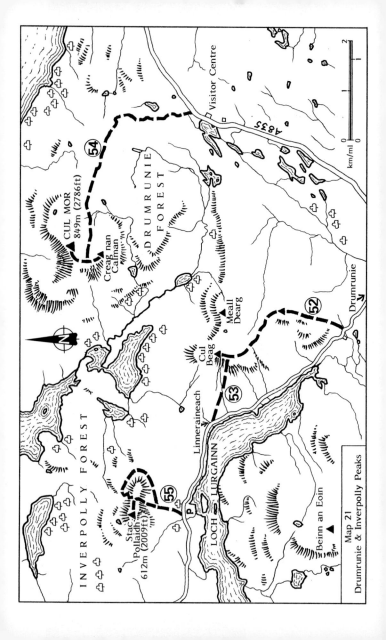

Visitor Centre

A835

2
1
0 km/ml
0

DRUMRUNIE FOREST

54

CUL MOR
849m (2786ft)

Creag nan
Calman

52

Drumrunie

Meall
Dearg

N

Cul
Beag

53

INVERPOLLY FOREST

Linneraineach

55

P

Stac
Pollaidh
612m (2009ft)

LOCH LURGAINN

Beinn an Eoin

Map 21
Drumrunie & Inverpolly Peaks

Plate 134 Stac Pollaidh and **Route 52** to the summit of Cul Beag seen from the moor

Plate 135 **Route 53** to Cul Beag seen across Loch Lurgainn

Plate 136 **Routes 52** and **53**—A hazy view of Stac Pollaidh from Cul Beag

Cul Mor

Cul Mor   2785 feet   849 metres

This is the most northerly peak in Wester Ross and rises steeply from the southern shore of Loch Veyatie. It looks its best when seen from Stac Pollaidh, but its twin summits, capped with quartzite, are also conspicuous objects in the view from Ledmore, which coign of vantage reveals the sharp rock pinnacle, known as Bod a'Mhiotailt, decking its north-western ridge. It may be climbed most easily from Knockanrock to the east, but is often scaled from Linneraineach, on Loch Lurgainn. The great disadvantage of the approach from Knockanrock is the circuit of several lochans at the peak's base. There is an immense corrie, known as Coire Gorm, on its northern precipitous front, which is encircled by a fine mural of sandstone cliffs and well worthy of appraisal.

Plate 137 The gullied western flanks of Cul Mor are well seen from Stac Pollaidh

Route 54. From Ullapool. Drive along the road to Ledmore and park your car near Knockanrock where a gate in the fence gives access to a good path westwards. When it peters out make for the col between twin peaks. Descend slightly to the west where a long line of sandstone crags rim the precipices facing Stac Pollaidh; note the wide gullies that split them and also the curious formations of sandstone hereabouts. Observe the strange elevation of the adjacent peak of Cul Beag and then climb to the cairn on the reigning peak. The panorama is extensive and noteworthy for the innumerable lochs and lochans that deck the landscape of both Wester Ross and Sutherland. The view to the north encompasses the entire ridge of Suilven, together with Canisp on its R, between which Quinag appears in the far distance. To the north-east the great bulk of Ben More Assynt is prominent and to the south-east appears the large group of hills dominated by Beinn Dearg. But the moorland to the west will hold your gaze, with the wedge of Stac Polaidh overlooking the maze of lochans, of which the largest is Loch Sionascaig, all of them backed by the blue of the Atlantic. Should you be lucky enough to visit this peak in the early days of spring, you may see a snow bunting which will hop around to pick up the crumbs from your lunch.

Cul Mor

Bod a'Mhiotailt

Plate 138 A distant view of **Route 54** and Elphin from above Cam Loch

Plate 54—The approach to the col between the twin peaks of Cul Mor

Plate 140 **Route 54**—The shattered western front of Cul Mor

Plate 141 **Route 54 — Stùlsan and Quinag from Cùl Mòr**

Plate 142 **Route 54**—Coire Gorm

Plate 143. **Route 54.** Ben More Assynt from the summit cairn on Cul Mor

Stac Pollaidh

Stac Pollaidh   2008 feet   612 metres

This little peak, with its bristling summit ridge of sandstone pinnacles, is the favourite of all mountaineers visiting Coigach. It is 14 miles/22 km from Ullapool and rises above the narrow road skirting Loch Lurgainn, from which it may be climbed in about one hour. Bold and steep buttresses rise at each end of the mountain, and that at the western extremity is the higher. There is a conspicuous saddle at the eastern end and this may be attained over steep talus slopes or by the zigzags on its northern slopes, but almost any point on the ridge can be reached by a rough scramble over scree, followed by one or other of the several gullies that cleave the ridge.

A little tower, with drops on either side, stands between the ridge proper and the highest top, but aside from the latter's more open prospect of the sea to the west, it has no other scenic attraction. The best vista of the ridge, with its numerous towers and supporting spurs, is obtained from the end of the broad spur near the summit. The weird formations of sandstone are a great attraction and those crowning the terminal points of some of the very narrow spurs can only be reached by a sensational scramble. They assume changing shapes as the walker moves along the ridge above them, and one of the most remarkable, but easily missed, was the Lobster's Claw which some years ago crowned a slender pinnacle in one of the gullies but has now disappeared owing to erosion. If the crest of the ridge is traversed faithfully it makes an entertaining scramble, but a path below the pinnacles on the south side may be used to avoid the difficult bits. The whole of Stac Pollaidh is the delight of the alert photographer and is the most rewarding and sensational subject in all Scotland.

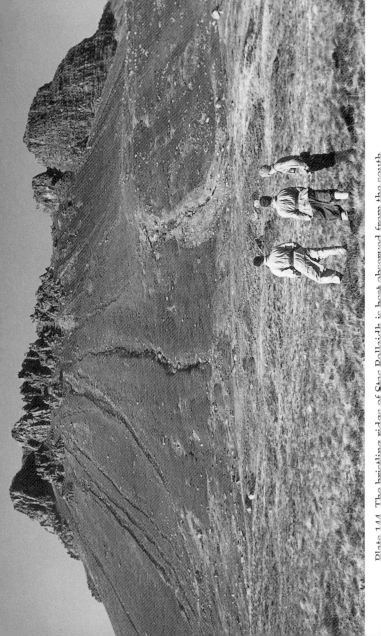

Plate 144 The bristling ridge of Stac Pollaidh is best observed from the south.

Route 55. The Traverse of Stac Pollaidh. Park your car in the car-park immediately below the peak, and then ascend the path above it to reach the level ground at the foot of the mountain. A recently restored path leads round the eastern buttress and up the zigzags on the northern slopes. On attaining the saddle, walk along to the cairn on the eastern buttress, which opens up fine prospect of both Cul Mor and Cul Beag. Then return to the saddle where you are confronted by a huge rock buttress which seems to bar your way. If you go to the L of it you will descend below the pinnacles, whereas by going down slightly to the R you will turn this obstacle and discover behind it a path that rises to the crest of the ridge.

The going is now delightful, with spacious prospects on either hand; those on the L include Beinn an Eoin and Ben Mór Coigach beyond Loch Lurgainn at your feet; those on the R reveal the innumerable blue lochans that characterise this part of Wester Ross and Sutherland, together with a wonderful view of the surprisingly long ridge of Suilven. On and on you go, enchanted by all you see both near and far, until you encounter the little tower which must be climbed if you wish to attain the summit cairn. Return the way you came, but walk out to the end of the first spur, now on your R, where in favourable conditions you will linger to enjoy the finest prospect of the unique sandstone pinnacles of Stac Pollaidh, backed by Cul Beag, with a lovely vista of Loch Lurgainn bounded by the white line of the road from Ullapool.

Plate 145 **Route 51.** The ___ ___ ___ of the summit ridge of Stob Bealláich.

Plate 146 **Route 55**—Cul Beag from the ridge

Plate 147 Beauly to ... : Cold Mar from the side

Plate 148 **Route 55**—Suilven appears between the two western towers

Suilven

Canisp

Plate 150 Weird pinnacles flank the south side of **Route 55**

Plate 151 **Route 55**—The elusive Lobster's Claw as it was in 1948

Suilven

Caisteal Liath	2399 feet	731 metres
Meall Mheadhonach	2300 feet	701 metres
Meall Bheag	2000 feet	610 metres

This wedge-shaped peak, rising in splendid isolation from the lochan-strewn moors of Sutherland, is perhaps the most famous in Scotland and a well-known problem for the walker. Seen from the east in the vicinity of Elphin, it presents a sharp, tapering and inaccessible appearance, whereas when observed from the west in the neighbourhood of Lochinver its rounded summit cannot fail to catch the eye and has given rise to its popular pseudonym, the Sugar Loaf. Its summit ridge is 1.5 miles/2.4 km in length, on which the most difficult peak to attain is the central one owing to the rim of guarding crags, below which the flanks of the hill fall so precipitously as to seem perpendicular. A strange feature that will surprise the walker is a stone wall spanning the ridge to the east of the Castle. Speculation suggests its erection to prevent deer from reaching the crowning peak and perhaps falling over its precipitous western front, but an opening has been left in its centre, possibly to allow access to sheep.

Suilven rises some 5 miles/8 km to the south-east of Lochinver, of which 2 miles/3.2 km consist of a road to Glencanisp Lodge, whence a stalkers' path continues to a point north of the peak. Thence a string of lochans on a shelf at its base lead to a wide and rough gully that rises to the ridge. The same point of ascent can be reached by a path from Little Assynt, or a similar gully on its south side can be reached from Inverkirkaig by following the river to Fionn Loch, whose long circuit leads to the base of this gully. The complete traverse of the ridge and its three peaks is a tit-bit for the rock climber and

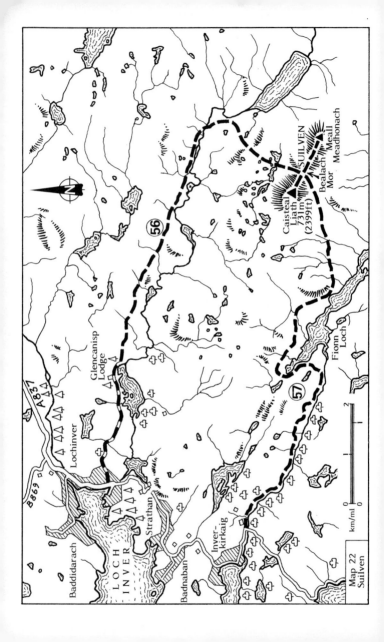

Baddidarach

B869

LOCH INVER

Lochinver

Badnaban

A837

strathan

Glencanisp
Lodge

Inver-
kirkaig

56

57

Fionn
Loch

Casteal
Liath
731m
(2399ft)

SUILVEN

Bealach
Mor

Meall
Meadhonach

N

km/ml
0   1   2
0

Map 22
Suilven

Caisteal Liath

Meall Mheadhonach

Meall Bheag

Plate 152 Suilven from Elphin

should be commenced with the ascent of one of the gullies or chimneys that split the western face of the Castle. The descent at the far end of the ridge presents no special difficulties.

Route 56. From Lochinver. Turn east up the narrow road between the houses facing the loch leading to Glencanisp Lodge. A car-park is signposted after 1 mile/1.6 km. Continue walking along the road to the gate into the lodge. Pass behind the north side of the lodge by a track to pick up the old stalkers' path. Proceed ahead past Suileag where the path from Little Assynt comes in on the L, and later after passing Lochan Buidhe the path crosses the river by a bridge and continues to recross it before Loch an Gainimh. Head south on a well-trodden and boggy path to gain the attractive lochans on the shelf at the base of the peak. Then scale the wide gully opposite by an eroding zigzag path to attain the Bealach Mor at its centre.

After a short rest turn east and traverse the airy crest of the ridge until you reach the gap beneath Meall Mheadhonach. Cross it and climb slightly to the south, taking every care on the steep sandstone slopes until you attain the rim of crags guarding its summit. Scramble up them without looking down and on reaching the cairn scan the splendid prospect to the east, noting the proximity of the adjacent Canisp. Continue along the ridge to Meall Bheag whose cairn is reached by a sensational ascent over a succession of sandstone terraces on the north side of this peak.

Then retrace your steps to the Bealach Mor, whence climb the broader ridge to the summit, Caisteal Liath; its spacious grassy summit opens up a marvellous panorama of hill and sea, in which the Coigach Peaks are prominent to the south, and Quinag to the north. Note also the vista along the ridge to the east and the vast array of blue lochans that dapple the landscape in every direction. These routes are for experienced walkers only and should not be attempted by the ordinary pedestrian.

Meall Mheadhonach

Caisteal Liath

Plate 153 Suilven and Lochinver

Bealach Mor

Plate 155 **Route 56** ascends the gully to Bealach Mor

Plate 155 Basalt. Mull County of Caithness. See Plate 40.

Plate 157 **Route 56** to Meall Mheadhonach

Plate 158 **Route 56** to Caisteal Liath

Plate 159 **Route 56**—A higher viewpoint reveals the wall on Caisteal Liath

Plate 160 **Route 56**—Meall Mheadhonach from Caisteal Liath

Route 57. From Inverkirkaig. Drive round the coast from Lochinver and park your vehicle in the car-park near the bridge over the River Kirkaig. Follow the path on the ʀ bank of the stream through scenery that is softer than that of Route 56. Note the beautiful falls on the ʀ and continue ahead to Fionn Loch. If you have not made arrangments to use the locked boat, you must bear north and walk round its shore on a well-trodden path. From the loch's northern shore turn north at a suitable point and head for the centre of Suilven. Then scale its long gully to join Route 56 at the Bealach Mor.

Plate 161 **Route 57**—Suilven from Fionn Loch

Quinag

Sail Gharbh	2651 feet	808 metres
Sail Gorm	2546 feet	776 metres
Spidean Coinich	2508 feet	764 metres
Centre Top	2448 feet	746 metres
Creag na h'Iolaire Ard	2339 feet	713 metres

The three fronts of this striking Y-shaped peak present an entirely different aspect of the mountain, and the most picturesque view of it is that of Spidean Coinich and the summit ridge ending at Sail Gharbh. It is observed at its finest from the head of Loch Assynt and includes a glimpse of Ardvreck Castle in the middle distance. The long western ridge terminating at Sail Gorm is well seen from the foot of Loch Assynt and also from the wild hill road to the east of Drumbeg, which reveals its facade of terraced sandstone seamed with deep gullies, some of which prove to be spectacular on closer acquaintance. The two old and abrupt northern sentinels of the Y dominate the views from Kylesku and Loch a'Chairn Bhain, and clearly disclose the immense Barrel Buttress between deep and nearly vertical gullies as the outstanding feature of Sail Gharbh; it is the main resort of the rock climber on this mountain, although ascents have been made by buttress and gully on the western face of Sail Gorm. The chief characteristic of the summit ridge is the broad flat pavement that terminates so precipitously at Sail Gharbh, and the castellated eminences that crown the subsidiary ridge ending at Sail Gorm.

Quinag consists mainly of purplish-red sandstone and is poised upon an uneven floor of Lewisan gneiss which is the chief geological feature of Sutherland; it rises to a height of some 2000 feet/600 m on the north face of Sail Gorm. White Cambrian quartzite caps the highest point of the eastern ridge,

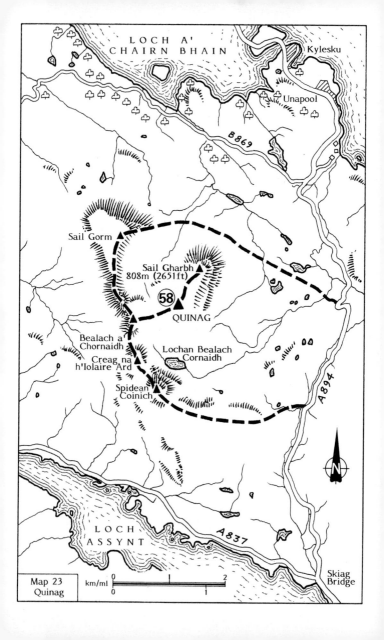

LOCH A'
CHAIRN BHAIN

Kylesku

Unapool

B 869

Sail Gorm ▲

Sail Gharbh
808m (2651ft) ▲

58

▲
QUINAG

Bealach a
Chornaidh ▲

Lochan Bealach
Cornaidh

Creag na
h'Iolaire Ard

Spidean
Coinich ▲

A 894

N

LOCH
ASSYNT

A 837

Skiag
Bridge

Map 23
Quinag

km/ml
0   2
0   1

Plate 162 An islet in Loch Assynt

Plate 163 Quinag and Ardvreck Castle from the head of Loch Assynt

covers the summit of Spidean Coinich, and extends eastwards down its slopes to the Allt Sgiathaig.

The ideal centre for its exploration is Inchnadamph, but those walkers with transport may reach it from Lochinver or Drumbeg.

Route 58. Quinag from Inchnadamph.

Start from a large parking place on the east side of the road 4 miles/6.4 km north of Inchnadamph near the highest point on the road between Skiag Bridge and Kylesku. Ascend the broad ridge to Spidean Coinich, with views of Lochan Bealach Cornaidh in the immense corrie on the R. This peak opens up a magnificent vista of Loch Assynt and a view of the full length of Suilven in the south. Traverse Creag na h'Iolaire Ard to reach to Bealach a'Chornaidh at the base of the Y and on attaining the Centre Top bear R for Sail Gharbh, noting the blue sea lochs ahead and the quartzite peak of Glas Bheinn on the R. Retrace your steps to the Centre Top and then traverse the eminences on the ridge to Sail Gorm, which unfolds a fine panorama of the deeply indented coastline of Sutherland to the west. Reverse the route, or return to the Centre Top and descend to Lochan Bealach Cornaidh to pick up a good path back to the car. Walkers should bear in mind that this route is a long and strenuous undertaking.

Those desiring to shorten the traverse by omitting Spidean Coinich may do so by following the good path mentioned above which starts slightly to the north and leads to Lochan Bealach Cornaidh.

Spidean Coinich

Sail Gorm

Plate 164. The western ridge of Quinag from the foot of Loch Assynt

Plate 165 **Route 58**—Sail Gharbh and Sail Gorm seen from a roadside lochan

Sail Gorm

Sail Gharbh

Plate 166 Quinag from Loch a'Chairn Bhain. Note the Barrel Buttress on Sail Gharbh.

Plate 167 **Route 58** to Spidean Coinich

Plate 168 **Route 58** The head of Loch Assynt from Spidean Coinich

Plate 169 **Route 58**—Suilven from Spidean Coinich

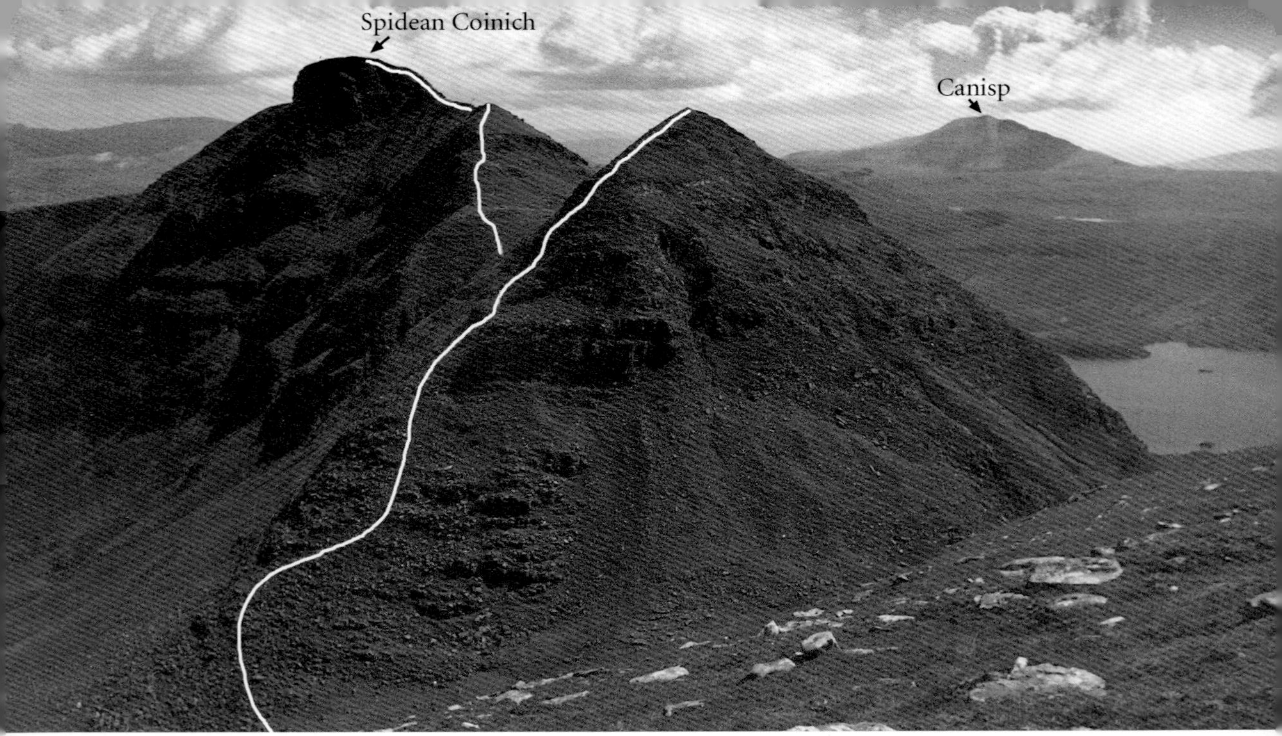

Canisp

Spidean Coinich

Plate 170. **Route 58.** Looking back from the centre top across the Bealach a'Chornaidh

Plate 171 **Route 58**—South western aspect of the summit ridge of Quinag

Canisp

Spidean Coinich

Plate 172. **Route 58** Crenellated gneiss spurs on the ridge to Sail Garbh

Plate 173 **Route 58**—A spectacular gully on the ridge of Sail Gorm

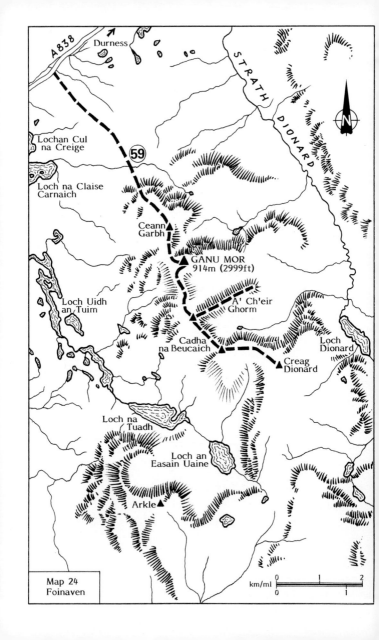

A838

Durness

Lochan Cul
na Creige

Loch na Claise
Carnaich

59

Ceann
Garbh

GANU MOR
914m (2999ft)

STRATH DIONARD

N

Loch Uidh
an Tuim

A' Ch'eir
Ghorm

Cadha
na Beucaich

Loch
Dionard

Creag
Dionard

Loch na
Tuadh

Loch an
Easain Uaine

Arkle

Map 24
Foinaven

km/ml   0   1   2
         0   1

Foinaven

Ganu Mor	2980 feet	908 metres
Ceann Gabh	2952 feet	900 metres
A'Ch'eir Ghorm	2843 feet	867 metres
Top South of Tower	2644 feet	806 metres
Creag Urbhard	2552 feet	778 metres

The remote situation of this peak precludes the possibility of its ever becoming as popular with walkers as those in the Central Highlands, but like its near neighbour, Arkle, it consists of quartzite and its lofty undulating ridge is on this account worthy of a special visit. It straddles the vast moors, with their hundreds of blue lochans, to the east of Rhiconich and is separated from the more northerly peaks of Sutherland by the long, wild and forlorn stretches of Strath Dionard. It may be conveniently approached from the Durness road some 3 miles/4.8 km to the north-east of Rhiconich, but can also be reached by an adventurous tramp through Strath Beag to the south of Loch Eriboll. To reach Foinaven, climb the mountain, traverse its long summit ridge, and visit its north-eastern spurs is a tough proposition for the fittest of mountaineers. But its bewildering state of erosion should be a sufficiently powerful magnet to attract those who wish to observe for themselves one of the most remarkable peaks in Scotland. For to sit alone on its crest and listen to the falling of its disintegrated quartzite blocks is one of the most eerie experiences in Britain.

Route 59. Foinaven from Rhiconich. Drive towards Durness and park your car at a convenient spot to the north of Lochan Cul na Creige. Make for the first top by crossing the gradually rising moor and avoid all boggy ground in the advance. Ascend the steep, grassy slopes of Ceann Garbh and follow the ridge

Plate 174. Foinaven dominates the wilds of Sutherland, and Loch Laxford on a left

to the highest peak of Ganu Mor. Continue along its crest at least as far as the pass of Cadha na Beucaich, which is guarded by a tower, and if time is not pressing and the weather is favourable turn the latter on the R, cross the pass and bear L for Creag Urbhard to examine its precipitous cliffs. On your return walk turn R to visit the central spur of A'Ch'eir Ghorm and just listen to the falling blocks of quartzite. Then regain the ridge and descend from Ceann Garbh to your car. The wide panorama is interesting because it includes a fine prospect of Ben Hope to the east and Arkle very near in the south, with Ben Stack peeping over its R shoulder. But it is the western vista that will hold your gaze, as the whole of the vast landscape is dappled with innumerable blue lochans which lead the eye to the illimitable stretches of the Atlantic.

Walkers who are staying at Kinlochbervie and have made the long traverse of Foinaven should take an off-day and visit SANDWOOD BAY. This is considered by many as the most beautiful in all Scotland and lies to the south of Cape Wrath; it is only accessible by foot. The bay is characterised by a vast sweep of golden sands, which are hemmed in on the south by lofty red cliffs, at the end of which stands a conspicuous stack known as Am Buachaille.

The best way to reach it is to follow a single-track road as far as some cottages at Blairmore and pass through a gate on the R beyond them which gives access to the moor. 2 miles/3.2 km of rough cart track and an equal distance thence of boggy track, passing a series of lochans, attains a broad ridge, beyond which Sandwood Bay comes into view below. The track runs down to the sands and it is perhaps 0.5 mile/0.8 km across them to the succession of long rolling breakers. The bay is a lovely retreat, but to some conveys a sense of haunting. However, photographers who reach it on a sunny summer morning, when the light is on the curving cliffs, will be rewarded by a scene of exquisite beauty.

Arkle

Cadha na Beucaich

Plate 177 Route 58. View of the site of Eirig_____ as seen M

Plate 176 **Route 59**—Retrospect of Ganu Mor from the ridge

Plate 177. **Route 59.** Looking across A'Ch'air Chasm to Ben Hope

Plate 178 **Route 59**—Cadha na Beucaich is the last gap in the ridge

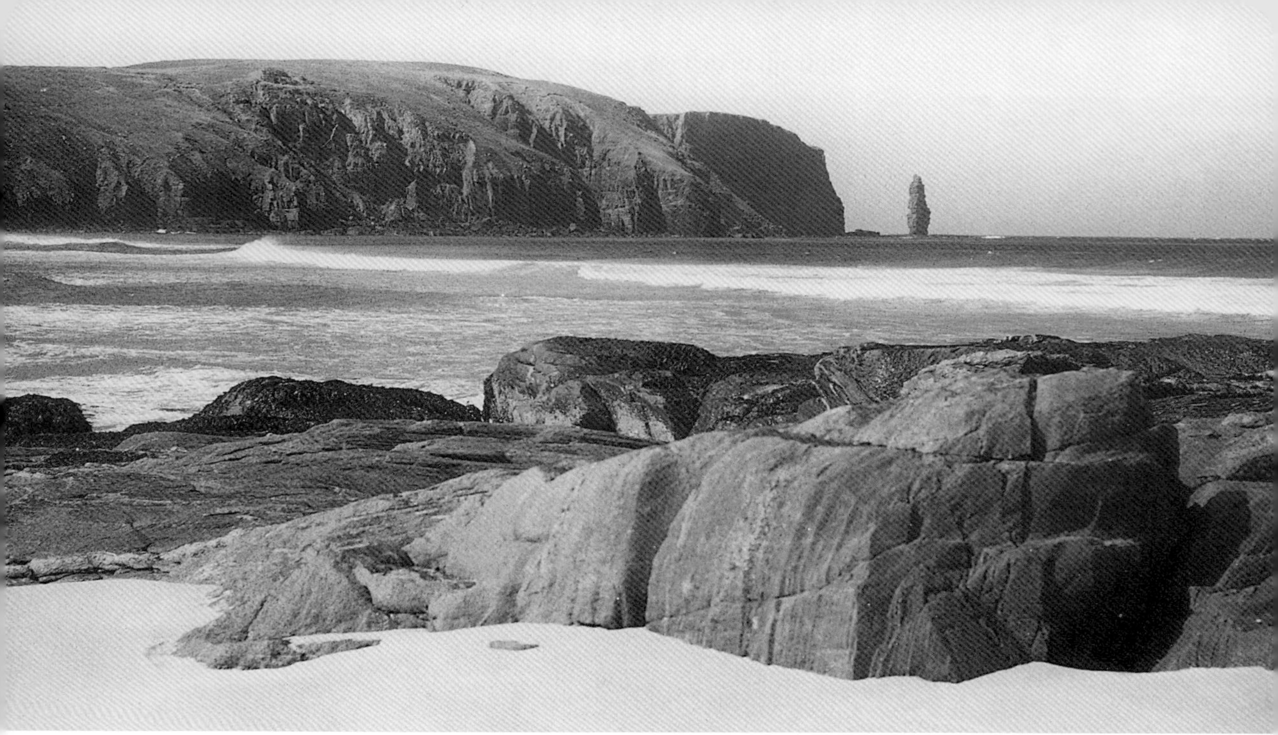

Plate 179 Sandwood Bay

Ben Hope

Ben Hope   3041 feet   927 metres

This mountain is the most northerly Munro in Scotland and rises some 1.5 miles/2.4 km to the south-east of the head of Loch Hope. Its most imposing elevation is revealed from the north in the vicinity of Hope Lodge because its precipitous, rocky north-western front is only seen to advantage from this angle. To the south and east its slopes are gentler and smoother, and cradle two small lochs and a number of lochans. The latter arc is clearly disclosed from the summit of Ben Loyal, while its western cliffs are well seen, and are indeed conspicuous, in the spacious views from Foinaven. They rise in two well-defined terraces; the lower of about 1000 feet/300 m is well shagged with trees, and the upper of about 2000 feet/600 m is split up into numerous rocky buttresses.

Ben Hope may be reached by the wild moorland road that runs from Altnaharra to Hope Lodge, and the first section of about 12 miles/19.3 km affords an almost adventurous drive owing to its passing places, which are few and far between. The second section begins at the conspicuous broch of Dun Dornaigil, and wends its way below the cliffs past Cashel Dhu, and thereafter through the trees fringing Loch Hope.

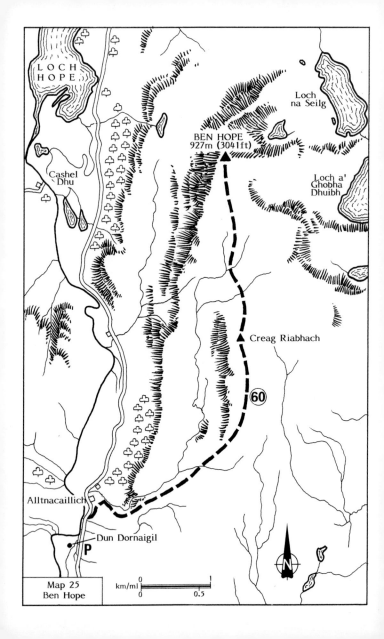

LOCH HOPE

Loch na Seilg

BEN HOPE
927m (3041ft)

Loch a'
Ghobha
Dhuibh

Cashel
Dhu

Creag Riabhach

60

Alltnacaillich

Dun Dornaigil

P

N

Map 25
Ben Hope

km/ml
0
0
0.5
1

Route 60. Ben Hope from Dun Dornaigil. Start at a car park near Dun Dornaigil just south of Altnacaillich. Follow the road north and pick up a small track that heads rightwards, skirting the farm, towards the Allt na Caillich. This burn descends from the moor and its L bank affords the easiest approach to the south ridge of the mountain. This is broad and relatively smooth, and rises at an easy gradient to the summit where the cairn is poised on its northern tip, surrounded on three sides by abysmal drops. The panorama on a clear day is extensive, in which the sea and sea lochs to the north, and the innumerable lochans in other directions, charm the eye. Ben Loyal is prominent to the east; Ben Klibreck in the south-east; Ben Hee in the south and the several peaks of the Reay Forest in the west.

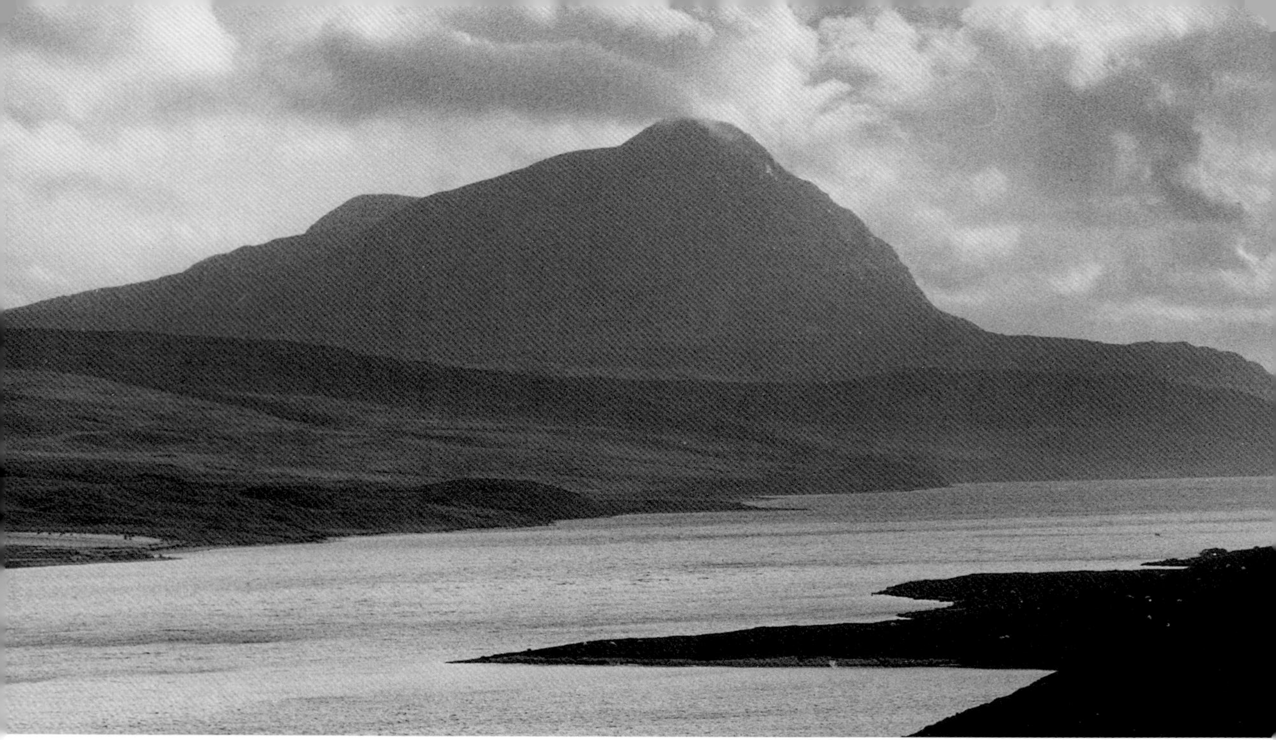

Plate 180 Ben Hope and Loch Hope from near Hope Lodge

Ben Loyal

An Caisteal	2506 feet	764 metres
Heddle's Top	2440 feet	744 metres
Carn an Tionail	2349 feet	716 metres
Sgor Chaonasaid	2335 feet	712 metres
Sgor a'Bhatain	2296 feet	700 metres
Sgor a'Chleirich	2175 feet	663 metres

This individual mountain rises from the swelling moorland some 5 miles/8 km to the south of Tongue and its western front, when seen from the vicinity of Lochan Hakel, makes one of the most beautiful pictures in Britain. Known also as the 'Queen of Scottish Peaks', it is admired alike by artists and photographers, and its particular splendour is due to the graceful pendent ridges that join its four western peaks of granite; they impart to the whole of it a grandeur that is altogether out of proportion to its height.

Walkers driving eastwards across the boggy uplands of A'Mhoine catch glimpses of the peak, but it is only on coming down to sea level at the Kyle of Tongue that its real stature is evident. If one avoids crossing the bridge over the Kyle of Tongue and follows the old road, the peak looks its best on attaining higher ground near Lochan Hakel, whose blue suddenly appears below the road on the R, when the full elevation is revealed in all its glory. And strangely enough, when the mountain is seen from the Altnaharra–Tongue road which skirts its eastern flanks, all its distinguishing features are hidden from view and completely belie its real charm.

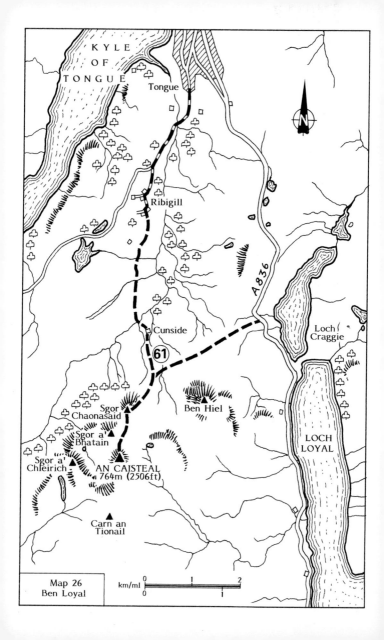

KYLE
OF
TONGUE

Tongue

Ribigill

Cunside

(61)

A 836

Loch
Craggie

Sgor
Chaonasaid

Ben Hiel

Sgor a'
Bhatain

Sgor a'
Chleirich

AN CAISTEAL
764m (2506ft)

Carn an
Tionail

LOCH
LOYAL

N

Map 26
Ben Loyal

km/ml   0   1   2
         0   1

Route 61. Ben Loyal from Tongue. This peak can be climbed from almost any point on the engirdling moor, but is usually ascended from Cunside Cottage which is about 1.5 miles/2.4 km to the south of the large farm of Ribigill: the latter is reached by a by-road that forks to the L from the Lairg road some 2 miles/3.2 km to the south of the village. Its prominent northern outpost of Sgor Chaonasaid is rocky and precipitous and should be avoided by all save the experienced rock climber. It is best to ascend the grassy slopes to the east of this sentinel and to then proceed due south along the gradually rising ridge to the commanding summit of An Caisteal. The same point of ascent may be reached with equal facility from the road beside Loch Craggie. The summit plateau is disappointing and reminds one of the Dartmoor tors rather than of the typical Scottish peak, and a good day is required to explore the whole of it and to visit all its tops. The panorama is stupendous and does not differ much from that of its near neighbour, Ben Hope, save that the eastern prospect comprises the wastes of Sutherland and Caithness, which are dappled with the gleaming blue of innumerable lochs and lochans.

Sgor Chaonasaid

An Caisteal

Plate 181 Ben Loyal from a roadside location

Plate 182 **Route 61**—Ben Hope from the summit of Ben Loyal

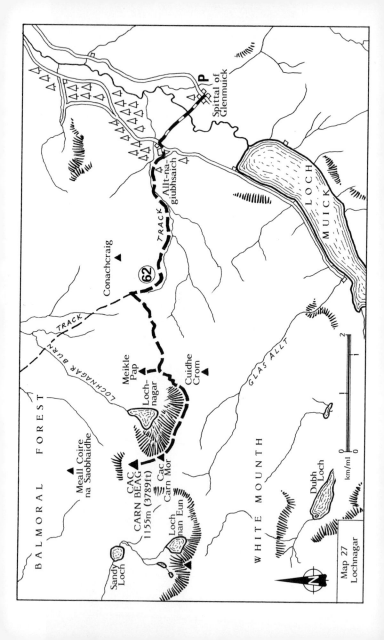

P

Spittal of Glenmuick

Allt-na-giubhsaich

TRACK

Conachcraig

62

TRACK

LOCHNAGAR BURN

BALMORAL FOREST

Meall Coire na Saobhaidhe

Meikle Pap

Loch-nagar

Cuidhe Crom

GLAS ALLT

L O C H   M U I C K

CAC CARN BEAG
1155m (3789ft)

Cac Carn Mor

Loch nan Eun

Sandy Loch

W H I T E   M O U N T H

Dubh Loch

km/ml

0   1   2

Map 27
Lochnagar

N

Lochnagar

Cac Carn Beag	3789 feet	1155 metres
Cac Carn Mor	3773 feet	1150 metres
The Stuic	3571 feet	1088 metres
Cuidhe Crom	3552 feet	1083 metres
Carn an t-Sagairt Mor	3435 feet	1047 metres
Carn an t-Sagairt Beag	3424 feet	1044 metres
Meikle Pap	3215 feet	980 metres
Meall Coire na Saobhaidhe	3195 feet	974 metres
Little Pap	3136 feet	956 metres

On a clear spring day the walker travelling westwards from Aberdeen may catch a glimpse of the great snow-covered summit of Lochnagar before he reaches Ballater. But if he wishes to obtain a better view of it he should make for the bridge over the Dee where the vast plateau of the White Mounth will be seen rising above the nearer and more shapely Coyles of Muick. If he drives along Deeside he will notice the group from time to time, and not the least interesting of these prospects is obtained from the low hills to the north of Balmoral, whilst at Invercauld Bridge, further to the west, the mountain with its small conical summit is a conspicuous feature above the trees fringing the river.

Lochnagar dominates the Royal Forest of Balmoral and although its highest peak is only the thirtieth in order of altitude in Scotland, the shapeliness of its foothills, combined with the superb crescent of cliffs forming its great eastern corrie, raise it to an important place in the fine mountain scenes in Britain. Its precipices consist of coarse red granite which weathers both horizontally and vertically, and these lines of weakness impart to the cliffs an illusion of gigantic masonry. In course of time the upper blocks become dangerously under-

Cuidhe Crom

Corrie

Meikle Pap

Plate 183 Lochnagar from the Spittal of Glen Muick

cut and ultimately fall to the floor of the corrie some 1200 feet/ 370 m below. They are thus a risky venue for the rock climber, but the mountaineer who revels in sensational snow ascents will find the prodigious gully known as the Black Spout an attractive and satisfying problem. The ascent of the mountain presents no difficulties or dangers if the eastern corrie is avoided, and climbers should keep well away from the snow cornices on the upper plateau owing to their unknown dimensions. The summit of Lochnagar is some 14 miles/22.5 km from Ballater and about 5 miles/8 km from the Spittal of Glen Muick, so that even with transport to its base, the ascent requires a full day for the complete enjoyment of all its majestic scenes.

Route 62. Lochnagar from Ballater. Drive to the Spittal of Glen Muick and park your car. Then follow the path on the R where a bridge across the River Muick gives direct access to the Allt na-guibhsaich which is the starting point of the ascent. Take the path through the conifers and on emerging in the open moorland keep to it high above the L bank of the burn. Bear R to round the shoulder of Conachcraig, with views of the Meikle Pap overhead and on its R of the distant summits of Beinn a'Bhuird and Ben Avon. At this point the way can be confusing because the track falls on the far side of the ridge, whence, however, it branches to the L for the Meikle Pap. Thereafter the route is clear and at a height of 2800 feet/853 m you encounter the Foxes Well, marked by a small cairn and affording the last drink of water on this ascent. On reaching the col the steep zigzags of the Ladder rise to the L, but before tackling them turn R and climb to the summit of the Meikle Pap for the magnificent view of the long line of precipices engirdling the corrie, in which the Black Spout is prominent and also the dark lochan cradled at its base. Now retrace your steps to the col and climb the Ladder, eventually to pass the Red Spout on the R on your way to Cuidhe Crom which is an excellent viewpoint

Cac Carn Beag

Plate 184. Lochnagar from the old Invercauld Bridge

Black Spout

Cac Carn Beag

Plate 185 **Route 62**—The Corrie from Cuidhe Crom

and worthy of a halt. Then continue your walk along the rim of the precipices and if they are snowbound make generous use of your ice axe. In due course you will encounter the subsidiary peak of Cac Carn Mor, from which it is only a short step to the higher Cac Carn Beag.

Here you will find the excellent indicator, erected by the Cairngorm Club in July 1924, with whose help you should have no difficulty in identifying many of the distant peaks, and on a clear day even the summit of Ben Nevis. Note also, but much nearer at hand to the south-west, the tremendous corrie dominated by the Stuic, a fine buttress above Loch nan Eun, and when retracing your steps look into the grim depths of the Black Spout before descending to your car.

At Cac Carn Mor walkers will notice a track coming up from the south-west, which is the usual route of ascent from Braemar by way of Loch Callater.

Plate 186 **Route 62**—Looking across the exit of Black Spout to Cac Carn Beag

Plate 187 **Route 62**—The Stuic and Loch Nan Eun from the summit

Plate 188 **Route 62**—Cloud over Cac Carn Mor

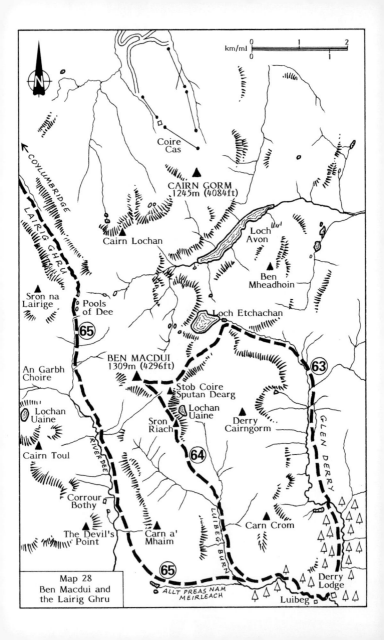

km/ml

0   1   2

0   1

N

← COYLUMBRIDGE

LAIRIG GHRU

Coire Cas

▲ CAIRN GORM
1245m (4084ft)

▲ Cairn Lochan

Loch Avon

▲ Ben Mheadhoin

▲ Sron na Lairige

Pools of Dee

65

Loch Etchachan

63

An Garbh Choire

▲ BEN MACDUI
1309m (4296ft)

Stob Coire Sputan Dearg

Lochan Uaine

Sron Riach

▲ Derry Cairngorm

GLEN DERRY

Lochan Uaine

▲ Cairn Toul

RIVER DEE

64

Corrour Bothy

▲ The Devil's Point

▲ Carn a' Mhaim

LUIBEG BURN

▲ Carn Crom

Derry Lodge

65

ALLT PREAS NAM MEIRLEACH

Luibeg

Map 28
Ben Macdui and
the Lairig Ghru

Ben Macdui

Ben Macdui	4295 feet	1309 metres
Stob Coire Sputan Dearg	4098 feet	1249 metres
Beinn Mheadhoin	3878 feet	1182 metres
Derry Cairngorm	3789 feet	1155 metres
Carn Etchachan	3674 feet	1120 metres
Sron Riach	3642 feet	1110 metres
Carn a'Mhaim	3402 feet	1037 metres
Lochan Uaine	3225 feet	983 metres
Loch Etchachan	3058 feet	932 metres
Carn Crom	2920 feet	890 metres
Loch A'an (Loch Avon)	2375 feet	724 metres

Ben Macdui is the highest mountain in the Cairngorms and the second highest in Scotland. Together with its outlier Cairn Gorm, it forms the massive group of hills rising between Glen Derry and the Lairig an Laoigh on the east and the Lairig Ghru on the west. The summit is scarcely well proportioned and consists of a flattish rounded top which perhaps presents its most graceful aspect when seen from Cairn Gorm to the north. The two peaks are connected by a broad high plateau which nowhere falls below the 3600 feet/1097 m contour. The supporting slopes of Ben Macdui are set at a gentle angle, excepting on the west, where they fall steeply to the Lairig Ghru. The ascent of this mountain, therefore, presents no difficulites but vast distances have to be covered to attain its cairn.

Two famous lochs lie in the heart of the group: Loch A'an (Loch Avon) and Loch Etchachan; the former is set deep in the hills amid one of the most impressive and sombre amphitheatres in the Highlands and is so remote, that were it not for the rough cave under the Shelter Stone where a night may be spent, it is doubtful if many walkers would ever see it. The

Plate 189 The satellites of Ben Macdui from Black Bridge

latter, lying in more open ground, is of considerably less interest, and is passed in the Glen Derry ascent of Ben Macdui.

As the crow flies the summit is actually nearer to Aviemore than Braemar, but unless its ascent is combined with that of Cairn Gorm, the expedition is lacking in interest. Those walkers wishing to undertake it should drive to Coire Cas, take the chair-lift to a point about 500 feet/150 m below the summit of Cairn Gorm, cross over the summit and down to the top of Fiacaill a'Choire Chais and then cross the plateau by way of Cairn Lochan to Ben Macdui, descending by way of Creag an Leth-choin (Lurcher's Crag) into the Lairig Ghru and Rothie-murchus, Route 65, or as an alternative follow Route 67 which takes in the Shelter Stone. The mountain, however, is more usually ascended from Braemar by way of Derry Lodge, beyond which there is a choice of two routes. The more popular of these is through Glen Derry and Coire Etchachan, a total distance of approximately 10 miles/16 km, but the more direct approach by Glen Luibeg and the fine ridge of Sron Riach is more interesting, revealing and 2 miles/3.2 km shorter.

Route 63. From Braemar by Glen Derry. Start as for Route 64 at the Derry Gates (locked) on the north side of the River Dee east of Linn of Dee and follow the track north alongside the Lui Water to cross a bridge and thence to Derry Lodge. Take the path going due north from the lodge, and after passing through the ancient forest of gnarled pines cross the Derry Burn and keep to the R of the gloomy glen until the cliffs of Beinn Mheadhoin appear ahead, a distance of about 6 miles/ 9.7 km. Now follow the L fork and climb the track that rises through the deep trough of Coire Etchachan past the basic Hutchison Memorial bothy until you reach easier ground where Loch Etchachan reposes amid a wilderness of rock and scree and reveals to the north the rounded summit of Cairn Gorm. Turn to the L and keep to the track that skirts the cliffs enclosing Coire Sputan Dearg, whence bear R and walk up the

Beinn Mheadhoin

Plate 190 **Route 63** Beinn Mheadhoin from the last trees in Glen Derry

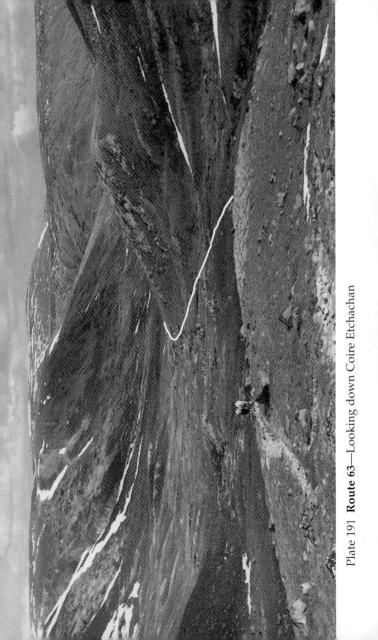

Plate 191 **Route 63**—Looking down Coire Etchachan

stony slopes to the cairn on the skyline. Ben Macdui, like Lochnagar, has an indicator erected in 1925 by the Cairngorm Club, from which you should be able to identify many of the surrounding hills on a clear day. However, the nearer tops that stretch from Cairn Toul to Braeriach on the other side of the Lairig Ghru to the west will hold your gaze, and the view of them is one of the grandest in the country. You will be impressed by the vastness of An Garbh Coire, with its sharp pointed summit of Sgor an Lochain Uaine, known also as the Angel's Peak, rising steeply on the L and just to the R of Cairn Toul. The skyline to the R encompasses Braeriach, which is supported by Coire Bhrochain, and then falls to Sron na Lairige and Rothiemurchus.

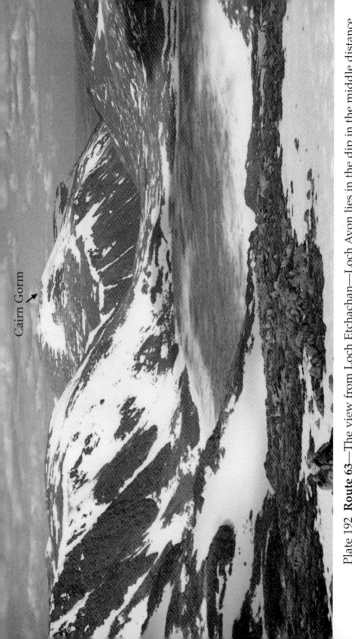

Cairn Gorm

Plate 192 **Route 63**—The view from Loch Etchachan—Loch Avon lies in the dip in the middle distance

Plate 194 **Route 63**—Cairn Toul, Sgor an Lochain Uaine and An Garbh Coire from Ben Macdui

Plate 195 **Route 63**—Braeriach and Coire Bhrochain from Ben Macdui

Route 64. From Braemar by Sron Riach. Start as for the previous route but continue west past Derry Lodge and across the bridge over the Derry Burn towards Glen Luibeg. Follow the Lairig Ghru path westwards through the trees with Carn a'Mhaim towering ahead on the R. In about 2 miles/3.2 km the path forks before reaching the Luibeg Burn and here you take the branch on the R and walk northwards following the burn through thick heather across the lower slopes of Carn Crom with a grand view ahead of Sron Riach. After crossing the Luibeg Burn the gradient increases and a stiff pull up the ridge will place you on its lofty crest where you will be rewarded by a magnificent prospect of Cairn Toul on the L, beyond the long shoulder of Carn a'Mhaim. Bear R now for the cliffs above Coire Sputan Dearg and if it is snowbound keep well away from the cornices overhanging the lip of the corrie, below which on the R you look down on the lonely Lochan Uaine, the second highest in the Cairngorms. On attaining the red granite blocks surmounting Stob Coire Sputan Dearg, turn L and walk up the easy stony slopes to Ben Macdui.

Plate 196 **Routes 64** and **65**—The path from Derry Lodge goes towards Carn a'Mhaim

Plate 197   **Route 64**—Stob Coire Sputan Dearg from Glen Luibeg

Plate 109 **Route 64** – Càrn Toul and Càrn an t-Sabhail in from Sgòr Phàrt.

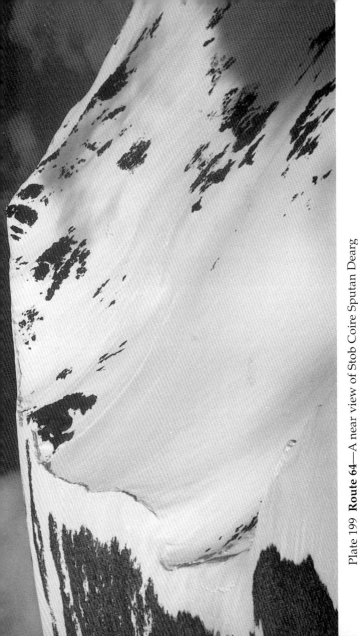

Plate 199 **Route 64**—A near view of Stob Coire Sputan Dearg

Peaks enclosing the Lairig Ghru

from north to south

ROTHIEMURCHUS

Carn Eilrig	2434 feet	742 metres	Castle Hill	2388 feet	728 metres
Carn Odhar	2408 feet	734 metres	Creag a'Chalamain	2582 feet	787 metres
Sron na Lairige	3884 feet	1184 metres	Creag an Leth-choin – Lurcher's Crag	3455 feet	1053 metres
Braeriach	4252 feet	1296 metres			
Sgor an Lochain Uaine (or Angel's Peak)	4127 feet	1258 metres	Ben Macdui	4295 feet	1309 metres
Cairn Toul	4235 feet	1291 metres			
The Devil's Point	3294 feet	1004 metres	Sron Riach	3642 feet	1110 metres
Creaghan nan Gabhar	2369 feet	722 metres	Carn a'Mhaim	3402 feet	1037 metres
Sgor Mor	2667 feet	813 metres			
Sgor Dubh	2431 feet	741 metres	Carn Crom	2920 feet	890 metres

DERRY LODGE

The Lairig Ghru

The Lairig Ghru is the finest and most popular of the passes in the Cairngorms and its traverse one of the most arduous in the whole of Britain. The best long distance view of it is from Speyside where it appears as a gigantic V-shaped opening between Ben Macdui and Braeriach. The approaches at either end are full of variety and interest, but the pass itself is the very epitome of austerity, barrenness and gloom. Its passage is not the longest expedition in the district but is enough to test the stamina of the fittest. The distance from Braemar to Aviemore is 27 miles/43 km, but it is not everyone who walks the whole way. A lift to Linn of Dee shortens it by 7 miles/11 km and another from Coylumbridge takes off a further 2 miles/3.2 km, but the other 18 miles/29 km cannot be reduced by any form of transport.

A point not to be lost sight of by those undertaking this walk is that no accommodation exists along the route although two small and spartan bothies offer shelter (Corrour NN 981958 and Garbh Coire NN 959986). On a fine and warm summer night this is not a serious matter, but in bad weather, not uncommon in the Lairig Ghru, shelter may be urgently required.

It is a matter of opinion which direction affords the more fascinating walk through the pass; but it is always an advantage to go from south to north, because on a good day the sunlight reveals the topography of the landscape more clearly. In the reverse direction not only is the sun in one's eyes, but its rays are refracted by the moisture and dust in the atmosphere, when one's full appreciation of the scenery is undoubtedly marred.

Plate 200. **Routes 64 and 65.** Deer in the vicinity of Derry Lodge

Route 65. From Linn of Dee to Coylumbridge. Start at the
Derry Gates (locked) on the north side of the River Dee east of
Linn of Dee and follow the track north alongside the Lui Water
to cross a bridge and thence to Derry Lodge. Follow the path
into Glen Luibeg to the fork in the Lairig Ghru path where the
flat expanse of sand and boulders marks the cloudburst of
1829. Take the L branch and go ahead to cross the bridge over
the Luibeg Burn and then ascend the rather steep spur of Carn
a'Mhaim. From the brow of the hill you should turn round to
admire the retrospect of the hills about Derry Lodge, to the R
of which you will perceive the summit of Lochnagar rising
above the vast expanse of moorland. The going is now easy
but rather wet for more than a mile/1.6 km, and as you round
the flanks of Carn a'Mhaim the prospect ahead of Glen Dee
and to the west the green floor of Glen Geusachan, over-
shadowed by Beinn Bhrotain and the Devil's Point, increases
in grandeur with every step. Threading the heather on your L
runs the Allt Preas nam Meirleach, which rises in a small group
of lochans. If you can spare the time, it is worthwhile ascending
to see them because they make a charming foreground to the
Devil's Point and Cairn Toul, the two superb peaks rising
across the glen.

   During this part of the tramp you will have wondered how
much further you have to go before sighting the pass itself, but
before swinging round the bend which discloses it, your gaze
will be riveted upon the magnificent symmetrical cone of the
Devil's Point whose shapely top and rifted supporting crags
make such a fine picture of mountain grandeur. Then, quite
suddenly, the Lairig Ghru will be revealed stretching away to
the north and you will doubtless pause to admire its stupendous proportions. On the L, and just beyond the Devil's Point,
the skyline is crowned by Cairn Toul, its flanks sweeping down
in one unbroken line past the overhanging corrie to the river,
2400 feet/730 m below. Behind it there is a glimpse of Coire
Bhrochain immediately beneath Braeriach, and this merges

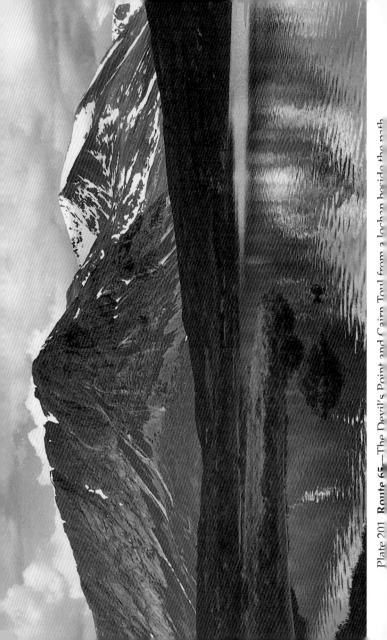

Plate 201 **Route 65**—The Devil's Point and Cairn Toul from a lochan beside the path.

Plate 202   **Route 65**—Looking north through the Lairig Ghru

with Sron na Lairige whose slopes fall towards the pass. On the R the featureless flanks of Ben Macdui are connected by a high rock ridge whose crest terminates with Carn a'Mhaim. The rough track now drops slightly and then runs almost level for 1.5 miles/2.4 km, passing the Corrour bothy on the L between the Devil's Point and Cairn Toul.

When you arrive opposite the latter you will realise the vastness of the distance which separates it from Braeriach, and a little further along the pass you will see Sgor an Lochain Uaine (Angel's Peak) high up to the south of the great amphitheatre of An Garbh Coire. If you scan the cliffs forming its crest you may be able to pick out the white line of the infant Dee descending from the Wells of Dee on the summit plateau of Braeriach. Thereafter the pass narrows and on approaching the highest point it levels out, being almost choked in places by the large boulders that have fallen from the hillsides. Here you will encounter the Pools of Dee, whose symmetry deceptively suggests the hand of man, and beyond them you will soon thankfully attain the highest point of the Lairig at an altitude of 2733 feet/833 m. The descent is at an easy gradient for the first 1.5 miles/2.4 km and then its narrow confines end below Creag an Leth-choin (Lurcher's Crag) high up on the R. Looking back, the pass presents a picture of wild desolation, but this aspect is softened in the advance northwards by occasional glimpses of Speyside far below.

The track drops rapidly, but there are still 2 miles/3.2 km of wilderness before the first tree heralds the approach to Rothiemurchus. It is worth pausing at this point to gaze upon the vast expanse of forest stretching away for miles to the banks of the Spey and frowned upon on the L by the conical sentinel of Carn Eilrig. This coign of vantage is a good one for the appraisal of the gigantic proportions of the Lairig Ghru, now left behind, where the apparent overhang of the Lurcher is well seen high up on the L.

If you delight in the beauty of trees you will revel in the

stately gathering which characterises Rothiemurchus, and if
you are fortunate you may catch a glimpse of the tiny crested
tit that lines its nest with deer's hair and makes its home
hereabouts. Here and there you will notice a windswept birch,
but it is the Scots Pines which are so magnificent. After 2
miles/3.2 km or so of the shady forest you will come to a fork
in the track. The R branch goes to Loch Morlich, the middle
one to the River Luineag, some 2 miles/3.2 km west of Loch
Morlich, and the L branch, your direction, to Coylumbridge. It
descends at first to join the R bank of the Allt Druidh, the burn
which rises in the Lairig Ghru, and you advance past its
junction with the larger stream of Am Beanaidh coming down
from Gleann Einich. You will pass through a deserted clearing
in the forest, carpeted with springy turf, and in a short distance
reach the iron footbridge erected in 1912 by the Cairngorm
Club, which spans the river below the ford. To give walkers an
idea of the distances they still have to cover in either direction,
the Cairngorm Club thoughtfully placed a tablet on the parapet
of their bridge and it gives the following approximate distances
and times:

To

Aviemore	1½ hours	4 miles
Coylumbridge	¾ hour	2 miles
Lairig Ghru summit	3 hours	5½ miles
Derry Lodge	6½ hours	14 miles
Linn of Dee	8 hours	18 miles
Braemar	10 hours	24½ miles

Beyond the bridge the path divides again; the L branch leads
to Loch an Eilein and by road to Inverdruie and thence to
Aviemore, while the R fork continues through forest by the L
bank of Am Beanaidh to Coylumbridge and civilisation.

Plate 203 **Route 65**—A wild retrospect near the summit of the pass

Plate 204 **Route 65**—An unsolved mystery in the Lairig Ghru

Plate 205 **Route 65** The first tree in Rothiemurchus

Plate 206 **Route 65**—The last glimpse of the Lairig Ghru from Rothiemurchus

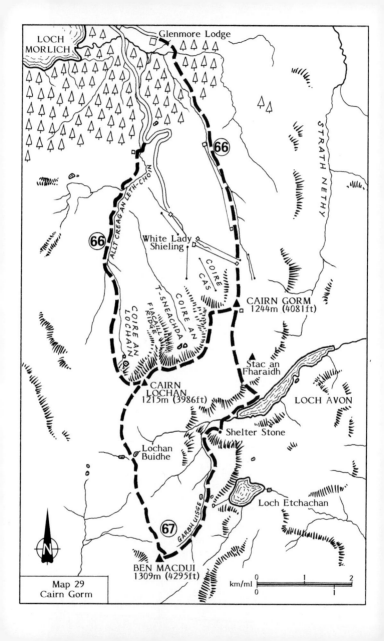

LOCH
MORLICH

Glenmore Lodge

STRATH NETHY

66

66

ALLT CREAG AN LETH-CHOIN

White Lady
Shieling

COIRE
CAS

COIRE AN
T-SNEACHDA

FIACAILL RIDGE

COIRE AN
LOCHAIN

CAIRN GORM
1244m (4081ft)

Stac an
Fharaidh

LOCH AVON

CAIRN
LOCHAN
1215m (3986ft)

Shelter Stone

Lochan
Buidhe

GARBH UISGE

Loch Etchachan

67

BEN MACDUI
1309m (4295ft)

N

Map 29
Cairn Gorm

km/ml
0   1   2
0   1

Cairn Gorm

Cairn Gorm	4081 feet	1244 metres
Cairn Lochan	3986 feet	1215 metres
Stob Coire an t-Sneachda	3856 feet	1176 metres
Fiacaill Arête	3691 feet	1125 metres
Creag an Leth-choin	3455 feet	1053 metres
Loch A'an (Loch Avon)	2375 feet	724 metres

Cairn Gorm is the lowest of the 4000 foot/1219 m peaks that make up the mountains that have become known as the Cairngorms; their correct name being Rhuadh Liath. Owing to its position almost at the northern end of the chain, it commands one of the finest prospects in the region. From Speyside it has some semblance of shapeliness, although it is rounded and far from striking except when seen from the vicinity of Grantown. If, however, its ascent on foot is combined with the high ridge walk to Cairn Lochan, the immense cliffs of the latter will make up for any tameness which may characterise its peer. Moreover, it is the most accessible of these great mountains; its ascent on foot is the shortest and easiest, and in consequence the most popular of them all. Development within Coire Cas for skiing means the average pedestrian can drive up to Coire Cas at an altitude of 2150 feet/655 m. It is then even possible to take the chair-lift and be borne aloft to within a few hundred feet of the summit. In fact, the only footwork involved is from the upper station to the cairn on Cairn Gorm itself.

Route 66 is included on the assumption that walkers will scorn the ascent by the chair-lift and use their well-shod feet as the only means of progress from start to finish. However, since Route 67 is a much longer and more strenuous expedition for one day, then use of both car and lift may be considered by all, save of course by the toughest of mountaineers.

All walkers who traverse the Cairn Gorm-Ben Macdui Plateau should remember that the following bothies have been removed over the past twenty years:

Curran situated beside Lochan Buidhe at MR 983010;

El Alamein on the north ridge of Cairn Gorm at MR 016054;

St Valery on the cliffs above the west end of Loch Avon at MR 002022;

Jean's Hut in Coire an Lochain.

Route 66. Cairn Gorm from Aviemore. Drive past the Forestry Commission caravan and camping park at Loch Morlich, stopping for a moment *en route* to admire the beauty of the loch, backed by the ridge you will eventually traverse, and park at a purpose-made car-park in the meadow after the bridge over the Abhainn Ruigh-cunachan. Put on your walking boots, shoulder your rucksack and proceed on your way joyfully, ignoring completely all pressing offers of a lift up to Coire Cas! Walk up the ski road through the remnants of the one-time fine forest of pines to the first hairpin bend. A good path branches off up the hill and crosses the road on its way towards the perched block of Clach Bharraig on the left skyline. Scramble up to it and note the splendid retrospect of Loch Morlich, and then pick up the nearby path for the summit of your peak, passing in its higher reaches the upper station of the chair-lift with its nearby rebuilt Ptarmigan Restaurant.

The summit of Cairn Gorm is littered with great boulders and its cairn opens up a spacious prospect round the northern arc, in which Loch Morlich immediately catches the eye by reason of its intense blue set amid the green and brown trees of the engirdling forest. To the west the whole of Rothiemurchus is laid bare, backed by the winding Spey, Loch Alvie and the Monadh Liath. To the east the Moray Firth can be seen in the far distance, fringed with golden sands, and beyond it on the skyline rise the peaks of Sutherland and Caithness. To the south-west Braeriach tops the skyline above the summit of

Cairn Gorm   Coire Gas   Coire an t-Sneachda   Coire an Lochain

Plate 207 Seen from Loch Morlich, **Route 66** follows the skyline to the right, there is now much new forestry on the far side of the loch

Cairn Toul

Angel's Peak

Braeriach

Cairn Lochan

Faicaill Ridge

Plate 208 **Route 66** seen from Cairn Gorm

Cairn Lochan, and to the L its lofty ridge sweeps down to the Angel's Peak and Cairn Toul. Ben Macdui is prominent in the south, with Derry Cairngorm on its east and the tors of Beinn Mheadhoin clearly disclosed on the skyline further to the L; while to the east a grand array of peaks, which include Ben Avon and Lochnagar, close in the view.

Now walk due west off your peak and continue round the rim of Coire Cas, and then turn south along the lip of Coire an t-Sneachda whose shattered cliffs fall steeply on your R. Continue past the little col and climb steadily towards Cairn Lochan, passing the top of the Fiacaill Ridge on your R; its narrow escarpment forms the eastern wall of Coire an Lochain and is crowned by one of the few spectacular rock arêtes in the Cairngorms. The cairn on the latter peak stands on the very edge of the cliffs, which you circle to reach their western side. From this coign of vantage you obtain the finest view of their peculiar architecture. They consist of granite, weathered both vertically and horizontally and are a splendid example of this type of titanic masonry. Continue your walk by descending the ridge that falls to the north, Maidan Creag an Leth-choin, and look back from time to time to get a comprehensive view of the precipitous cliffs, below which lies the famous 'Great Slab' together with the two black lochans in the bottom of the corrie. At the base of the ridge you will encounter the rippling Allt Creag an Leth-choin, which you follow to a choice of paths on the west side of Allt Mor all the way back to the hairpin in the road and hence your car.

Plate 200 **Route 66** The summit cairn is perched on the edge of the cliffs of Càrn Làrban

Plate 210 **Route 66**—Looking back into Coire an Lochain

Route 67. Cairn Gorm to Ben Macdui by the Shelter Stone.
This route is for the experienced walker and should be severely
left alone by the ordinary pedestrian, who might find himself
in difficulties among the rocky escarpments surrounding Loch
Avon. From the ski area car-park, use the chair-lift to reach the
top of Cairn Gorm quickly. Then descend due south from the
cairn into the grassy depression of Coire Raibeirt which is
hemmed in on the east by Stac an Fharaidh and on the west by
the Stag Rocks. Follow a path down the east side of the burn.
On reaching Loch Avon bear west round its shore, and cross
the Garbh Uisge which flows into the head of the loch. It may
be necessary to cross further upstream for dry feet, though this
is sometimes impossible during winter or spring melt periods.
Just to the south, lying amongst the jumble of boulders at the
base of the giant Shelter Stone Crag, you will discover the
cottage-sized block of rock known as the Shelter Stone; a howff
which is situated amid some of the grandest rock scenery in
Scotland and which may still contain a visitors' book for you
to sign.

Scramble up beside the burn for some 1000 feet/300 m,
taking in a zigzag course to ease the angle of ascent, and on
reaching more level ground, where two tributaries of the burn
emerge, bear L for the top of the cliff overhanging the Shelter
Stone for the magnificent vista of Loch Avon. Now return to
the stream and follow it to its source below Ben Macdui. On
leaving the cairn retrace your steps for a short distance and
then keep to the higher contours, going north past Lochan
Buidhe, until you eventually reach Cairn Lochan. Finally walk
round the edge of the three corries back to Cairn Gorm and so
to your car.

Plate 211 **Route 67**—The Cairn Gorm upper chair lift and White Lady Sheiling

The Storr

The Storr	2359 feet	719 metres
Old Man of Storr	160 feet	49 metres

Walkers proceeding from Kyleakin to Sligachan in the Isle of Skye will get their first glimpse of this remarkable peak as they skirt the peninsula between Loch Ainort and Loch Sligachan, and on a clear day will easily perceive its fantastic buttresses topping the Trotternish skyline. But since it rises from the ridge over 6 miles/9.7 km to the north of Portree, those who wish to explore it must drive to its base at Loch Leathan, whence the formidable cliffs are easily attained, the Sanctuary and the Old Man visited and the lofty summit ridge traversed in an easy day. However, the finest view of the Storr is revealed from the head of Loch Fada, a treasured resort of the trout fisherman, from which excellent coign of vantage its deeply cleaved buttresses and nearby Old Man stand up superbly on the skyline.

While the ordinary pedestrian can safely explore the bizarre rock scenery surrounding the Sanctuary and its many weird pinnacles, the traverse of the summit ridge should only be attempted by the experienced walker who will revel in the grandeur of the rock architecture and of the mainland peaks that rise across the Sound of Raasay, in which he should have no difficulty in identifying Slioch and the Torridon Peaks. However, although only 160 feet/49 m high the ascent of the Old Man of Storr is quite a different problem, and it was only climbed for the first time in July 1955, by D. Whilans, J. Barber and G. J. Sutton.

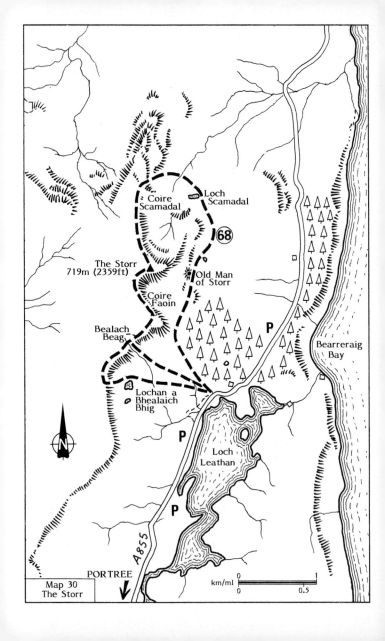

Coire
Scamadal

Loch
Scamadal

68

The Storr
719m (2359ft)

Old Man
of Storr

Coire
Faoin

Bealach
Beag

Bearreraig
Bay

P

Lochan a
Bhealaich
Bhig

P

Loch
Leathan

P

N

A855

PORTREE

km/ml

0   1

0   0.5

Map 30
The Storr

Plate 213 The Storr from Loch Fada

Route 68. The Traverse of the Storr. Drive north from Portree and park towards the end of Loch Leathan. Ascend from the south-western corner of the plantation beside a small burn and follow this through the woods to reach the strange collection of rocks guarding the Sanctuary. The Old Man is worth climbing up to if only to examine closely its undercut structure of trap rock. Then pass round it to take a look at the nearby leaning Needle and make your way through the boulders at the base of the cliffs into Coire Scamadal with its tiny lochan. Here you will find a break in the lower cliffs through which you can gain the ridge whence proceed carefully to the L and climb along the crest of the buttresses and skirt the yawning gullies through which you will occasionally glimpse the Old Man of Storr far below. After passing the summit cairn the ridge bends to the L round the enclosing walls of Coire Faoin and as you descend it you will obtain a splendid vista of the whole of the wild Sanctuary and its pinnacles backed by the blue sea. The easiest descent is to follow the line of cliffs to the south when you will eventually reach a trickling burn that has worn its way through them to the grassy plateau at their base and beside which runs a sketchy track whence a walk across the moor will lead back to your car. However if you have a steady head you may prefer to descend the sensational path that winds its way down the north face of the last buttress and ends at the pinnacles guarding the Sanctuary.

Plate 214 Close-up of the Old Man of Storr

Plate 215. **Beacle 60.** Looking across the Sanctuary to the peaks on the mainland.

Quiraing

Meall na Suiramach	1781 feet	543 metres
The Needle	180 feet	55 metres

From afar this remote peak in the Isle of Skye looks quite uninteresting, as its eastern front appears as a broken wall of rock that frowns upon the lochan-strewn moorland sloping down to Staffin Bay. But on closer inspection it will be found not only to consist of the weirdest collection of perpendicular buttresses and pinnacles in Britain, but also to hide away in its uppermost recesses an oval Table covered with smooth, sheep-cropped grass of vivid hue, which might well make an excellent putting green situated in one of the most spectacular amphi-theatres in the country. Moreover, its approach reveals on the R a detached and seemingly inaccessible pyramid of sheer rock known as the Prison, which when scaled at the back affords the finest prospect of the precipices and the Needle opposite.

The easiest and most pleasant way of reaching Quiraing is from the 7 miles/11.3 km of twisting, hilly road between Staffin and Uig which passes over a low break in the Trotter-nish backbone at an altitude of 853 feet/260 m. Here you will find a car-park which is less than 2.5 miles/4 km from the junction with the main road to Staffin and about a mile/1.6 km to the south of Quiraing. Walkers staying at Flodigarry, to the north of Staffin, may take a more or less direct line across the ups and downs of the moor and reach the Table by a stone shoot that issues from a narrow gully between its guarding pinnacles.

The grassy eminence of Meall na Suiramach is one of the more northerly of the Trotternish backbone and from afar is seen to dominate the shattered cliffs of Quiraing. Those who have explored this bizarre collection of pinnacles and buttresses

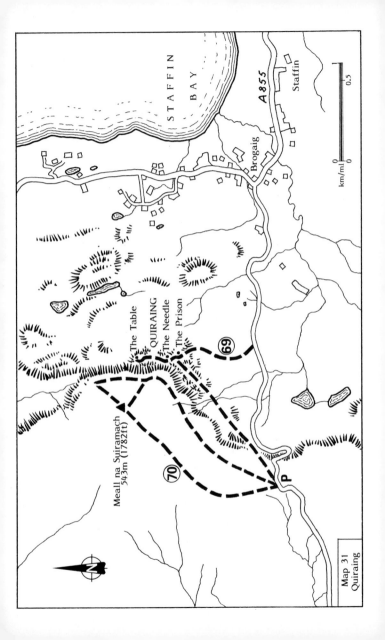

STAFFIN BAY

Staffin

A855

Brogaig

The Table
QUIRAING
The Needle
The Prison

69

Meall na Suiramach
543m (1782ft)

70

P

N

km/ml
0   0.5

Map 31
Quiraing

will have been impressed by the sheer rock walls enclosing the Table on the west. They are the only unscalable guardians of the peak, as on all other sides grassy slopes, dappled with heather and bracken, lead up to the cairn. It is a rare experience to see a walker ascending the broad southern ridge which reveals a magnificent prospect of the sea far below and of the mainland peaks to the east, but culminates in a spectacular bird's-eye view of Quiraing.

Route 69. Quiraing from Staffin. From the car-park at the col on the Staffin to Uig road, a sketchy track starts on the other side of the road, and after a few ups and downs falls to the gently rising shelf which gives easy and direct access to the Prison. Do not attempt to scale its precipitous western front, but instead ascend its grassy flanks to reach a rake that rises to the R, beyond which contour round to the L behind the first pinnacle until you attain the saddle that joins it to the second. The exceedingly steep and slippery grass here requires care in this short ascent, but the rewards are immense as the whole of the buttresses and pinnacles on the other side of the stony intervening gap are laid bare from this superlative coign of vantage. Now retrace your steps to the path and climb the steep track that rises to the L of the Needle, which is 180 feet/55 m high. Keep to the track as it threads the gloomy recesses between the gaunt pinnacles and buttresses until the Table appears ahead. Go round it to the L where you will find a way winding aloft to its grassy top, which is one of the most amazing situations in all our homeland hills. Behind you rise the unscalable walls of the Meall na Suiramach, while in all other directions you look through the gaps between the pinnacles; to the L to the sea and its islands, and to the R to the Trotternish ridge trailing away to the south, both of which are enlivened by the glint of light on the many lochans strewn on the extensive moorland below.

The Needle was climbed on August 19th, 1977, by a youth

Plate 216 The approach to the Prison by **Route 69**

Plate 217 The Needle from the Prison

Plate 218 **Route 69**—Looking down on the Needle and Prison from the Central Gully

of 16½ years. Kevin R. Bridges began the very dangerous ascent by climbing a crack on its east face, above which he found the rock very fractured and loose. A traverse L and a groove led to a sound flake belay on the south-east arête, but his brother, Michael, who followed to this point considered it too risky to continue. Kevin climbed directly above the belay for some 25 feet/8 m, and then traversed R to the north-east arête and continued to a grassy ledge immediately below the summit. He placed four slings linked together round the top and abseiled down after leaving a small cairn there. The current rock climbing guidebook to Skye grades the climb as HVS and states that it is included 'as more of a warning than as a recommendation'.

Plate 219 **Route 69** terminates on the flat grassy top of the Table

Plate 220 **Route 69** —One of the many views from the Table

Route 70. Meall na Suiramach from Staffin. The most convenient starting point for this ascent is from the same car-park as for Quiraing. As there is no track you just cross the road and go straight up the slopes opposite which involve a hard slog of some 600 feet/180 m. Thence you bear R and on reaching the crest of the broad ridge walk along to the cairn after a total ascent of less than 1000 feet/300 m. Now turn R and carefully approach the edge of the vast sanctuary cradling the Table, a sensational prospect that may come as a surprise even to those who are familiar with this weird scene from below. Continue your exploration by strolling to the R along the edge of the precipices, noting Staffin Bay beyond the pinnacles and finally the upper section of the Needle from a dizzy point where the cliffs bend away to the south. Return along the declining grass slopes and eventually down the steep ground to your car.

Plate 221 The table from the highest point of **Route 70**

Plate 222 The rock pinnacles surrounding the Sanctuary from **Route 70**

Plate 223 Looking down on the Needle and Prison from **Route 70**

Sgurr a'Bhasteir

Sgurr a'Fionn
Choire

Am Basteir

Sgurr nan Gillean

Sgurr Beag

Plate 224 The northern peaks of the Cuillin from the Sligachan Burn

The Peaks of the North Cuillin

Sgurr nan Gillean	3163 feet	964 metres
Bruach na Frithe	3143 feet	958 metres
Sgurr a'Fionn Choire	3067 feet	935 metres
Am Basteir	3064 feet	934 metres
Bhasteir Tooth	3005 feet	916 metres
Sgurr a'Bhasteir	2949 feet	899 metres
Bidein Druim nan Ramh	2851 feet	869 metres
Sgurr na Bhairnich	2825 feet	861 metres
An Caisteal	2723 feet	830 metres
Sgurr Beag	2507 feet	764 metres
Sgurr na h-Uamha	2415 feet	736 metres

Everyone who visits the misty Isle of Skye to climb in the famous Cuillin looks forward with great anticipation to catching the first glimpse of these peaks, which only come into view on the approach to Sligachan. And the excitement increases during the first ascent, which may well be that of Sgurr nan Gillean which acts as a powerful magnet to all who stay at the Sligachan Hotel. Climbed by one or other of the routes that lead to its shapely tapering summit, it is well known to mountaineers who have tasted its pleasures and also the safety of the black gabbro of which it is composed. But of all the peaks in Scotland, those which so liberally deck the Main Ridge usually involve more rock climbing, and other than Bruach na Frithe are not for the ordinary pedestrian. The rewards from the summit of Sgurr nan Gillean are immense; for much of the wild grandeur of the Main Ridge is revealed to the gaze as it swings round in a great bend to the south, with here and there a glimpse of the distant sea; as well as a spacious panorama of the Trotternish backbone to the north and of the softer lines of the Red Hills to the east, with, on their R, a magnificent prospect of the rock architecture of both Clach Glas and Bla Bheinn.

Sligachan is splendidly situated for the walker who desires to explore the northern peaks of the Cuillin, and even those as far south as Bidein Druim nan Ramh may be reached and climbed in a day by a strong party. But as most of the southern peaks are so to speak on the doorstep of Glen Brittle, they are most conveniently ascended from this well-known centre. Moreover, easy as it looks from afar, no inexperienced walker should venture on the Main Ridge, save the above-mentioned Bruach na Frithe on a clear day, as the peaks themselves are not only often difficult of access, but they are also subject to immersion by the mists which are not uncommonly encountered in this region. In such conditions and without an intimate knowledge of the safe ways off this terrain, an adventure could easily result in accident or tragedy.

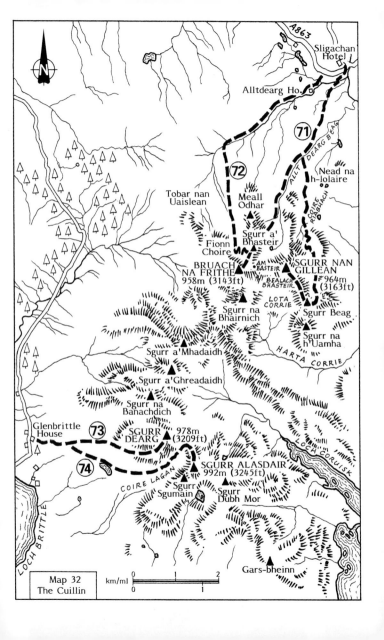

N

A863

Sligachan
Hotel

Alltdearg Ho.

71

ALLT DEARG BEAG

72

Nead na
h-Iolaire

COIRE
RIABHACH

Tobar nan
Uaislean

Meall
Odhar

Fionn
Choire

Sgurr a'
Bhasteir

BRUACH
NA FRITHE
958m (3143ft)

AM
BASTEIR

SGURR NAN
GILLEAN
964m
(3163ft)

BEALACH
BHASTEIR

LOTA
CORRIE

Sgurr na
Bhairnich

Sgurr Beag

Sgurr na
h'Uamha

Sgurr a'Mhadaidh

HARTA
CORRIE

Sgurr a'Ghreadaidh

Sgurr na
Banachdich

LOCH CORUISK

Glenbrittle
House

73

SGURR
DEARG
978m
(3209ft)

74

COIRE LAGAN

Sgurr
Sgumain

SGURR ALASDAIR
992m (3245ft)

Sgurr
Dubh Mor

LOCH BRITTLE

Gars-bheinn

Map 32
The Cuillin

km/ml   0   1   2

         0   1

Plate 225 **Route 71**—Clach Glas, Bla Bheinn and Glen Sligachan from Coire Riabhaich

Sgurr nan Gillean

Route 71. The Tourist Route from Sligachan. Leave the hotel by the Dunvegan road and take the path on the L which leads to the derelict power house. Cross the burn by a bridge and follow its meanderings across the moor in a direct line with your peak. Throughout this part of the walk the profile of Sgurr nan Gillean does not change much except to become slightly foreshortened, and since the Pinnacle Ridge rises on this side of it you cannot see the deep clefts that make it so spectacular. When you encounter the rippling Allt Dearg Beag, keep beside it for some distance until you reach a cairn which marks your way, and here turn L to cross it and make for the dip west of Nead na h'Iolaire. This section of the track is sketchy, but clearer on reaching the cairn overlooking Coire Riabhaich, whence you bear to the R and climb steadily while circling the corrie, with its gleaming lochan on your L, and the striking view of Bla Bheinn which dominates Glen Sligachan. On leaving the corrie the track steepens and the hard collar-work begins. Cairns in plenty mark your course and you twist in and out of the wilderness of boulders and scree lying at the base of the Pinnacle Ridge, now on your R. Ahead towers the shattered but almost horizontal skyline of the South-East Ridge, up which you scramble over steep scree to reach the cairn on its crest.

While this is the shortest way to reach the ridge, it is more interesting and revealing to bear to the south and take a diagonal course for the diminutive peak of Sgurr Beag, because it opens up a more comprehensive view of Sgurr nan Gillean and its satellites. Its graceful pointed summit towers into the sky overhead and is flanked on the R by the Pinnacle Ridge whose deep rifts are now clearly visible, while on the L the sharply indented Main Ridge trails away to the south on the

Plate 226 The lowly ... ... of Bowmont Water ... Cheviot ... Gill ... of ... from the ... Br... on the ... Ayshire Hills.

other side of the abysmal depths of Lota Corrie. If you have
time in hand it is worthwhile to walk to the end of the ridge
where you will encounter the remarkable pyramid of Sgurr na
h-Uamha, poised above Harta Corrie, but unless you are an
experienced climber do not attempt to scale it. Now retrace
your steps to the foot of your peak where the final ascent
begins. At first the going is rough but easy and you keep to the
Lota Corrie side of its crest. A few cairns indicate your way
until the ridge steepens, whence you will appreciate the
wonderful adhesive properties of gabbro. Up and up you go,
making liberal use of your hands to ensure safe progress, and
bear to the R near the top where you will find a short hiatus
over which you step boldly on to the summit platform with its
small cairn. The last hundred feet or so have been an exciting
scramble, with terrific drops on either side, and you will be
glad to rest for a while by the summit cairn to admire the vast
prospect of peak and sea that stretches all around you. Moreover, you will probably agree that this platform which is
poised in the sky conveys the sense of isolation better than that
of any other peak you have climbed, since no part of its
supporting ridges can be seen as you sit by the cairn and you
feel aloof from the turmoil of life far below.

The first thing to catch your eye may well be the Pinnacle
Ridge to the north, of which you now have a bird's-eye view,
and where you can easily pick out the fourth pinnacle, known
as Knight's Peak, whose traverse is the key to the successful
ascent of the whole ridge. Beyond it you will enjoy the vista of
the coastline of Skye stretching from Loch Sligachan at your
feet to the further tip of Trotternish, in which the Storr is the
most conspicuous feature on a clear day. To the R you may
speculate on the names of the various islands and the peaks on
the mainland. To the south you look across Lota Corrie to the
declining Druim nan Ramh, and beyond it to Sgurr Alasdair
and its satellites, in which the lofty and difficult ridge of the
Dubhs is prominent. To the east Marsco stands well in front of

the Red Hills in which the graceful cone of Glamaig may charm your eye, and to the south-east Bla Bheinn rises finely above the remote stretches of Glen Sligachan. To the west and south the Main Ridge forms a semicircle to merge with Sgurr Alasdair, and you may find it of interest to name the many peaks that deck this famous playground of the rock climber. The best descent is to retrace your route down the South-East Ridge.

Plate 227 Sgurr a'Bhasteir and Macleod's Tables from the summit

Sgurr a'Fionn
Choire

Bruach na Frithe

Am Basteir

Plate 228 The western ridge of Sgurr nan Gillean

Bruach na Frithe

This peak cannot be seen from Sligachan as it is hidden behind the nearer Sgurr a'Bhasteir and the best distant view of it is included in the due western prospect from Sgurr nan Gillean. From this lofty coign of vantage the Main Ridge slopes down to the Bealach a'Bhasteir, rises along the very thin crest of Am Basteir and then turns sharp L to take in the rocky bulge of Sgurr a'Fionn Choire, above which Bruach na Frithe dominates the skyline. It is, however, a prominent object in the view to the south from the path rising to the Bealach a'Mhaim, from which it is usually climbed. Its ascent is nothing more than a strenuous walk for the ordinary pedestrian, and may be combined to advantage with a visit to Sgurr a'Bhasteir. The easiest route is by way of Fionn Choire first over grass which in the spring is dotted with Alpine flowers, then through a maze of boulders to the path ascending the scree which terminates on the Main Ridge at the Bealach nan Lice, whence the track on the R rises to the summit. But experienced walkers have two alternative approaches which are not difficult, include a good scramble and are thus of greater interest. One of them takes in Coir' a'Tobar nan Uaislean which is joined to the peak by a broken ridge that forms the southern wall of Fionn Choire; the other necessitates a visit to Coire na Creiche and its continuation Coir' a'Tarneilear, whence the gash to the L of An Caisteal is ascended and the ridge followed to the L again over Sgurr na Bhairnich to Bruach na Frithe. The fine situation of this peak is such that it opens up one of the grandest vistas of the twisting ridge to the south, which is surmounted by many of the familiar peaks so readily reached from Glen Brittle.

Route 72. The Ascent from Sligachan. Leave the hotel by the Dunvegan road and turn L along the track past Alltdearg House and up the L bank of the cascading Allt Dearg Mor. This rises to the Bealach a'Mhaim and reveals splendid views on the L of the northern peaks of the Cuillin. Cross the burn, whence follow the rather sketchy track over grass, moss and stones into the mouth of Fionn Choire. This is bounded on the L by Meall Odhar and the ridge connecting it with Sgurr a'Bhasteir, and on the R by the ridge taking root at Tobar nan Uaislean already mentioned. For some distance the floor of the corrie is grassy and in great contrast to most of the other stony corries in the Cuillin; it is famous for its spring Alpines. On attaining its upper reaches steep scree and boulders replace the gentler grass and the prospect on either hand is grim as you mount the zigzags that terminate on the ridge at the Bealach nan Lice. At this point the gap between the cliffs is narrow and guarded by a small rock pinnacle on the L, beyond which to the south-east you may pick out on a clear day the strange pyramid of Sgurr na h-Uamha on the L and Sgurr na Stri on the R at the head of Loch Coruisk, backed by the glittering sea. Now turn sharp R and follow the well-trodden track over Sgurr a'Fionn Choire to the summit of your peak. The splendour of the spacious panorama will attract your eye, but your gaze will be held by the twisting ridge to the south, which, however, is best photographed before attaining the cairn. You may be able to identify the peaks on the three great bends in the ridge, as follows: the first section on the L ends at Sgurr na Bhairnich; it then turns to the R over An Caisteal and Bidein Druim nan Ramh to Sgurr a'Mhadaidh; where it again bends to the L over Sgurr a'Ghreadaidh, Sgurr Dearg and Sgurr Alasdair to Garsbheinn where the last section is partly hidden by the Dubhs ridge. This coign of vantage is a good one for the view of Bla Bheinn because the whole of its western front is seen above the gap between Sgurr Beag and Sgurr na h-Uamha.

Now, retrace your steps to the bealach and bear R to view

Sgurr a'Bhasteir

Bruach na Frithe

Fionn Choire

Plate 229 **Route 72**—The entrance to Fionn Choire from Bealach a'Mhaim

Plate 230 Route 72 Bruach na Frithe from Sgurr na Bhairnich

Ghreadaidh

Dearg

Alasdair

Dubhs

Gars-bheinn

Plate 231 **Route 72**—The twisting main ridge to the south of Bruach na Frithe

Bla Bheinn

Plate 232 **Route 72** passes Am Basteir and the Bhasteir Tooth

the detached Bhasteir Tooth, known also as the Executioner, and its adjoining Am Basteir, both of which are the playground of the rock climber and conspicuous on the skyline when viewed from Sligachan. Immediately opposite, the south ridge of Sgurr a'Bhasteir takes root and if care is taken no difficulty should be encountered in making its ascent. From its lofty summit you obtain the most spectacular prospect of the Pinnacle Ridge of Sgurr nan Gillean on the other side of Coire a'Bhasteir, and if you are a photographer the best time to make the exposure is between 3 and 4 p.m. in the spring. At this hour the westering sunlight skims across your subject to impart both contrast and detail.

The ordinary pedestrian should descend by way of a return to Bealach nan Lice and Fionn Choire, but experienced walkers may prefer to scramble down the north-east ridge of the peak and pick up the moorland path beside the Allt Dearg Beag for Sligachan. However, the best round trip is to ascend the ridge from Tobar nan Uaislean, visit Sgurr a'Bhasteir and return through the Fionn Choire.

Plate 233 **Route 72** The pinnacle ridge of Sgurr nan Gillean from Sgurr a'Bhasteir.

The Peaks of the South Cuillin

Sgurr Alasdair	3254 feet	992 meters
Inaccessible Pinnacle	3235 feet	986 metres
Sgurr Thearlaich	3209 feet	978 metres
Sgurr Dearg	3209 feet	978 metres
Sgurr a'Ghreadaidh	3192 feet	973 metres
Sgurr na Banachdich	3166 feet	965 metres
Stone Shoot	3136 feet	956 metres
An Stac	3130 feet	954 metres
Sgurr Mhic Choinnich	3110 feet	948 metres
Sgurr Sgumain	3107 feet	947 metres
Sgurr Dubh Mor	3097 feet	944 metres
Sgurr Dubh an Da Bheinn	3077 feet	938 metres
Sgurr Thormaid	3038 feet	926 metres
Sgurr nan Eag	3031 feet	924 metres
Sgurr a'Mhadaidh	3012 feet	918 metres
Gars-bheinn	2936 feet	895 metres
Sgurr Thuilm	2890 feet	881 metres
Sgurr a'Choire Bhig	2871 feet	875 metres
Sron na Ciche	2818 feet	859 metres
Thearlaich-dubh Gap	2805 feet	855 metres
Sgurr Dubh Beag	2401 feet	732 metres
Sgurr Coir'an Lochain	2392 feet	729 metres
Sgurr nan Gobhar	2067 feet	630 metres
Sgurr na Stri	1621 feet	494 metres

Walkers who wish to see more clearly the topography of this section of the Main Ridge could not do better than drive down to the campsite at Glen Brittle. For the rising ground behind the shop is crowned by the more distant ridge from Sgurr na Banachdich to Sron na Ciche, with the great mass of Sgurr Dearg dominating the scene. Banachdich appears on the L and

Plate 234 The main ridge from the campsite at Glen Brittle

Sgurr Mhic Choinnich, Sgurr Alasdair, Sgurr Sgumain and Sron na Ciche on the R. The next section from Dearg to Sgurr nan Gobhar encloses Coire na Banachdich and is well seen from Glen Brittle on a sunny afternoon. However, the most spectacular section from Sgurr Thuilm to Bruach na Frithe, which encloses Coire na Creiche, is revealed to perfection from where the rising Glen Brittle road emerges from the glen on the journey over to Carbost. The triangular peak in the centre is Sgurr an Fheadain, split in the middle by the famous Waterpipe Gully, and dominated by Bidein Druim nan Ramh on the skyline. The two inner corries are Coir' a'Tarneilear on the L and Coire a'Mhadaidh on the R.

Plate 235 Coire na Banachdich from the Memorial Hut, Glen Brittle

Sgurr Dearg

This peak rises immediately to the east of Glen Brittle and is bounded on the L by Coire na Banachdich and on the R by Coire Lagan. Seen from Glen Brittle on a sunny evening, it rises between Sgurr na Banachdich on the L and Sgurr Alasdair on the R, when the view of it is wholly magnetic and will be remembered with delight by all those walkers who have spent an invigorating day on the Main Ridge, of which this peak is a part. Its flat summit ridge is characterised by the narrow and slightly leaning obelisk known as the Inaccessible Pinnacle which affords the most attractive rock climbing problem on this mountain. Both ends of the adjacent ridge reveal the splendour of its neighbouring peaks, and include the narrow and sensational crest of Sgurr na Banachdich and the grandeur of the northern precipices of Sgurr Alasdair. But even on a calm day the ascent of Sgurr Dearg, though not difficult, requires care; therefore the ordinary pedestrian should not venture upon it unless in the company of an experienced walker, because the long precipitous shoulder connecting it with Sron Dearg is narrow in places and a steady head is essential.

Route 73. The Ascent from Glen Brittle. Leave Glen Brittle by the Coire Lagan path, and after passing the waterfall of Eas Mor on the L, advance straight towards the shoulder of the mountain. Here masses of scree make the ascent rather trying, but on reaching a conspicuous dyke below the first point on the ridge the going becomes easier. Beyond this small summit the angle is reduced and you cross a vast expanse of scree while making direct to Sron Dearg, which looks like a titantic castle poised high on the ridge and extending right across it. The views on the L down into Coire na Banachdich are impressive, while those of Sron na Ciche on the R reveal its

Plate 236 Coire na Croiche - consult p.487 for details.

whole front clearly, especially the Terrace which rises diagonally from L to R. There is no easy way to the top of Sron Dearg, although you may be tempted to go over to the R, and when you attain its cairn the narrow shattered continuation of the ridge is seen ahead. On tackling this you will pass some sensational drops and one or two places which are rather slippery, but this long shoulder is soon traversed and you then walk forward to the summit ridge of your mountain.

The most magnificent prospect is on your R where you look across Coire Lagan to its engirdling ridge dominated by Sgurr Alasdair, the highest peak in the Cuillin. This superb skyline from L to R includes Sgurr Mhic Choinnich and Sgurr Thearlaich. The whole of the great Stone Shoot is visible and, to the R of the reigning peak, Sgurr Sgumain seems to be leaning over towards Sron na Ciche further to the R. Looking now to the L of this group you may be impressed by the bold outline of An Stac, but your gaze will rest upon the Inaccessible Pinnacle whose curving crest terminates abruptly upon the summit ridge. Continuing your stroll, now on the Main Ridge, you soon come to the northern tip of Sgurr Dearg which discloses the most striking prospect of Sgurr na Banachdich, right from the bealach at your feet to its summit, with Sgurr Thormaid, the Three Teeth and Sgurr a'Ghreadaidh on its R and above them a glimpse of Sgurr Thuilm.

If you are with a party of climbers, they may prefer to return to Glen Brittle by way of Coire na Banachdich where a knowledge of the intricacies of the route is necessary, otherwise it is safer to descend the way you came.

Coire na
Banachdich

Sron Dearg

Plate 237 **Route 73**—Sgurr Dearg from Eas Mor

Plate 238 **Route 73**—The Inaccessible Pinnacle

Plate 239 **Route 73**—The ridge to Sgurr na Banachdich

Mhic Coinnich   Thearlaich   Alasdair   Sgumain

Plate 240 **Route 73**—Sgurr Alasdair and satellites from Sgurr Dearg

Sgurr Alasdair

This is the highest peak in the Cuillin and when seen from Glen Brittle its pointed summit is conspicuous on the skyline, together with that of its satellite, Sgurr Sgumain, below which the ridge falls to the R to the almost level top of Sron na Ciche. The finest view of it is obtained from Sgurr Dearg, but its importance in the landscape is also disclosed from Sgurr nan Eag to the south, when it is seen beyond the shining surface of the lonely loch on the floor of Coir' a'Ghrunnda. In this prospect, however, its precipitous front is confused and much shattered, whereas Sgurr Thearlaich on its R indicates the narrowness of the cat-walk down to Sgurr Mhic Choinnich. The summit of Sgurr Alasdair is the smallest in this range of hills and there is barely room for the walker to sit down beside the cairn.

It is usually climbed from Coire Lagan by the great Stone Shoot, whose ascent is extremely arduous, and on reaching the col a short knife-edge of basalt connects it with the peak. It is taken in during the complete traverse of the Main Ridge, when it is reached from the col below the Dubhs by way of the Thearlaich-Dubh Gap, but as this is a tricky problem it is only tackled by experienced rock climbers. Another route involving some scrambling is by the ascent of the South-West Ridge, but since there is a very awkward *mauvais pas* at its base, which must be climbed before the ridge proper can be tackled, it should be severely left alone by the ordinary pedestrian.

Route 74. The Ascent from Glen Brittle. Follow the well-trodden path from Glen Brittle right into the gloomy recesses of Coire Lagan and then walk over to the bottom of the Stone Shoot. Go first close to the crags on the R, and when you reach the band of rock near the middle of the shoot, go over to the L

Thearlaich

Alasdair

Sguimain

Coir'a'Ghrunnda

Plate 241 **Route 74**—The dominating peak of the Cuillin seen from Sgurr nan Eag

Plate 242 **Route 74**—Mist in the Great Stone Shoot

close to the rock wall, at which point you enter the grim portals of the shoot. This is the easiest course to take and the higher you get the smaller the stones, but by keeping close to one side or the other, where the stones do not roll so readily, progress is much facilitated. On emerging at the col there is a dramatic change of scene; for you are confronted by a splendid prospect of the Dubhs, with Gars-bheinn on their R, and if you go over to the far edge of the col you will get a glimpse of the Thearlaich-Dubh Gap below on the L. The backward vista down the Stone Shoot is impressive, as it conveys a matchless conception of the wild amphitheatre of mountains that enclose the corrie at your feet.

Now tackle the narrow arête, using your hands to ensure safe progress, until you step finally on to the tiny summit of your dominating peak. Looking round the vast panorama, you will immediately note the narrow arm of rock that stretches westwards for a few feet, and then the side of the peak plunges down at a sensational angle in one seemingly unbroken preci-pice right to the floor of Coire Lagan. To the south-west the spectacular ridge falls to the col, and rises again to Sgurr Sgumain with Loch Brittle and the illimitable sea in the background. To the north, and immediately overlooking the Stone Shoot, stands Sgurr Thearlaich whose cairn is only 50 feet/15 m below and tops the cat-walk that falls steeply to the col below Sgurr Mhic Choinnich. Beyond this there is the finest view of Sgurr Dearg, whose seamed flanks drop sensationally into Coire Lagan, and to the R of it the ridge trails away to the north to end with the shapely peak of Sgurr nan Gillean. The magic of this superb panorama is completed by the lovely lines of Bla Bheinn to the east and enhanced by the background in many directions of the blue sea, dappled with islands, and stretching to infinity.

If you have lingered on Sgurr Alasdair to revel in these scenes of mountain grandeur you will descend from the peak late in the day to Coire Lagan, accompanied by the clatter of rolling stones. And here, amid this desolation of rock and scree you may well linger again, standing beside the still lochan that is held in the grip of the hillside by a gigantic boilerplate, from which the seaward panorama stands out in stark contrast to this mountain wilderness. Below you lies the long arm of Loch Brittle with Rhum and Canna floating serenely on the surface of the rippling ocean, relieved here and there by the white sail of a ship, or the smoke trail of a steamer. And if the evening is still with an unflecked sky stretching from the sunrise to the sunset, you will stand spellbound while you watch and wait. For the blue of the heavens will slowly change through every colour of the spectrum as the sun sinks towards the Atlantic away to the west, while the crags around you will be trans-muted from pink to gold until day passes into night. Then the jagged skyline will be silhouetted against the twinkling stars and you will stumble down the rough track back to Glen Brittle, perhaps in the ghostly light of the silvery moon, but with your being saturated with the magic and mystery of the incomparable Cuillin.

NOTE: Owing to limited space only four of the peaks of the Cuillin have been included in this volume, but interested readers may consult the author's *Magic of Skye*, which contains a complete description of the Main Ridge, together with numerous photographs illustrating its fine topography and climbing problems from start to finish.

Plate 243 Cuillin panorama from the north

Two panoramas of the Cuillin

Owing to the twisting elevations of the Main Ridge of the Cuillin it is impossible to see the whole of it from any one viewpoint. The photograph below reveals only the most northerly section, from Sgurr nan Gillean to Sgurr na Banachdich and Sgurr nan Gobhar, and can be seen on a clear day, preferably by afternoon lighting, from the Sligachan–Dunvegan road. After driving up the two bends above Drynoch at the head of Loch Harport the road straightens out and there is a car-park on the L. Walk up to the nearby eminence and there it is!

The peaks from L to R are as follows:

Pinnacle Ridge to Sgurr nan Gillean
Ridge rising to Sgurr a'Bhastier
Am Bastier and Sgurr a'Fionn Choire above
Fionn Choire
Ridge of Tobar nan Uaislean rising to
Bruach na Frithe
An Caisteal
Bidein Druim nan Ramh above
Sgurr an Fheadain and the Waterpipe Gully
Four peaks of Sgurr a'Mhadaidh
Sgurr a'Ghreadaidh
Sgurr Thuilm
Sgurr Dearg
Sgurr na Banachdich falling to
Sgurr nan Gobhar

However, the most spectacular view is from Elgol, but even here the southern section of the ridge is partially obscured by Gars-bheinn. Seen under the most favourable conditions, occasionally with snow on the peaks, it is the most magnificent scene in Britain, enhanced by the blue of Loch Scavaig in the immense foreground. To reach Elgol involves a longish hilly drive, with the unveiling of many beautiful scenes on the way. The most arresting is that of Bla Bheinn from Loch Slapin and includes the adjacent Clach Glas whose traverse is beloved by the rock climber. After driving round the head of the loch there is a fine retrospect from the point where it narrows, and a few miles further along beyond Kilmarie a gate and a stile appear on the R. Thence a path leads to Camasunary and Loch Coruisk for direct access to the Cuillin. And finally there is the superb spectacle on reaching Elgol, considered by many as one of the finest in the world.

Plate 244 Bla Bheinn, Clach Glas and Sgurr nan Each from Loch Slapin

Plate 245 The Bla Bheinn Ridge from the path to Camasunary

Plate 246 A superb vista of the Cuillin from Elgol

Sense on the Scottish Hills

"Look well to each step"

Climb if you will, but remember that courage and strength are nought without prudence, and that a momentary negligence may destroy the happiness of a lifetime. Do nothing in haste; look well to each step; and from the beginning think what may be the end.

Edward Whymper

1. Seek advice daily about local conditions and problems. Beware of avalanches and dangerous corniced ridges. Pay attention to weather forecasts. If bad stay in the valleys; conditions on Scottish tops can become Arctic.
2. Never go alone, but keep parties small, with an experienced leader. Don't separate. Leave a note of route planned and report forced changes at earliest opportunity.
3. Plan your expedition with a safety margin and turn back while there is yet time. Before starting note local rescue posts.
4. Wear tricouni nailed boots in winter or crampons: vibrams are dangerous on snow and ice.
5. Carry an ice-axe and practise braking. Also reserve food, torch, whistle and watch.
6. Wear warm and windproof clothes. Carry extra for tops, halts and cold.
7. Take a 1 inch map and know how to use it with a suitable compass (e.g. prismatic or "Silva").
8. If lost or caught in a blizzard, keep calm; seek or build temporary shelter. Vital energy can be lost fighting the wind—a dangerous foe.

9. If there is an accident send written message to nearest rescue post, giving accident position accurately. One member should stay with victim.

10. Learn life-saving first aid and carry simple first aid kit.

Copies of *Mountain Rescue & Cave Rescue* can be obtained from Mountain Rescue Committee, Hill House, Cheadle Hulme, Stockport, Cheshire.

Issued by the Mountain Rescue Committee of Scotland. Hamish MacInnes, Secretary, Glencoe.

This **Route Card** is reproduced with the permission of the Chief Constable of Inverness-shire and is similar to others in use elsewhere in Scotland. The idea is sound and if adopted and used consistently by all climbers and walkers throughout our mountainous country it could be the means of facilitating any call for Mountain Rescue. I hope the English and Welsh Police will favour its use and distribute the Route Card widely wherever climbers and mountain walkers are lodged. It is, of course, most important that NO DIGRESSION is made from the stated route, otherwise in the event of an accident searchers would be unable to locate the victim.

Let us know
when you go
on our hills

Names and Addresses: Home Address and Local Address	Route
Time and date of departure;	Bad Weather Alternative:
Place of Departure and Registered Number of Vehicle (if any)	
Estimated time of Return:	Walking/Climbing (delete as necessary)

GO UP WELL EQUIPPED · TO COME BACK SAFELY

Please tick items carried:

Emergency Food	Torch	Ice Axe
Waterproof Clothing (Colour ·	Whistle	Crampons
Winter Clothing (Colour ·	Map	Polybag
	Compass	First Aid

Please complete and leave with Police, landlady, warden etc.
Inform landlady or warden to contact Police if you are overdue.

PLEASE REPORT YOUR SAFE RETURN.

Index

Bold type denotes main references